YOU'VE

GOT

JOKES

YOU'VE GOT JOKES

Platinum Press, LLC
2011

ISBN—13:978-1-879582-73-6

Printed and bound in The United States of America

9 8 7 6 5 4 3

CONTENTS

BUSINESS JOKES

A young executive was leaving the office late one evening when he found the CEO standing in front of a shredder with a piece of paper in his hand.

"Listen," said the CEO, "this is a very sensitive and important document here, and my secretary has gone for the night. Can you make this thing work for me?"

"Certainly," said the young executive. He turned the machine on, inserted the paper, and pressed the start button.

"Excellent, excellent!" said the CEO, as his paper disappeared inside the machine. "I just need one copy . . ."

An accountant dies and goes to Heaven. He reaches the pearly gates and is amazed to see a happy crowd all waving banners and chanting his name.

After a few minutes St. Peter comes running across and says, "I'm sorry I wasn't here to greet you personally. God is looking forward to meeting such a remarkable man as yourself."

The accountant is perplexed. "I've tried to lead a good life, but I am overwhelmed by your welcome," he tells St. Peter.

"It's the least we can do for someone as special as you are. Imagine, living to the age of 123 and still looking so young," says St. Peter.

The man looks even more dumbfounded and replies, "123 years old? I don't know what you mean. I'm only 40."

St. Peter replies, "But that can't be right - we've seen your time sheets!"

The stockbroker received notice from the IRS that he was being audited. He showed up at the appointed time and place with all his financial records, then sat for what seemed like hours as the accountant pored over them.

Finally the IRS agent looked up and commented, "You must have been a tremendous fan of Sir Arthur Conan Doyle."

"Why would you say that?" wondered the broker.

"Because you've made more brilliant deductions on your last three returns than Sherlock Holmes made in his entire career."

Bill Gates dies and Satan greets him: "Welcome Mr. Gates, we've been waiting for you. This will be your home for all eternity. You've been selfish, greedy and a big liar all your life. Now, since you've got me in a good mood, I'll be generous and give you a choice of three places in which you'll be locked up forever.

Satan takes Bill to a huge lake of fire in which millions of poor souls are tormented and tortured. He then takes him to a massive coliseum where thousands of people are chased about and devoured by starving lions. Finally, he takes Bill to a tiny room in which there is a bottle of the finest wine sitting on a table. To Bill's delight, he sees a PC in the corner. Without hesitation, Bill says "I'll take this option."

"Fine," says Satan, allowing Bill to enter the room. Satan locks the room after Bill.

As he turns around, he bumps into Lucifer. "That was Bill Gates!" crted Lucifer. "Why did you give him the best place of all!"

"That's what everyone thinks" snickered Satan.

"The bottle has a hole in it!"

"What about the PC?"

"It's got Windows 95!" laughed Satan.

"And it's missing three keys."

"Which three?"

"Control, Alt and Delete."

Two friends meet in the office of one of them, a notorious techo-geek.

"Hey, bud, how are ya?"

"I'm good. Congratulations, that new secretary of yours is beautiful!"

"Well, I'm glad you like her. Believe it or not, she's a robot!

"No way, how could that be?"

"Way! She's the latest model from Japan. Lemme tell you how she works. If you squeeze her left tit, she takes dictation. If you squeeze her right tit, she types a letter. And that's not all, she can have sex, too!"

"Holy shit! You're kidding, right?"

"No, she's something, huh? Tell you what, you can even borrow her"

"So, his friend takes her into the restroom and is in there with her for a whille. Suddenly, he hears him screaming "Eeeeyaaaaa! Heeelp Ooooooh! Aaaaaaah? Eeeeeeeeeeaaargghhhh!"

The guy says, "Shit! I forgot to tell him her ass is a pencil sharpener!"

At a recent computer expo, Bill Gates reportedly compared the computer industry with the auto industry and stated, "If GM had kept up with technology like the computer industry has, we would all be driving $25.00 cars that got 1,000 miles to the gallon."

In response to Bill's comments, General Motors issued a press release stating: If GM had developed technology like! Microsoft, we would all be driving cars with the following characteristics

1. For no reason whatsoever, your car would crash twice a day.

2. Every time they repainted the lines in the road, you would have to buy a new car.

3. Occasionally your car would die on the highway for no reason. You would have to pull to the side of the road, close all of the windows, shut off the car, restart it, and reopen the windows before you could continue. For some reason you would simply accept this.

4. Occasionally, executing a maneuver such as a left turn would cause your car to shut down and refuse to restart, in which case you would have to reinstall the engine.

5. Macintosh would make a car that was powered by the sun, was reliable, five times as fast and twice as easy to drive - but would run on only five percent of the roads.

6. The oil, water temperature, and alternator warning lights would all be replaced by a single "This Car Has Performed An Illegal Operation" warning light.

7. The airbag system would ask "Are you sure?" before deploying.

8. Occasionally, for no reason whatsoever, your car would lock you out and refuse to let you in until you simultaneously lifted the door handle, turned the key and, grabbed hold of the radio antenna.

9. Every time a new car was introduced car buyers would have to learn how to drive all over again because none of the controls would operate in the same manner as the old car

10. You'd have to press the "Start" button to turn the engine off.

Employee. . . . . "I'm sorry but I can't come in today..
My doctor says I suffer from Anal Glaucoma."
Boss. . . . . "Anal Glaucoma? What's that?"
Employee. . . . "I just can't see my ass coming to work!"

Dear Staff,

DRESS CODE

It is advised that you come to work dressed according to your salary. If we see you wearing Prada sneakers & carrying a Gucci bag we assume you are doing well financially and therefore you do not need a raise. If you dress poorly, you need to learn to manage your money better, so that you may buy nicer clothes and therefore you do not need a raise.

If you dress in-between, you are right where you need to be and therefore you do not need a raise.

PERSONAL DAYS:

Each employee will receive 104 personal days a year. These are called Saturday & Sunday.

LUNCH BREAK:

Skinny people get 30 minutes for lunch as they need to eat more so that they can look healthy.

Normal size people get 15 minutes for lunch to get a balanced meal to maintain their average figure.

Fat people get 5 minutes for lunch, because that's all the time needed to drink a SlimFast and take a diet pill.

SICK DAYS:

We will no longer accept a doctor statement as proof of sickness. If you are able to go to the doctor, you are able to come to work.

RESTROOM USE:

Entirely too much time is being spent in the restroom. There is now a strict 3-minute time limit in the stalls.

At the end of three minutes, an alarm will sound, the toilet paper roll will retract, the stall door will open and a picture will be taken.

After your second offense, your picture will be posted on the company bulletin board under the "Chronic Offenders" category.

SURGERY:

As long as you are an employee here, you need all your organs.

You should not consider removing anything.

We hired you intact. To have something removed constitutes a breach of employment.

Thank you for your loyalty to our company. We are here to provide a positive employment experience.

Therefore, all questions, comments, concerns, complaints, frustrations, irritations, aggravations, insinuations, allegations, accusations, contemplation, consternation and input should be directed elsewhere.

In prison . . . You spend the majority of your time in a 8 × 10 cell
At work. . . . You spend most of your time in a 6 × 8 cubicle

In prison. . . . You get 3 meals a day
At work . . . You get only a break for one meal and you have to pay for it

In prison . . . You get time off for good behavior
At work . . . You get rewarded for good behavior with more work

In prison . . . A guard locks and unlocks all the doors for you
At work. . . . You must carry around a security card and unlock and open all the doors yourself

In prison . . . You can watch television and play games
At work . . . You get fired for watching television and playing games

In prison . . . You have your own toilet
At work . . . You have to share

In prison. . . . They allow family and friends to visit
At work . . . You cannot even speak to family and friends

In prison . . . All expenses are paid by taxpayers, no work required
At work. . . . You get to pay all the expenses and then they deduct from your salary to pay for prisoners

In prison. . . . You spend most of your life looking through bars from the inside wanting to get out
At work. . . . You spend most of your time waiting to get out and go inside bars

In prison . . .There are wardens who are often sadistic
At work . . . They are called Supervisors

In prison . . . You have unlimited time to read e-mail jokes
At work. . . . You get fired if you get caught

I was having trouble with my computer. So I called Harold, the computer guy, to come over. Harold clicked a couple of buttons and solved the problem. He gave me a bill for a minimum service call.

As he was walking away, I called after him, “So, what was wrong?”

He replied, “It was an ‘ID ten T’ error.”

I didn't want to appear stupid, but I nonetheless inquired, "An ID ten T error? What's that, in case I need to fix it again?"

Harold grinned. "Haven't you ever heard of an ID ten T error before?"

"No," I replied.

"Write it down," he said, "and I think you'll figure it out."

So I wrote it down.

I D 1 0 T

Over the past few years, scientists say they've been developing what they say is a revolutionary new kind of baby bottle. It's a baby bottle actually shaped like a woman's breast.

If that's true, forget baby bottles, make beer bottles.

An optometrist was instructing a new employee on how to charge a customer.

"As you are fitting his glasses, if he asks how much they cost, you say '$75.'

If his eyes don't flutter, say, 'For the frames. The lenses will be $50.'

If his eyes still don't flutter, you add 'Each.'"

This good looking man walks into an agent's office in Hollywood and says "I want to be a movie star."

Tall, handsome and with experience on Broadway, he had the right credentials.

The agent asked, "What's your name?"

The guy said, "My name is Penis van Lesbian."

The agent said, "Sir, I hate to tell you, but in order to get into Hollywood, you are gonna have to change your name."

"I will NOT change my name! The van Lesbian name is centuries old, I will not disrespect my grandfather by changing my name. Not ever."

The agent said, “Sir, I have worked in Hollywood for years . . . you will NEVER go far in Hollywood with a name like Penis van Lesbian! I’m telling you, you will HAVE TO change your name or I will not be able to represent you.”

“So be it! I guess we will not do business together” the guy said and he left the agent’s office.

FIVE YEARS LATER. . . . .

The agent opens an envelope sent to his office. Inside the envelope is a letter and a check for $50,000. The agent is awestruck, who would possibly send him $50,000?

He reads the letter enclosed . . .

“Dear Sir,

Five years ago, I came into your office wanting to become an actor in Hollywood, you told me I needed to change my name. Determined to make it with my God-given birth name I refused. You told me I would never make it in Hollywood with a name like Penis van Lesbian.

After I left your office, I thought about what you said. I decided you were right. I had to change my name. I had too much pride to return to your office, so I signed with another agent. I would never have made it without changing my name, so the enclosed check is a token of my appreciation.

Thank you for your advice.

“Dick Van Dyck”

A customer sent an order to a distributor for a large amount of goods totaling a great deal of money. The distributor noticed that the previous bill hadn’t been paid. The collections manager left a voice-mail for them saying, “We can’t ship your new order until you pay for the last one.”

The next day the collections manager received a collect phone call, “Please cancel the order. We can’t wait that long.”

A customer at a counter of a lawn ornament shop said to the cashier, “Give me four of those pinwheels, two of those pink flamingos, two of the sunflowers, and one of those bent-over grandmas in bloomers".

The cashier replied, "That'll be eight dollars for the pinwheels, ten dollars for the flamingos, six dollars for the sunflowers, and an apology for my wife!"

The owner of a small business was confused about paying an invoice, so he decided to ask his secretary for some mathematical help.

He called her into his office and said, "You graduated from The University and I need some help.

If I were to give you $20,000, minus 14%, how much would you take off?"

The secretary thought a moment, then replied, "Everything but my earrings."

A customer wanted to ask his attractive waitress for a date, but couldn't get her attention. When he was able to catch her eye, she quickly looked away. Finally he followed her into the kitchen and blurted out his invitation. To his amazement she readily consented. He said, "Why have you been avoiding me all this time? You wouldn't even make eye contact."

"Oh," replied the waitress, " I thought you wanted more coffee."

A plumber was called to a woman's apartment to repair a leaking pipe. When he arrived he was pleased to discover that the woman was quite a luscious, well-stacked babe, and during the course of the afternoon the two became extremely friendly.

About 5.30 p.m. the phone rang, disturbing the bedroom activities. "That was my husband," she said, "He's on his way home, but is going back to the office around 8. Come back then, dear, and we can take up where we left off."

The union plumber looked at the woman in disbelief. "What? On my own time??"

I can't say I've ever gotten a shave from a barber, but I've seen others who have. I was in a shop once, and an obviously new barber nicked a customer several times while giving him a shave.

The new barber, in an effort to smooth things over asked solicitiously, "Do you want your head wrapped in a hot towel?"

"No thanks." said the customer. "I'll carry it home under my arm."

After every flight, Qantas pilots fill out a form, called a "gripesheet," which tells mechanics about problems with the aircraft. The mechanics correct the problems, document their repairs on the form, and then pilots review the gripe sheets before the next flight. Never let it be said that ground crews lack a sense of humor. Here are some actual maintenance complaints submitted by Qantas' pilots (marked with a P) and the solutions recorded (marked with an S) by maintenance engineers.

P: Left inside main tire almost needs replacement.
S: Almost replaced left inside main tire.

P: Test flight OK, except auto-land very rough.
S: Auto-land not installed on this aircraft.

P: Something loose in cockpit.
S: Something tightened in cockpit.

P: Dead bugs on windshield.
S: Live bugs on back-order.

P: Autopilot in altitude-hold mode produces a 200 feet per minute descent.
S: Cannot reproduce problem on ground.

P: Evidence of leak on right main landing gear.
S: Evidence removed.

P: DME volume unbelievably loud.

S: DME volume set to more believable level.

P: Friction locks cause throttle levers to stick.
S: That's what friction locks are for.

P: IFF inoperative in OFF mode.
S: IFF always inoperative in OFF mode.

P: Suspected crack in windshield.
S: Suspect you're right.

P: Number 3 engine missing.
S: Engine found on right wing after brief search.

P: Aircraft handles funny.
S: Aircraft warned to: straighten up, fly right, and be serious.

P: Target radar hums.
S: Reprogrammed target radar with lyrics.

P: Mouse in cockpit.
S: Cat installed

P: Noise coming from under instrument panel. Sounds like a midget pounding on something with a hammer.
S: Took hammer away from midget.

The phone rang as I was sitting down to my evening meal, and as I answered it I was greeted with "Is this Karl Brummer". Not sounding anything like my name, I asked who is calling.

The telemarketer said he was with The ABC Company or something like that. Then I asked him if he knew Karl personally and why was he calling this number.

I then said off to the side, "get some pictures of the body at various angles and the blood smears", I then turned back to the phone and advised the caller that he had entered a murder scene and must stay on the line because we had already traced this call and he would be receiving a summons to testify in this murder case.

I questioned the caller at great length as to his name, address, phone number at home, at work, who he worked for, how he knew the dead guy and could he prove where he had been about one hour before he made this call.

The telemarketer was getting very concerned and his answers

were given in a shaky voice. I then told him we had located his position and the police were entering the building to take him into custody, at that point I heard the phone fall and the scurrying of his running away.

My wife asked me as I returned to our table why I had tears streaming down my face and so help me, I couldn't tell her for about fifteen minutes I was laughing so much. My meal was cold, but it was the best meal in a long, long time.

A dedicated Teamsters union worker was attending a convention in Las Vegas and decided to check out the brothels. When he got to the first one, he asked the Madam, "Is this a union house?" "No," she replied, "I'm sorry it isn't." "Well, if I pay you $100, what cut do the girls get?" "The house gets $80 and the girls get $20," she answered. Mightily offended at such unfair dealings, the union man stomped off down the street in search of a more equitable, hopefully unionized shop.

His search continued until finally he reached a brothel where he asked if this was a union house? The Madam responded, "Why yes sir, this is a union house. We observe all union rules." The man asked, "And if I pay you $100, what cut do the girls get?" She said, the girls get $80 and the house gets $20." "That's more like it!" the union man said. He handed the Madam $100, looked around the room, and pointed to a stunningly attractive blonde. "I'd like her," he said. "I'm sure you would, sir," said the Madam. Then she gestured to a 92-year old woman in the corner, "but Ethel here has 67 years seniority and according to union rules, she's next."

A guy walks into the local welfare office, marches straight up to the counter and says, "Hi . . . You know, I just HATE drawing welfare. I'd really rather have a job."

The social worker behind the counter says, "Your timing is excellent. We just got a job opening from a very wealthy old man who wants a chauffeur and bodyguard for his beautiful nymphomaniac daughter. You'll have to drive around in his

Mercedes, but he'll supply all of your clothes and because of the long hours, meals will be provided. You'll be expected to escort her on her overseas vacation trips and will have to satisfy all her sexual urges. You'll be provided a two-bedroom apartment above the garage. The starting salary is $200,000 a year.

"The guy, wide-eyed, says, "You're bullshittin' me!"

The social worker says, "Yeah, well . . . you started it

I urgently needed a few days off work, but I knew the boss would not allow me to take a leave. I thought that maybe if I acted "CRAZY" then he would tell me to take a few days off. So I hung upside down from the ceiling and made funny noises.

My coworker, asked me what I was going. I told her that I was pretending to be a light bulb so that the boss would think I was "CRAZY" and give me a few days off.

A few minutes later the boss came into the office and asked "What are you doing?" I told him I was a light bulb. He said "You are clearly stressed out. Go home and recuperate for a couple of days. "I jumped down and walked out of the office. When my coworker (the blonde) followed me, the boss said to her, "And where do you think you're going?" She said, "I'm going home too, I can't work in the dark!"

A little old lady answered a knock on the door one day, only to be confronted by a well-dressed young man carrying a vacuum cleaner.

"Good morning," said the young man. "If I could take a couple of minutes of your time, I would like to demonstrate the very latest in high-powered vacuum cleaners." "Go away," said the old lady. "I haven't got any money, I'm broke!" As she proceeded to close the door, the young man wedged his foot in the door and pushed it wide open. "Don't be too hasty," he said. "Not until you have at least seen my demonstration." And with that, he emptied a bucket of horse manure on to her hallway carpet.

"If this vacuum cleaner does not remove all traces of this horse manure from your carpet, Madam, I will personally eat the remainder. The old lady stepped back and said, "Well I hope you've got a damned good appetite, because they cut off my electricity this morning."

You Know You're Living In 2009, if:

1. You accidentally enter your password on the microwave.

2. You haven't played solitaire with real cards in years.

3. You have 15 phone numbers to reach your family of 3.

4. You e-mail your friend who works at the desk next to you.

5. Your reason for not staying in touch with friends is that they do not have e-mail addresses.

6. When you go home after a long day at work you still answer the phone in a business manner.

7. When you make phone calls from home, you accidentally dial "9" to get an outside line.

8. You've sat at the same desk for four years and worked for three different companies.

10. You learn you've been laid off on the 11 o'clock news.

11. Your boss doesn't have the ability to do your job.

12. Contractors outnumber permanent staff and are more likely to get long-service awards.

13. You read this entire list, and kept nodding and smiling.

A sales rep, an administration clerk, and the manager are walking to lunch when they find an antique oil lamp.

They rub it and a Genie comes out.

The Genie says, "I'll give each of you just one wish."

"Me first! Me first!" says the admin clerk. "I want to be in the Bahamas, driving a speedboat, without a care in the world." Puff! She's gone.

"Me next! Me next!" says the sales rep. "I want to be in Hawaii, relaxing on the beach with my personal masseuse, an endless supply of Pina Coladas and the love of my life." Puff! He's gone.

"OK, You're up," the Genie says to the manager. The manager says, "I want those two back in the office after lunch."

A businessman on his deathbed called his friend and said, "Bill, I want you to promise me that when I die you will have my remains cremated."

"And what," his friend asked, "do you want me to do with your ashes?"

The businessman said, "Just put them in an envelope and mail them to the Internal Revenue Service. Write on the envelope, "Now, you have everything."

PLEASE READ THE FOLLOWING SIX STATEMENTS AND THE AMAZING CONCLUSION TO WHICH THEY LEAD:

1. The sport of choice for the urban poor is BASKETBALL.
2. The sport of choice for maintenance level employees is BOWLING.
3. The sport of choice for front-line workers is FOOTBALL.
4. The sport of choice for supervisors is BASEBALL.
5. The sport of choice for middle management is TENNIS.
6. The sport of choice for corporate officers is GOLF.

AMAZING CONCLUSION:

The higher you are in the corporate structure, the smaller your balls become.

2 MINUTE MANAGEMENT COURSE

LESSON ONE:

An eagle was sitting on a tree - resting . . . doing nothing. A small rabbit saw the eagle and asked him, "Can I also sit like you and do nothing"? The eagle answered, "Sure, why not"? So, the rabbit sat on the ground below the eagle and rested.

Suddenly, a fox appeared, jumped on the rabbit and ate it.

Management Lesson . . . To be sitting and doing nothing, you must be sitting very, very high up.

LESSON TWO:

A turkey was chatting with a bull. "I would love to be able to get to the top of that tree; but, I haven't got the energy", sighed the turkey. "Well, why don't you nibble on some of my droppings?", replied the bull . . ." they're packed with nutrients". The turkey pecked at a lump of dung and found it actually gave him enough strength to reach the lowest branch of the tree. The next day, after eating some more dung, he reached the second branch. Finally, on the fifth day, he found himself proudly perched at the top. There, he was promptly spotted by a farmer who shot him out of the tree.

Management Lesson . . . Bull shit might get you to the top; but, it won't keep you there.

LESSON THREE:

A little bird was flying South for the winter. It was so cold, the bird's wings froze and he fell to the ground in a large field.

While he was lying there, a cow came by and dropped some dung on him.

As the frozen bird lay there in the pile of cow dung, it began to realize how warm it was.

The dung was actually thawing him out!

The bird lay there all warm and happy, and soon began to sing for joy.

A passing cat heard the bird singing and came to investigate.

Following the sound, the cat discovered the bird under the pile of cow dung and promptly dug him out and ate him.

Management Lessons . . .

1.) Not everyone who shits on you is your enemy.

2.) Not everyone who gets you out of shit is your friend.

3.) And, when you're in deep shit keep your mouth shut!!!

You're at a party with a bunch of friends and see a gorgeous girl. One of your friends goes up to her and pointing at you says, "He's fantastic in bed."

That's Advertising.

You see a gorgeous girl at a party. You go up to her and get her telephone number. The next day you call and say, "Hi, I'm fantastic in bed." That's Telemarketing.

You're at a party and see a gorgeous girl. You get up and straighten your tie, you walk up to her and pour her a drink. You open the door for her, pick up her bag after she drops it, offer her a ride, and then say, "By the way, I'm fantastic in bed."

That's Public Relations.

You're at a party and see a gorgeous girl. She walks up to you and says, I hear you're fantastic in bed."

That's Brand Recognition.

All the organs of the body were having a meeting, trying to decide who was the one in charge.

"I should be in charge," said the brain, "because I run all the body's systems, so without me nothing would happen".

"I should be in charge" said the blood, "because I circulate oxygen all over, so without me you'd all waste away."

"I should be in charge," said the stomach, "because I process food and give all of you energy."

"I should be in charge," said the legs, "because I carry the body wherever it needs to go."

"I should be in charge," said the eyes, "because I allow the body to see where it goes."

"I should be in charge," said the rectum, "because I'm responsible for waste removal."

All the other body parts laughed at the rectum and insulted him. So in a huff, he shut down tight. Within a few days, the brain had a terrible headache, the stomach was bloated, the legs got wobbly, the eyes got watery and the blood was toxic. They all decided that the rectum should be the boss.

The Moral of the story?

The asshole is usually in charge.

A businessman tells his friend that his company is looking for a new accountant.

His friend asks, "Didn't your company hire a new accountant a few weeks ago?"

The businessman replies, "That's the accountant we're looking for."

We've just been informed that the Internal Revenue Service has simplified its 1040 forms for next year in the spirit of becoming a "kinder, gentler" IRS. It goes like this:

(A) How much did you make last year?______

(B) How much do you have left?______

(C) Send in amount on line B.

Q: What is the definition of an accountant?

A: Someone who solves a problem, you didn't know you had, in a way you don't understand.

Q: What does an accountant do for birth control?

A: He talks about his business.

Q: What is an extroverted accountant?

A: One who looks at your shoes while he's talking to you instead of his own.

Q: What is an insolvency practitioner?

A: Someone who arrives after the battle and bayonets all the wounded.

Q: Why did the auditor cross the road?

A: Because he looked in the file and that's what they did last year.

Q: What do accountants suffer from that ordinary people don't?

A: Depreciation.

Q: What is the difference between a lawyer and an accountant?

A: The accountant knows he is boring.

Q: How was copper wire invented?

A: Two accountants were arguing over a penny.

Q: When does a person decide to become an accountant?

A: When he realizes he doesn't have the charisma to succeed as an undertaker.

Q: What's the definition of a good tax accountant?

A: Someone who has a loophole named after him.

Q: What's an accountant's idea of trashing his/her hotel room?

A: Refusing to fill out the guest comment card.

Q: What's a shy and retiring accountant?

A: An accountant who is a half a million shy and that's why he's retiring.

Q: What's an actuary?

A: An accountant without the sense of humor.

Q: Why do some accountants decide to become actuaries?

A: They find bookkeeping too exciting.

Q: What is GAAP (generally accepted accounting principles)?

A: The difference between accounting theory and practice.

Top 20 Sayings we'd like to see on those office inspirational posters:

1. Rome did not create a great empire by having meetings, they did it by killing all people who opposed them.
2. If you can stay calm, while all around you is chaos . . . then you probably haven't completely understood the seriousness of the situation.
3. Doing a job RIGHT the first time gets the job done. Doing the job WRONG fourteen times gives you job security.
4. Eagles may soar, but weasels don't get sucked into jet engines.
5. Artificial Intelligence is no match for Natural Stupidity
6. A person who smiles in the face of adversity . . . probably has a scapegoat.
7. Plagiarism saves time.
8. If at first you don't succeed, try management.
9. Never put off until tomorrow what you can avoid all together.
10. TEAMWORK . . . means never having to take all the blame yourself.
11. The beatings will continue until morale improves.
12. Never underestimate the power of very stupid people in large groups.
13. We waste time, so you don't have to.
14. Hang in there, retirement is only fifty years away!
15. Go the extra mile. It makes your boss look like an incompetent slacker.

16. A snooze button is a no substitute for no alarm clock at all.
17. When the going gets tough, the tough take a coffee break.
18. INDECISION is the key to FLEXIBILITY.

Boss Asks Employee:
"Do you believe that there is life after death?"
Employee Answers:
"Certainly not, there's no proof of it", he replied.
Boss Tells Employee:
"Well, there is now. After you left early yesterday to go to your brother's funeral, he came here looking for you."

MEDICAL JOKES

Doctor Ricciardi who was known for miraculous cures for arthritis had a waiting room full of people when a little old lady, completely bent over in half, shuffled in slowly, leaning on her cane. When her turn came, she went into the doctor's office, and, amazingly, emerged within half an hour walking completely erect with her head held high.

A woman in the waiting room who had seen all this walked up to the little old lady and said, "It's a miracle! You walked in bent in half and now you're walking erect. What did that doctor do?"

She answered, "Miracle, shmiracle. . he gave me a longer cane."

Q: I've heard that cardiovascular exercise can prolong life; is this true?

A: Your heart is only good for so many beats, and that's it . . . don't waste them on exercise. Everything wears out eventually. Speeding up your heart will not make you live longer; that's like saying you can extend the life of your car by driving it faster. Want to live longer? Take a nap.

Q: Should I cut down on meat and eat more fruits and vegetables?

A: You must grasp logistical efficiencies. What does a cow eat? Hay and corn! And what are these? Vegetables! So a steak is nothing more than an efficient mechanism of delivering vegetables to your system. Need grain? Eat chicken. Beef is also a good source of field grass (green leafy vegetable). And a pork chop can give you 100% of your recommended daily allowance of vegetable products.

Q: Should I reduce my alcohol intake?

A: No, not at all. Wine is made from fruit. Brandy is distilled wine, that means they take the water out of the fruit so you get even more of the goodness that way. Beer is also made out of grain. Bottoms up!

Q: How can I calculate my body/fat ratio?

A: Well, if you have a body and you have fat, your ratio is one to one. If you have two bodies, your ratio is two to one, etc.

Q: What are some of the advantages of participating in a regular exercise program?

A: Can't think of a single one, sorry. My philosophy is: No Pain . . . Good!

Q: Aren't fried foods bad for you?

A: YOU'RE NOT LISTENING!!! . . . Foods are fried these days in vegetable oil. In fact, they're permeated in it. How could getting more vegetables be bad for you?

Q: Will sit-ups help prevent me from getting a little soft around the middle?

A: Definitely not! When you exercise a muscle, it gets bigger. You should only be doing sit-ups if you want a bigger stomach.

Q: Is chocolate bad for me?

A: Are you crazy? HELLO Cocoa beans! Another vegetable!!! It's the best feel-good food around!

Q: Is swimming good for your figure?

A: If swimming is good for your figure, explain whales to me.

A guy is going on an ocean cruise, and he tells his doctor that he's worried about getting seasick. The doctor says, "Just eat two pounds of stewed tomatoes before you leave the dock." The guy says, "Will that keep me from getting sick, Doc?" The doctor says, "No, but it'll look real pretty in the water."

A guy goes in to see a psychiatrist. He says, "Doc, I can't seem to make any friends. Can you help me, you fat slob?"

Jim and Edna were both patients in a mental hospital. One day while they were walking past the hospital swimming pool, Jim suddenly jumped into the deep end. He sank to the bottom of the pool and stayed there. Edna promptly jumped in to save him. She swam to the bottom and pulled Jim out.

When the head doctor became aware of Edna's heroic act she immediately ordered her to be discharged from the hospital, as she now considered her to be mentally stable. When she went to tell Edna the news she said, "Edna, I have good news and bad news. The good news is you're being discharged, since you were able to rationally respond to a crisis by jumping in and saving the life of the person you love, I have concluded that your act displays sound mindedness.

The bad news is, Jim, hung himself in the bathroom with his bathrobe belt right after you saved him. I am so sorry, but he's dead." Edna replied, "He didn't hang himself. I put him there to dry." "How soon can I go home?"

A man was just waking up from anesthesia after surgery, and his wife was sitting by his side. His eyes fluttered open and he said, "You're beautiful." Then he fell asleep again.

His wife had never heard him say that, so she stayed by his side. A few minutes later, his eyes fluttered open and he said, "You're cute!"

The wife was disappointed because instead of "beautiful," it was now "cute." She said, "What happened to 'beautiful'?"

The man replied, "The drugs are wearing off!"

The famous sex therapist was on the radio taking questions when a caller asked,

"Doctor, I want to know, why do men always want to marry a virgin?" To which the doctor handily responded, "To avoid criticism."

A cardiologist died and was given an elaborate funeral. A huge heart covered in flowers stood behind the casket during the service. Following the eulogy, the heart opened, and the casket rolled inside.

The heart then closed, sealing the doctor in the beautiful heart.

At that point, one of the mourners burst into laughter. When all eyes stared at him, he said, "I'm sorry, I was just thinking of my own funeral. I'm a gynecologist".

A sweet grandmother telephoned Mount Sinai Hospital.

She timidly asked, "Is it possible to speak to someone who can tell me how a patient is doing?"

The operator said "I'll be glad to help, Dear. What's the name and room number?"

The grandmother in her weak tremulous voice said, "Mary Schwartz, room 302."

The Operator replied, "Let me check. Oh, good news. Her records say that Mary is doing very well. Her blood pressure is fine; her blood work just came back as normal and her physician, Dr. Cohen, has scheduled her to be discharged Tuesday."

The Grandmother said, "Thank you. That's wonderful!, I was so worried! God bless you for the good news."

The operator replied, "You're more than welcome. Is Mary your daughter?"

The Grandmother said, "No, I'm Mary Schwartz in 302. No one tells me anything.

A physician claimed that the following are actual comments made by his patients (predominantly male) while he was performing their colonoscopies:

1. "Take it easy, Doc. You're boldly going where no man has gone before."
2. "Find Amelia Earhart yet?"
3. "Can you hear me NOW?"
4. "Oh boy! That was sphincterrific!"
5. "Are we there yet? Are we there yet? Are we there yet?"

6. "You know, in Arkansas we're now legally married."
7. "Any sign of the trapped miners. Chief?"
8. "You put your left hand in, you take your left hand out . . . "
9. "Hey! Now I know how a Muppet feels!"
10. "If your hand doesn't fit, you must quit!"
11. "Hey Doc, let me know if you find my dignity."
12. Could you write a note for my wife saying that my head is, in fact, not up there.

A lady walked into a pharmacy and spoke to the pharmacist. She asked, "Do you have Viagra?"

"Yes," he answered.

She asked, "Does it work?"

"Yes," he answered.

"Can you get it over the counter?" she asked.

"I can if I take two," he answered.

A man went to the pharmacy to pick up his Viagra prescription and exclaimed over the $10/pill price.

His wife, who was with him, had a different opinion: "Oh, $40 a year isn't too bad."

A patient complained to his doctor, "I've been to three other doctors and none of them agreed with your diagnosis."

The doctor calmly replied, "Just wait until the autopsy, then they'll see that I was right."

An elderly man went to his doctor and said, "Doc, I think I'm getting senile. Several times lately, I have forgotten to zip up."

"That's not senility," replied the doctor. "Senility is when you forget to zip, down."

A guy falls asleep on the beach for several hours and gets a horrible sunburn. He is taken to the hospital by ambulance and is promptly admitted after being diagnosed with second degree burns.

With his skin already starting to blister and noting the severe pain he is in, the doctor prescribes continuous intravenous feeding with saline, electrolytes, a sedative and a Viagra pill every four hours.

The nurse, who is rather astounded, asks, "What good will Viagra do for him now, Doctor?"

"It'll keep the sheets off his legs."

The owner of this drug store walks in to find a guy leaning heavily against a wall. The owner asks the clerk: "What's with that guy over there by the wall?"

The clerk responds: "Well, he came in there this morning to get something for his cough. I couldn't find the cough syrup, I gave him an entire bottle of laxative."

The owner, wide-eyed and excited shouts:

"You idiot! You can't treat a cough with a bottle of laxatives!" The clerk calmly responds: "Of course you can!

Look at him; he's afraid to cough!"

Joe had been having headaches for many years and his wife finally convinced him to see a neurologist.

The doctor said, "Joe, the good news is I can cure your headaches. The bad news is that, it will require castration. You have a very rare condition which causes your testicles to press on your spine, and the pressure creates one hell of a headache. The only way to relieve the pressure is to remove the testicles." Joe was shocked, and depressed. He wondered if he had anything to live for. He had no choice but to go under the knife.

When he left the hospital, he was without a headache for the first time in 20 years, but he felt like he was missing an important part of himself. As he walked down the street; he realized that he felt like a different person. He could make a new beginning, and live a new life. He saw a men's clothing store and thought, "That's what I need. . . a new suit." He entered the shop, and & told the salesman "I'd like a new suit."

The elderly salesman eyed him briefly, and said, "Let's see size 44 long."

Joe laughed, "That's right, how did you know?"

"Been in the business 60 years," the salesman said. Joe tried on the suit. It fit perfectly. As Joe admired himself in the mirror, the salesman asked, "How about a new shirt?"

Joe thought of a moment, and then said, "Sure."

The salesman eyed Joe, and said, "Let's see, 3 sleeves and 16 1/2 neck."

Joe was surprised, "That's right how did you know?"

"Been in the business 60 years." Joe tried on the shirt and it fit perfectly.

He walked comfortably around the shop, and the salesman asked, "How about some new underwear?"

Joe thought for a moment and said, "Sure." The salesman said, "Let's see . . . size 36."

Joe laughed, "Ah, ha, I've got you, I've worn a size 34 since I was 18 years old."

The salesman shook his head, "You can't wear a size 34. A size 34 would press your testicles up against the base of your spine and give you one hell of a headache."

When I was pregnant with my second child, I was certain that I wanted an epidural for pain management during childbirth. My doctor asked me at which stage of labor did I want the epidural administered.

I responded: "Just meet me in the parking lot!"

MEDICAL INSURANCE EXPLAINED

Q. What does HMO stand for?

A. This is actually a variation to the phrase, "HEY MOE". tTs roots go back to a concept pioneered by Moe of the Three Stooges, who discovered that a patient could be made to forget the pain in his foot if he was poked hard enough in the eye.

Q.I just joined an HMO. How difficult will it be to choose the doctor I want?

A. Just slightly more difficult, than choosing your parents. Your insurer will provide you with a book listing all the doctors in the plan. The doctors basically fall into two categories: those who are no longer accepting new patients, and those who will see you but are no longer participating in the plan. But don't worry, the remaining doctor who is still in the plan and accepting new patients has an office just a half-day's drive away and a diploma from a third world country.

Q. Do all diagnostic procedures require pre-certification?

A. No. Only those you need.

Q. Can I get coverage for my preexisting conditions?

A. Certainly, as long as they don't require any treatment.

Q. What happens if I want to try alternative forms of medicine?

A. You'll need to find alternative forms of payment.

Q. My pharmacy plan only covers generic drugs, but I need the name brand. I tried the generic medication, but it gave me a stomach ache. What should I do?

A. Poke yourself in the eye.

Q. What if I'm away from home and I get sick?

A. You really shouldn't do that.

Q. I think I need to see a specialist, but my doctor insists he can handle my problem. Can a general practitioner really perform a heart transplant right in his office?

A. Hard to say, but considering that all you're risking is the $20 co-payment, there's no harm in giving it a shot.

Q. Will health care be different in the next decade?

A. No, but if you call right now, you might get an appointment by then.

A couple of old gents were golfing one day, when one of the men mentioned that he was going to go to Dr. Markow for a new set of dentures in the morning.

His elderly friend remarked that he, too, had gone to the very same dentist two years before.

"Is that so?" The first old gentleman asked. "Did he do a good job?"

The second gent replied, "Well, I was on the golf course yesterday when a fellow on the next fairway hooked a shot. The ball must have been going at least 200 mph when it smacked me right in the testicles."

The first old guy was confused and asked, "What does that have to do with your dentures?"

The second man answered, "That was the first time in two yeas that my teeth didn't hurt."

A woman found out that her dog could hardly hear, so she took it to the veterinarian. He found that the problem was hair in its ears. He cleaned both ears and the dog could hear fine The vet then proceeded to tell that lady that, if she wanted to keep this from recurring, she should go to the store and get some 'Nair' hair remover and rub it in the dog's ears once a month.

The lady goes to the drug store and gets some 'Nair' hair remover. At the register, the druggist tells her, "If you're going to use this under your arms, don't use deodorant for a few days.'

The lady says: 'I'm not using it under my arms.'

The druggist says: 'If you're using it on your legs, don't shave for a couple of days.'

The lady says: 'I'm not using it on my legs either. If you must know, I'm using it on my Schnauzer.'

The druggist says: 'Stay off your bicycle for a week.

Two women were sitting in the doctor's waiting room comparing notes on their various disorders.

"I want a baby more than anything in the world," said the first, "But I guess it is impossible."

"I used to feel just the same way," said the second. "But then everything changed. That's why I'm here. I'm going to have a baby in three months."

"You must tell me what you did."

"I went to a faith healer."

"But I've tried that. My husband and I went to one for nearly a year and it didn't help a bit."

The other woman smiled and whispered, "Try going alone, next time, dearie."

This woman rushed to see her doctor, looking very much worried and all strung out. She rattles off: "Doctor, take a look at me. When I woke up this morning, I looked at myself in the mirror and saw my hair all wiry and frazzled up, my skin was all wrinkled and pasty, my eyes were bloodshot and bugging out, and I had this corpse-like look on my face! What's WRONG with me, Doctor!?"

The doctor looks her over for a couple of minutes, then calmly says: "Well, I can tell you that there's nothing wrong with your eyesight. . . ."

A man goes to a shrink and says, "Doctor, my wife is unfaithful to me. Every evening, she goes to Larry's bar and picks up men. In fact, She sleeps with anybody who asks her! I'm going crazy. What do you think I should do?" "Relax," says the Doctor, "Take a deep breath and calm down. Now, tell me, exactly where is Larry's bar?"

First year students at Medical School were receiving their first anatomy class with a real dead human body.

They all gathered around the surgery table with the body covered with a white sheet. The professor started the class by telling them, "In medicine, it is necessary to have two important qualities as a doctor. The first is that you should not be disgusted by anything involving the human body."

The Professor pulled back the sheet, stuck his finger in the anus of the corpse, withdrew it and stuck it in his mouth.

"Go ahead and do the same thing," he told his students. The students initially freaked out, hesitated for several minutes, but eventually took turns sticking a finger in the anus of the corpse and sucking on it.

When everyone finished, the Professor looked at the class and told them, "The second most important quality is observation. I stuck in my middle finger but sucked on my index finger. Now learn to pay attention!"

A middle-aged woman seemed sheepish as she visited her gynecologist.

"Come now," coaxed the doctor, "you've been seeing me for yeas. There's nothing you can't tell me."

"This one's kind of strange . . ."

"Let me be the judge of that," the doctor replied.

"Well," she said, "yesterday I went to the bathroom in the morning and I heard a plink-plink in the toilet; when I looked down, the water was full of pennies."

"I see."

"That afternoon I went again and there were nickels in the bowl."

"Uh-hu."

"That night," she went on, "there were dimes and this morning there were quarters!

You've got to tell me what's wrong with me!" she implored, "I'm scared out of my wits!" The gynecologist put a comforting hand on her shoulder. "There, there, it's nothing to be scared about . . ."

"You're simply going through your change."

Patient: I'm in a hospital! Why am I in here?

Doctor: You've had an accident involving a bus.

Patient: What happened?

Doctor: Well, I've got some good news and some bad news. Which would you like to hear first?

Patient: Give me the bad news first.

Doctor: Your legs were injured so badly that we had to amputate both of them.

Patient: That's terrible! What's the good news?

Doctor: There's a guy in the next ward who made a very good offer on your shoes.

This old man visits his doctor and after a thorough examination, the doctor tells him, "I have good news and bad news, what would you like to hear first?"

Patient: Well, give me the bad news first.

Doctor: You have cancer, I estimate that you have about two years left.

Patient: That's terrible! In two years, my life will be over! What kind of good news could you probably tell me, after this?

Doctor: You also have Alzheimer's. In about three months you are going to forget everything I told you.

A dentist, after completing work on a patient, came to him begging.

Dentist: Could you help me? Could you give out a few of your loudest, most painful screams?

Patient: Why? Doctor, it wasn't all that bad this time.

Dentist: There are so many people in the waiting room right now, and I don't want to miss the four o'clock train.

A patient has a sore throat and goes to a doctor to get treatment for it.

Doctor: Your tonsils gotta come out.

Patient: I wanna second opinion.

Doctor: Okay, you're ugly, too.

HUSBAND/WIFE JOKES

On a visit to Chicago, a woman was eager to visit a posh department store about a dozen blocks from her hotel. Her husband obligingly hailed a cab. "The lady wants to go to Neiman Marcus," he told the driver.

The cabby looked over his shoulder at them. "And the gentleman?" he asked. "Does he want to go to the bank?"

A woman came home, screeching her car into the driveway, and ran into the house. She slammed the door and shouted at the top of her lungs, "Honey, pack your bags. I won the lottery!"

The husband said, "Oh my God! What should I pack, beach stuff or mountain stuff?"

"Doesn't matter," she said. "Just get out."

Jack wakes up with a huge hangover after attending his company's Christmas Party. Jack is not normally a drinker, but the drinks didn't taste like alcohol at all. He didn't even remember how he got home from the party. As bad as he was feeling, he wondered if he did something wrong.

Jack had to force himself to open his eyes, and the first thing he sees is a couple of aspirins next to a glass of water on the side table. And, next to them, a single red rose! Jack sits up and sees his clothing in front of him, all clean and pressed. He looks around the room and sees that it is in perfect order, spotlessly clean. So is the rest of the house.

He takes the aspirins, cringes when he sees a huge black eye staring back at him in the bathroom mirror. Then he notices a note hanging on the corner of the mirror written in red with little hearts on it and a kiss mark from his wife in lipstick:

"Honey, breakfast is on the stove. I left early to get groceries to make you your favorite dinner tonight. I love you, darling! Love, Mary"

He stumbles to the kitchen and sure enough, there is hot breakfast, steaming hot coffee and the morning newspaper. His son is also at the table, eating. Jack asks, "Son . . . what happened last night?"

"Well, you came home after 3 A.M., drunk and out of your mind. You fell over the coffee table and broke it, and then you puked in the hallway, and got that black eye when you ran into the door."

Confused, he asked his son, "So, why is everything in such perfect order and so clean? I have a rose, and breakfast is on the table waiting for me??"

His son replies, "Oh THAT! . . . Mom dragged you to the bedroom, and when she tried to take your pants off, you screamed, 'Leave me alone, I'm married!!' "

She spent the first day packing her belongings into boxes, crates and suitcases. On the second day, she had the movers come and collect her things. On the third day, she sat down for the last time at their beautiful dining room table by candle-light, put on some soft background music, and feasted on a pound of shrimp, a jar of caviar, and a bottle of spring-water.

When she had finished, she went into each and every room and deposited a few half-eaten shrimp shells dipped in caviar into the hollow of the curtain rods. She then cleaned up the kitchen and left. When the husband returned with his new girlfriend, all was bliss for the first few days. Then slowly, the house began to smell.

They tried everything; cleaning, mopping and airing the place out. Vents were checked for dead rodents and carpets were steam cleaned. Air fresheners were hung everywhere. Exterminators were brought in to set off gas canisters, during which they had to move out for a few days and in the end they even paid to replace the expensive wool carpeting. Nothing worked.

People stopped coming over to visit. Repairmen refused to work in the house. The maid quit. Finally, they could not take the stench any longer and decided to move. A month later, even though they had cut their price in half, they could not find a buyer for their stinky house. Word got out and eventually even the local realtors refused to return their calls. Finally, they had to borrow a huge sum of money from the bank to purchase a new place.

The ex-wife called the man and asked how things were going. He told her the saga of the rotting house. She listened politely and said that she missed her old home terribly and would be willing to reduce her divorce settlement in exchange for getting the house back. Knowing his ex-wife had no idea how bad the smell was, he agreed on a price that was about 1/2 of what the house had been worth, but only if she were to sign the papers that very day. She agreed and within the hour his lawyers delivered the paperwork.

A week later the man and his girlfriend stood smiling as they watched the moving company pack everything to take to their new home . . . and to spite the ex-wife, they even took the curtain rods!!!!!!

The old man had died. A wonderful funeral was in progress and the country preacher talked at length of the good traits of the deceased, what an honest man he was, and what a loving husband and kind father he was. Finally, the widow leaned over and whispered to one of her children, "Go up there and take a look in the coffin and see if that's your pa."

A man asked his wife to pack for him, for a weekend fishing trip. She gladly obliged with clothes, toiletries, and the fishing gear he asked for: rods, reels, tackle box. At the last moment, he said, "Please pack my new silk pajamas, would you?"

This made her somewhat suspicious, but she did as he asked. When he returned, looking very refreshed, she asked if he caught a lot of fish. "Oh, yes," he said, "three walleyes, four or five bass . . . it was great . . . but, you know, you forgot to pack my new silk pajamas."

She smiled. "No, I didn't. They're in your tackle box."

A man is at work one day when he notices that his co-worker is wearing an earring. This man knows his co-worker to be a normally conservative fellow, and is curious about his sudden change in "fashion sense." The man walks up to him and says, "I didn't know you were into earrings."

"Don't make sure a big deal, it's only an earring," he replies sheepishly.

His friend falls silent for a few minutes, but then his curiosity prods him to say, "So, how long have you been wearing one?"

"Ever since my wife found it in my truck."

Jeff just found out that his wife is pregnant. He did the math, and according to her due date, Jeff was out of town at the time of conception.

He was amazed. He couldn't believe it. He will finally make it into the Guinness Book of World Records for impregnating his wife via phone sex!

The man approached a very beautiful woman in a large supermarket and asked, "I've lost my wife here in the supermarket. Can you talk to me for a couple of minutes?"

Woman: "Why?"

Man: "Because every time I talk to a beautiful woman, my wife appears out of nowhere."

Trying to sneak upstairs in the wee hours, the extremely drunk husband falls backwards down the many steps. He lands on his behind, smashing the two empty pints in his back pockets. So numb, he doesn't notice anything until he is undressing in the bathroom, and sees he has bloodied up his behind something terrible. He repairs the damage as best he can and sneaks into bed. Next morning, his wife wakes him up cheerfully, "Boy, you must've really tied one on last night."

"No way. I worked late and stopped for a couple beers, that's all!"

"OH, PLEASE!!"

"What? What makes you think I was drunk?":

"My first big clue?" replies the wife, "All the band-aids I found stuck to the bathroom mirror."

It was a terrible night, blowing cold and rain in a most frightful manner. The streets were deserted and the local baker was just about to close up shop when a little man slipped through the door. He carried an umbrella, blown inside out, and was bundled in two sweaters and a thick coat. But even so he still looked wet and bedraggled. As he unwound his scarf he said to the baker, "May I have two bagels to go, please?"

The baker in astonishment, "Two bagels? Nothing more?"

"That's right," answered the little man. "One for me and one for Gladys."

"Gladys is your wife?" asked the baker.

"What do you think," snapped the little man, "my mother would send me out on a night like this?"

The aged farmer and his wife were leaning against the edge of the pigpen when the old woman wistfully recalled that the next week would mark their golden wedding anniversary. "Let's have a party, Homer," she suggested. "Let's kill the pig."

The farmer scratched his grizzled beard. "Gee, Martha," he finally answered, "I don't see why the pig should take the blame for something that happened fifty years ago."

A man comes home from an exhausting day at work, plops down on the couch in front of the television, and tells his wife, "Get me a beer before it starts." The wife sighs and gets him a beer. Fifteen minutes later, he says, "Get me another beer before it starts." She looks cross, but fetches another beer and slams it down next to him. He finishes that beer and a few minutes later says, "Quick, get me another beer, it's going to start any minute."

The wife is furious. She yells at him, "Is that all you're going to do tonight? Drink beer and sit in front of that TV? You're nothing but a lazy, drunken, fat slob, and furthermore . . ."

The man sighs and says, "It's started . . ."

Sam had been a soldier at war for more than three years, during which he had been in many battles and won many decorations. He was finally discharged from service and returned home to a wife and son whom he hadn't seen in almost four years.

As he was walking up the path to his house, his young son spotted him and yelled, "Mommy, Mommy, here comes Daddy, and he's got a purple heart on!" to which the mother replied, "I don't give a damn what color it is! Let him in, and you go play at the Joneses' for a couple of hours."

A police officer pulls over a speeding car. The officer says, "I clocked you at 80 miles per hour, sir."

The driver says, "Gee, officer I had it on cruise control at 60, perhaps your radar gun needs calibrating."

Not looking up from her knitting the wife says: "Now don't be silly dear, you know that this car doesn't have cruise control."

As the officer writes out the ticket, the driver looks over at his wife and growls, "Can't you please keep your mouth shut for once?"

The wife smiles demurely and says, "You should be thankful your radar detector went off when it did."

As the officer makes out the second ticket for the illegal radar detector unit, the man glowers at his wife and says through clenched teeth, "Darn it, woman, can't you keep your mouth shut?"

The officer frowns and says, "And I notice that you're not wearing your seat belt, sir. That's an automatic $75 fine."

The driver says, "Yeah, well, you see officer, I had it on, but took it off when you pulled me over so that I could get my license out of my back pocket."

The wife says, "Now, dear, you know very well you didn't have your seat belt on. You never wear your seat belt when you're driving."

And as the police officer is writing out the third ticket the driver turns to his wife and barks, "WHY DON'T YOU PLEASE SHUT UP??"

The officer looks over at the woman and asks, "Does your husband always talk to you this way, Ma'am?"

"Only when he's been drinking."

A dog is truly a man's best friend. If you don't believe it, just try this experiment. Put your dog and your wife in the trunk of the car for an hour. When you open the trunk, which one is really happy to see you?

A woman walked into the kitchen to find her husband stalking around with a fly swatter. "What are you doing?" she asked.

"Hunting flies," he responded: "Oh, killing any?" she asked.

"Yep, 3 males, 2 females," he replied.

Intrigued, she asked.

"How can you tell them apart?"

He responded, "3 were on a beer can, 2 were on the phone."

A wife says to her husband, "Are you hungry for breakfast?" He replies, "No, it must be the Viagra." A few hours later, she says, "Do you want to eat lunch?" He answers, "No, it must be the Viagra." Later still, she asks him, "How about supper?" He replies, "No, it must be the Viagra." She says, "Get the Hell off me, I'm starving."

Fresh from my shower, I stand in front of the mirror, complaining to my husband that my breasts are too small. Instead of characteristically telling me it's not so, he uncharacteristically comes up with a suggestion: "If you want your breasts to grow, then every day take a piece of toilet paper and rub it between your breasts for a few seconds."

Willing to try anything, I fetch a piece of toilet paper and stand in front of the mirror, rubbing it between my breasts. "How long will this take?" I ask. "They will grow larger over a period of years," he replies.

I stop. "Do you really think rubbing a piece of toilet paper between my breasts every day will make my breasts larger over the years?" Without missing a beat he says, "Worked for your butt, didn't it?"

"Cash, check or charge?" the clerk asked, after folding items the woman wished to purchase. As she fumbled for her wallet he noticed a remote control for a television set in her purse.

"So, do you always carry your TV remote?" he asked.

"No," she replied, "but my husband refused to come shopping with me, so I figured this was the most evil thing I could do to him."

While attending a Marriage Seminar dealing with communication, Tom and his wife, Grace, listened to the instructor: "It is essential that husbands and wives know the things that are important to each other." He addressed the man, "Can you describe your wife's favorite flower?"

Tom leaned over, touched his wife's arm gently and whispered, "It's Pillsbury, isn't it?"

A man walks into a pharmacy and wanders up and down the aisles. The sales girl notices him and asks him if she can help him. He answers that he is looking for a box of tampons for his wife. She directs him down the correct aisle. A few minutes later, he deposits a huge bag of cotton balls and a ball of string on the counter. She says, confused, "Sir, I thought you were looking for some tampons for your wife?"

He answers, "You see, it's like this. Yesterday, I sent my wife to the store to get me a carton of cigarettes, and she came back with a tin of tobacco and some rolling papers—cause it's sooooo much cheaper. So, I figure if I have to roll my own . . . so does she.

A couple drove down a country road for several miles, not saying a word. An earlier discussion had led to an argument and neither of them wanted to concede their position. As they passed a barnyard of mules, goats, and pigs, the husband asked sarcastically, "Relatives of yours?"

"Yep," the wife replied, "in-laws."

A husband read an article to his wife about how many words women use a day . . . 30,000 to a man's 15,000. The wife replied, "The reason has to be because we have to repeat everything to men . . ." The husband then turned to his wife and asked, "What?"

A man said to his wife one day, "I don't know how you can be so stupid and so beautiful all at the same time." The wife responded, "Allow me to explain. God made me beautiful so you would be attracted to me; God made me stupid so I would be attracted to you!"

Husband and wife were in the midst of a violent quarrel, and hubby was losing his temper. "Be careful," he said to his wife. "You will bring out the beast in me." "So what?" his wife shot back, "Who is afraid of a mouse?"

A man and his wife were having an argument about who should brew the coffee each morning. The wife said, "You should do it, because you get up first, and then we don't have to wait as long to get our coffee."

The husband said, "You are in charge of cooking around here and you should do it, because that is your job, and I can just wait for my coffee."

Wife replies, "No, you should do it, and besides, it is in the Bible that the man should do the coffee."

Husband replies, "I can't believe that, show me."

So she fetched the Bible, and opened the New Testament and showed him at the top of several pages, that it indeed says . . . . . . "HEBREWS"

There was a man who worked all his life, had saved all of his money, and was a real "miser" when it came to his money. Just before he died, he said to his wife . . . "When I die, I want you to take all my money and put it in the casket with me. I want to take my money to the afterlife with me." And so he got his wife to promise him, with all of her heart, that when he died, she would put all of the money into the casket with him.

Well, he died. He was stretched out in the casket, his wife was sitting there dressed in black, and her friend was sitting next to her. When they finished the ceremony, and just before the undertakers got ready to close the casket, the wife said, "Wait just a moment!" She had a small metal box with her; she came over with the box and put it in the casket. Then the undertakers locked the casket down and they rolled it away. So her friend said, "Girl, I know you were not fool enough to put all the money in there with your husband."

The loyal wife replied, "Listen, I'm a Christian; I cannot go back on my word. I promised him that I was going to put that money into the casket with him."

"You mean to tell me you put that money in the casket with him!?!?"

"I sure did," said the wife. "I got it all together, put it into my account, and wrote him a check . . . If he can cash it, then he can spend it."

Bob works hard at the plant and spends two nights each week bowling and plays golf every Saturday. His wife thinks he's pushing himself too hard, so for his birthday she takes him to a local strip club.

The doorman at the club greets them and says, "Hey, Bob! How ya doin'?" His wife is puzzled and asks if he's been to this club before. "Oh, no," says Bob. "He's on my bowling team."

When they are seated, a waitress asks Bob if he'd like his usual and brings over a Budweiser. His wife is becoming increasingly uncomfortable and says, "How did she know that you drink Budweiser?"

"I recognize her, she's the waitress from the golf club. I always have a Bud at the end of the 1st nine, honey."

A stripper then comes over to their table, throws her arms around Bob, starts to rub herself all over him and says, "Hi Bobby. Want your usual table dance, big boy?"

Bob's wife, now furious, grabs her purse and storms out of the club. Bob follows and spots her getting into a cab. Before she slams the door, he jumps in beside her. Bob tries desperately to explain how the stripper must have mistaken him for someone else, but his wife is having none of it. She is screaming at him at the top of her lungs, calling him every 4-letter word in the book.

The cabby turns around and says, "Geez Bob, you picked up a real bitch this time."

Dear Abby:

My husband is not happy with my mood swings. The other day, he bought me a mood ring so he would be able to monitor my moods. When I'm in a good mood it turns green. When I'm in a bad mood it leaves a big red mark on his forehead. Maybe next time he'll buy me a diamond.

Sincerely,
Bitchy in Boston

Harry is unable to perform sexually. He goes to his doctor who tries a few things. Nothing works, so the doctor refers him to an

American Indian medicine man. The medicine man says, “I can cure this.” He throws a white powder in a flame. There is a flash of billowing blue smoke. He says, “This is powerful medicine. You can only use it once a year. You say ‘123’ and it will rise for as long as you wish.”

The guy asks, “What happens when it’s over, and I don’t want to continue?”

The medicine man replies, “All you or your partner has to say is ‘1234’ and it will go down. But be warned, it will not work again for another year.”

Harry rushes home, eager to try out his new powers and prowess. That night, ready to surprise Mary, he showers, shaves, and puts on an exotic shaving lotion. He gets into bed, and lying next to her, says “123.”

He suddenly becomes more aroused than anytime in his life, just as the medicine man had promised. Mary, who had been facing away, turns over and asks, “What did you say 123 for?” And that is why you should never end a sentence with a preposition.

Husband and wife in bed together. She feels his hand rubbing her shoulder.

She: “Oh, that feels good.” His hand moves to her breast.

“Gee, honey, that feels wonderful.” His hand moves to her leg.

“She: Oh, honey, don’t stop.”

But he stops.

She: “Why did you stop?”

He: “I found the remote.”

A woman arrived at the Gates of Heaven. While she was waiting for Saint Peter to greet her, she peeked through the gates. She saw a beautiful banquet table. Sitting all around were her parents and all the other people she had loved and who had died before her. They saw her and began calling greetings to her, “Hello - How are you! We’ve been waiting for you! Good to see you.”

When Saint Peter came by, the woman said to him, “This is such a wonderful place! How do I get in?”

"You have to spell a word," Saint Peter told her.

"Which word?" the woman asked.

"Love." The woman correctly spelled "Love" and Saint Peter welcomed her into Heaven. About a year later, Saint Peter came to the woman and asked her to watch the Gates of Heaven for him that day. While the woman was guarding the Gates of Heaven, her husband arrived. "I'm surprised to see you," the woman said. "How have you been?"

"Oh, I've been doing pretty well since you died," her husband told her. "I married the beautiful young nurse who took care of you while you were ill. And then I won the multi-state lottery. I sold the little house you and I lived in and bought a huge mansion. And my wife and I traveled all around the world. We were on vacation in Cancun and I went water skiing today. I fell and hit my head, and here I am. What a bummer! How do I get in?"

"You have to spell a word," the woman told him.

"Which word?" her husband asked.

"Czechoslovakia."

A funeral service is being held for a woman who has just passed away. At the end of the service, the pall bearers are carrying the casket out when they accidentally bump into a wall, jarring the casket. They hear a faint moan. They open the casket and find that the woman is actually alive! She lives for ten more years, and then dies. Once again, a ceremony is held, and at the end of it, the pall bearers are again carrying out the casket. As they carry the casket towards the door, the husband cries out, "Watch that wall!"

A husband in his back yard is trying to fly a kite. He throws the kite up in the air, the wind catches it for a few seconds, then it comes crashing back down to earth. He tries this a few more times with no success. All the while, his wife is watching from the kitchen window, muttering to herself how men need to be told how to do everything. She opens the window and yells to her husband, "You need a piece of tail." The man turns with a confused look on his face and says, "Make up your mind. Last night, you told me to go fly a kite."

An 80-year-old woman was arrested for shop lifting. When she went before the judge he asked her, "What did you steal?"

She replied: "a can of peaches." The judge asked her why she had stolen them and she replied that she was hungry. The judge then asked her how many peaches were in the can. She replied 6. The judge then said, "I will give you 6 days in jail."

Before the judge could actually pronounce the punishment the woman's husband spoke up and asked the judge if he could say something. He said, "What is it?"

The husband said, "She also stole a can of peas."

Three men were sitting together, bragging about how they had given their new wives duties. The first man had married a woman from Indiana. He bragged that he had told his wife she was going to do all the dishes and house cleaning that needed to be done at their house. He said that it took a couple of days, but on the third day he came home to a clean house, and the dishes were all washed and put away.

The second man had married a woman from Utah. He bragged that he had given his wife orders that she was to do all the cleaning, dishes, and the cooking. He told them that the first day he didn't see any results, but the next day it was better. By the third day, his house was clean, the dishes were done, and he had a huge dinner on the table.

The third man had married a Long Island girl. He said that he told her that her duties were to keep the house cleaned, dishes washed, lawn mowed, laundry washed, and hot foods on the table for every meal. He said the first day he didn't see anything, the second day he didn't see anything, but by the third day most of the swelling had gone down and he could see a little out of his left eye, just enough to fix himself a bite to eat, load the dishwasher, and telephone a landscaper.

John was on his deathbed and gasped pitifully. "Give me one last request, dear," he said.
"Of course, John," his wife said softly.
"Six months after I die," he said, "I want you to marry Bob."
"But I thought you hated Bob," she said.
With his last breath John said, "I do!"

An old man goes to the Wizard to ask him if he can remove a curse he has been living with for the last 40 years. The Wizard says, "Maybe, but you will have to tell me the exact words that were used to put the curse on you."
The old man says without hesitation, "I now pronounce you man and wife."

A wife was making a breakfast of fried eggs for her husband. Suddenly, her husband burst into the kitchen. "Careful," he said, "CAREFUL! Put in some more butter! Oh my GOD! You're cooking too many at once. TOO MANY! Turn them! TURN THEM NOW! We need more butter. Oh my GOD! WHERE are we going to get MORE BUTTER? They're going to STICK! Careful . . . CAREFUL! I said be CAREFUL! You NEVER listen to me when you're cooking! Never! turn them! Hurry up! Are you CRAZY? Have you LOST your mind? Don't forget to salt them. You know you always forget to salt them. Use the salt. USE THE SALT!!! THE SALT! THE SALT"!!!
The wife stared at him. "What in the world is wrong with you? You think I don't know how to fry a couple of eggs?"
The husband calmly replied, "I wanted to show you what it feels like when I'm driving."

One day, a man came home and was greeted by his wife dressed in a very sexy nightie. "Tie me up," she purred, "and you can do anything you want." So he tied her up and went fishing.

Saturday morning a man got up early, dressed quietly, slipped into the garage to load his clubs into the car, and proceeded to back out into a torrential down pour. There was snow mixed with the rain, and the wind was blowing 50 mph.

He pulled back into the garage, turned on the radio, and discovered that the weather would be bad throughout the day. He went back into the house, quietly undressed, and slipped back into bed. There he cuddled up to his wife's back, now with a different anticipation, and whispered, "The weather out there is terrible."

She sleepily replied, "Can you believe my stupid husband is out golfing in that shit."

A man dies "in the act" after taking Viagra and rigor mortis has set into his private parts. The funeral director can't get the coffin lid nailed on and has to discuss the alternatives with the man's beautiful young widow. "I'm afraid that the only way to get the lid on is either to pay about $3,000 for an extra large coffin or to amputate his member."

"Well, I have no more money," states the widow, "and it is against my religion for me to bury him in more than one piece."

The funeral director thinks about this and then comes up with the brain-wave: He'll amputate the member and then stick it up the deceased's backside, in which case a more expensive coffin is unnecessary and the husband will still be, in a manner of speaking, in the one piece. The widow reluctantly agrees.

On the day of the funeral, the deceased is displayed in an open casket. As the mourners file by, one mourner places flowers on the coffin and a drop of water from the flowers falls onto the deceased's face, looking for all the world like a teardrop.

The next mourner to file by is the widow. She looks down at her lifeless husband, notices the "teardrop" and says to him quietly, "See, I told you it hurts!"

Bob was in trouble. He forgot his wedding anniversary. His wife was really pissed. She told him "Tomorrow morning, I expect to find a gift in the driveway that goes from 0 to 200 in 6 seconds AND IT BETTER BE THERE!!"

The next morning he got up early and left for work. When his wife woke up, she looked out the window and sure enough there was a box gift-wrapped in the middle of the driveway. Confused, the wife put on her robe and ran out to the driveway, brought the box back in the house. She opened it and found a brand new bathroom scale.

Bob has been missing since Friday.

A very elderly couple is having an elegant dinner to celebrate their 50th wedding anniversary. The old man leans forward and says softly to his wife, "Dear, there is something that I must ask you. It has always bothered me that our tenth child never quite looked like the rest of our children. Now I want to assure you that these 50 years have been the most wonderful experience I could have ever hoped for, and your answer cannot take that all away. But, I must know, did he have a different father?"

The wife drops her head, unable to look her husband in the eye, she paused for moment and then confessed. "Yes. Yes, he did."

The old man is very shaken, the reality of what his wife was admitting hit him harder than he had expected. With a tear in his eye he asks, "Who? Who was he? Who was the father?"

Again, the old woman drops her head, saying nothing at first as she tried to muster the courage to tell the truth to her husband. Then, finally, she says: "You."

A woman pregnant with her first child paid a visit to her obstetrician's office. After the exam, she shyly said, "My husband wants me to ask you . . . ," to which the doctor replies, "I know, I know," placing a reassuring hand on her shoulder. "I get asked that all the time. Sex is fine until late in the pregnancy."

"No, that's not it," the woman confessed. "He wants to know if I can still mow the lawn."

At Saint Mary's Catholic Church they have a weekly husband's marriage seminar. At the session last week, the Priest asked Luigi, who was approaching his 50th wedding anniversary, to take a few minutes and share some insight into how he had managed to stay married to the same woman all these years.

Luigi replied to the assembled husbands. "Well, I've a-tried to treat-a her nice, spend the money on her, but best of all is that I took-a her to Italy for the 20th anniversary!"

The Priest responded, "Luigi, you are an amazing inspiration to all the husbands here! Please tell us what you are planning for your wife for your 50th anniversary."

Luigi proudly replied, "I'm a-gonna go and get her."

Three women: one engaged, one married, and one a mistress, are chatting about their relationships and decide to amaze their men . . . . that night all three will wear a black leather bra, stiletto's and a mask over their eyes. After a few days, they meet again.

The engaged girlfriend: "The other night, when my boyfriend came back home, he found me with the leather bodice, 5 inch stilettos and mask. He saw me and said: 'You are the woman of my life, I love you' . . . then we made love all night long."

The mistress: "Ah! Me, too. The other night I met my lover in the office and I was wearing the leather bodice, mega stilettos, mask over my eyes and a raincoat, when I opened the raincoat . . . he did not say anything . . . . but we had wild sex all night."

The married one: "The other night I sent the kids to stay at my mothers for the night. I got myself ready—leather bodice, super stilettos and mask over my eyes. My husband comes back from work, opens the door and says: 'Hi, Batman! What's for dinner?' "

A man walks into a bank, gets in line, an when it is his turn he pulls out a gun and robs the bank. To make sure he leaves no witnesses he turns around and asks the next customer in line, "Did you see me rob this bank?" The customer replies, "Yes," whereupon the robber shoots him in the head and kills him.

The robber quickly moves to the next customer in line and says to the man, "Did you see me rob this bank?" The man calmly responds, "No, but my wife did."

A woman awakes during the night to find that her husband was not in their bed. She puts on her robe and goes downstairs to look for him. She finds him sitting at the kitchen table with a hot cup of coffee in front of him. He appears to be in deep thought, just staring at the wall. She watches as he wipes a tear from his eye and takes a sip of his coffee.

"What's the matter, dear?" she whispers as she steps into the room. "Why are you down here at this time of night?"

The husband looks up from his coffee, "I am just remembering when we first met 20 years ago and started dating. You were only 16. Do you remember back then?" he asks solemnly.

The wife is touched to tears thinking that her husband is so caring, so sensitive. "Yes, I do" she replies.

The husband pauses. The words were not coming easily. "Do you remember when your father caught us in the back seat of my car?"

"Yes, I remember," said the wife, lowering herself into a chair beside him.

The husband continues. "Do you remember when he shoved the shotgun in my face and said, 'Either you marry my daughter, or I will send you to jail for 20 years?' "

"I remember that, too," she replies softly.

He wipes another tear from his cheek and says . . . "I would have gotten out today."

A Mexican maid asked for a pay increase. The wife was very upset about this and asked: "Now Maria, why do you think you deserve a pay increase?"

Maria: "Well, Senora. There are three reasons why I deserve a raise. The first is that I iron better than you."

Wife: "Who said you iron better than me?"

Maria: "Your husband said so."
Wife: "Oh."
Maria: "The second reason is that I am a better cook than you."
Wife: "Nonsense, who said you were a better cook than me?"
Maria: "Your husband did."
Wife: "Oh."
Maria: "My third reason is that I am a better lover than you."
Wife (really furious now): "Did my husband say that as well?"
Maria: "No, Senora. The gardener did."
She got the raise.

Two women friends had gone for a Girls Night Out, and had been decidedly over-enthusiastic on the cocktails. Incredibly drunk and walking home, they needed to pee. They were very near a graveyard and one of them suggested they do their business behind a head stone or something. The first woman had nothing to wipe with so she thought she'd take off her panties, use them, then throw them away.

Her friend, however, was wearing a rather expensive underwear set and didn't want to ruin hers but was lucky to salvage a large ribbon from a wreath that was on one of the graves and proceeded to wipe herself with that.

After finishing, they then made off for home. The next day the first woman's husband phoned the other husband and said, "These damn girls night out have got to stop. My wife came home last night without her panties."

"That's nothing," said the other husband. "Mine came back with a card stuck between the cheeks of her ass that said, 'From All of Us at the Fire Station, We'll Never Forget You.' "

This guy in a bar notices a woman, always alone, who comes in on a fairly regular basis. After the second week, he made his move. "No thank you," she said politely. "This may sound rather odd in this day and age, but I'm keeping myself pure until I meet the man I love."

"That must be rather difficult," the man replied.

"Oh, I don't mind too much," she said. "But, it has my husband pretty upset."

One evening a husband and wife were about to go to a costume party. The wife knew her husband was going to be dressed like Gumby, but she hadn't chosen her costume yet. When it was time to leave for the party the wife decided she wanted to stay home, because of her awful headache. But she insisted that her husband still go and have fun.

After he left she took a nap. She woke up an hour later and felt good enough to go to the party. When she got there she saw her husband (the only man dressed like Gumby) flirting and dancing with many girls. She got very upset, and decided to "test" him. She approached him (he, of course, doesn't recognise her). They started flirting and dancing. She was acting really sexual (for she knows it's her husband). Anyway, they end up having sex in the back of some car (no, he still doesn't realize who she is). When they're done he goes back to the party, but she races home. When at home she gets back in bed and starts reading a book (so as not to look suspicious). Not long after, he arrives home as usual.

She asks him how the party went, and he replies, "oh, you know, same old stuff. Me and the guys played cards and had a couple beers, but you gotta hear what happened to the guy who borrowed my costume . . .

My wife and I were watching "Who Wants to Be a Millionaire" while we were in bed. I turned to her and said, "Do you want to have sex?"

"No." she answered.

I then said, "Is that your final answer?"

"Yes." she replied.

Then I said, "I'd like to phone a friend."

That's the last thing I remember.

Couples who have lived together a long time have their own way of communicating. A woman overheard her aunt and uncle one day: "What are you looking for in that closet?" she asked. "Nothing," he answered. "Well, it's not in there. Look under the bed."

As husbands and wives will, from time to time, my wife and I were having the discussion about what would happen in the eventuality that one of us would predecease the other like . . . tomorrow night. The usual "would you remarry?" questions were asked and answered.

I asked my wife, "If there was a nuclear war tomorrow, and you were the last woman alive on the face of the Earth, would you help procreate the species? Assume there were 10 men that were a mixture of reasonably attractive, and totally repugnant."

My wife asked, "Are you alive or dead?"

"Where I was standing at the moment the war broke out is now a smoking hole," I informed her.

A few moments of consideration. "Yes, reluctantly, if I were the last woman on the face of the Earth, and the survival of the species depended on it, I'd have to do what was necessary."

I was wandering into the kitchen to refill my drink when I heard this, muttered under her breath: ". . . bet your ass, I'd set myself up as Queen, though."

The young girl said to her rather hip new priest, "Father, is it a sin to have sex before receiving Communion?"

The priest replied, "Only if you don't block the aisle."

A man placed some flowers on the grave of his dearly departed mother and started back toward his car when his attention was diverted to another man kneeling at a grave. The man seemed to be praying with profound intensity and kept repeating, "Why did you have to die? Why did you have to die?"

The first man approached him and said, "Sir, I don't wish to interfere with your private grief, but this demonstration of pain is more than I've ever seen before. For whom do you mourn so deeply? A child? A parent?"

The mourner took a moment to collect himself, then replied, "My wife's first husband."

What makes these questions so difficult is that every one is guaranteed to explode into a major argument if the man answers incorrectly (i.e., tells the truth). Therefore, as a public service, each question is analyzed below, along with possible responses.

QUESTION #1: WHAT ARE YOU THINKING ABOUT?

The proper answer to this, of course, "I'm sorry if I've been quiet dear. I was just reflecting on what a warm, wonderful, thoughtful, caring, intelligent woman you are, and how lucky I am to have met you."

This response obviously bears no resemblance to the true answer, which most likely is one of the following:

1. Hockey.
2. Sex.
3. How fat you are.
4. How much prettier she is than you.
5. How I would spend the insurance money if you died.

Perhaps the best response to this question was offered by Al Bundy, who once told Peg, "If I wanted you to know what I was thinking, I would be talking to you!"

Question #2: Do You Love Me?

The proper response is: "YES" or, if you feel a more detailed answer is in order, "Yes, dear."

Inappropriate responses include:

1. Oh Yeah, shit loads.
2. Would it make you feel better if I said yes?
3. That depends on what you mean by love.
4. Does it matter?
5. Who? Me?

Question #3: Do I Look Fat?

The correct answer is an emphatic: "Of course not!" Among the incorrect answers are:

1. Compared to what?
2. I wouldn't call you fat, but you're not exactly thin.
3. A little extra weight looks good on you.
4. I've seen fatter.
5. Could you repeat the question? I was just thinking about how I would spend the insurance money if you died.

Question #4: Do You Think She's Prettier Than Me?

Once again, the proper response is an emphatic: "Of course not!"

Incorrect responses include:

1. Yes, but you have a better personality.
2. Not prettier, but definitely thinner.
3. Not as pretty as you were when you were her age.
4. Define pretty.
5. Could you repeat the question? I was just thinking about how I would spend the insurance money if you died.

Question #5: What Would You Do If I Died?

A definite no-win question. The real answer, of course, is, "Buy a Corvette and Boat." No matter how you answer this, be prepared for at least an hour of follow-up questions, usually along these lines:

Woman: Would you get married again?

Man: Definitely not!

Woman: Why not? Don't you like being married?

Man: Of course I do.

Woman: Then why wouldn't you remarry?

Man: Okay, I'd get married again.

Woman: You would? (WITH A HURT LOOK ON HER FACE) Would you sleep with her in our bed?

Man: Where else would we sleep?

Woman: Would you put away my pictures, and replace them with pictures of her?

Man: That would seem like the proper thing to do.

Woman: And would you let her use my golf clubs?

Man: She can't use them; she's left-handed.

Woman: —silence—

Man: Crap.

A husband is at home watching a football game when his wife interrupts, "Honey, could you fix the light in the hallway? It's been flickering for weeks now."

He looks at her and says angrily, "Fix the light? Now? Hellooo . . . does it look like I have a G.E. logo printed on my forehead? I don't think so."

"Well then, could you fix the fridge door? It won't close right."

To which he replied, "Fix the fridge? Does it look like I have Westinghouse written on my forehead? I don't think so."

"Fine," she says, "then could you at least fix the steps to the front door? They're about to break."

"I'm not a damn carpenter and I don't want to fix steps," he says. "Does it look like I have Ace Hardware written on my forehead? I don't think so . . . I've had enough of you. I'm going to the bar!"

So he goes to the bar and drinks for a couple hours. He starts to feel guilty about how he treated his wife, and decides to go home and help out. As he walks into the house he notices the steps are already fixed. As he enters the house, he sees the hall light is working. As he goes to get a beer, he notices the fridge door is fixed.

"Honey, how'd all this get fixed?"

She said, "Well, when you left I sat outside and cried. Just then a nice, well-built, young man asked me what was wrong, and I told him. He offered to do all the repairs, and all I had to do was either go to bed with him or bake a cake."

He said, "So, what kind of cake did you bake him?"

She replied, "Hellooo . . . Do you see Betty Crocker written on my forehead?"

A woman was out golfing one day when she hit her ball into the woods. She went into the woods to look for it and found a frog in a trap. The frog said to her, "If you release me from this trap, I will grant you 3 wishes." The woman freed the frog. The frog said, "Thank you, but I failed to mention that there was a condition to your wishes, whatever you wish for, your husband will get 10 times more or better!"

The woman said, "That would be okay." For her first wish, she wanted to be the most beautiful woman in the world. The frog warned her, "You do realize that this wish will also make your husband the most handsome man in the world, an Adonis, that women will flock to."

The woman replied, "That will be okay because I will be the most beautiful woman and he will only have eyes for me."

So, KAZAM-she's the most beautiful woman in the world! For her second wish, she wanted to be the richest woman in the world. The frog said, "That will make your husband the richest man in the world and he will be ten times richer than you."

The woman said, "That will be okay because what's mine is his and what's his is mine."

So, KAZAM she's the richest woman in the world!

The frog then inquired about her third wish, and she answered, "I'd like a mild heart attack."

A woman was leaving a convenience store with her morning coffee when she noticed a most unusual funeral procession approaching the nearby cemetery. A long black hearse was followed by a second long black hearse about 50 feet behind the first one.

Behind the second hearse was a solitary woman walking a pit bull on a leash. Behind her, a short distance back, were about 200 women walking single file.

The woman couldn't control her curiosity. She respectfully approached the woman walking the dog and said, "I am so sorry for your loss, and I know now is a bad time to disturb you, but I've never seen a funeral like this. Whose funeral is it?"

"My husband's."

"What happened to him?"

The woman replied, "My dog attacked and killed him."

She inquired further, "Well, who is in the second hearse?"

The woman answered, "My mother-in-law. She was trying to help my husband when the dog turned on her."

A poignant and thoughtful moment of silence passed between the two women. "Can I borrow the dog?"

Morris returns from a long business trip and finds out that his wife has been unfaithful during his time away.

"Who was it!!!???" he yells. "That alta kakker Goldstein?"

"No," replied his wife. "It wasn't Goldstein."

"Was it Feldman, that dirty old man?"

"No, not him."

"Aha! Then it must have been that idiot Rabinovich!"

"No, it wasn't Rabinovich either . . ."

Morris was now fuming. "What's the matter?" he cried. "None of my friends are good enough for you?"

An Irish woman of advanced age visited her physician to ask for help in reviving her husband's libido. "What about trying Viagra?" asked the doctor.

"Not a chance," she said. "He won't even take an aspirin."

"Not a problem," replied the doctor. "Give him a Viagra. Drop it into his coffee. He won't even taste it. Give it a try and call me in a week to let me know how things went."

It wasn't a week later that she called the doctor, who inquired as to progress. The poor dear exclaimed, "Oh, faith, bejaysus and begorrah! T'was horrid. Just terrible, doctor!"

"Really? What happened?" asked the doctor.

"Well, I did as you advised and slipped it in his coffee and the effect was almost immediate. He jumped hisself straight up, with a twinkle in his eye, and with his pants a-bulging fiercely! With one swoop of his arm, he sent the cups and tablecloth flying, ripped me clothes to tatters and took me then and there, making wild, mad, passionate love to me on the tabletop! It was a nightmare, I tell you, an absolute nightmare!"

"Why so terrible?" asked the doctor, "Do you mean the sex your husband provided wasn't good?"

"Oh, no, no, no, doctor, the sex was fine indeed! 'Twas the best sex I've had in 25 years! But sure as I'm sittin' here, I'll never be able to show me face in Starbucks again!"

Woman's Perfect Breakfast

She's sitting at the table with her gourmet coffee. Her son is on the cover of the Wheaties box. Her daughter is on the cover of Business Week. Her boyfriend is on the cover of Playgirl. And her husband is on the back of the milk carton.

"Pastor," said Mary, "I wonder if we could make a change in the wording of our ceremony."

"Yes, Mary," replied the pastor, "it is sometimes done. What do you have in mind?"

"Well," said Mary, "I'd like to alter the 'until death do us part' section to read, 'Substantial penalty for early withdrawal.' "

Bill: It was really bad in divorce court today with me and my wife.

Doug: How's that?

Bill: Well, she cried, and the judge wiped her tears with my checkbook!

A man was sitting on the edge of the bed, observing his wife, looking at herself in the mirror. Since her birthday was not far off he asked what she'd like to have for her Birthday.

"I'd like to be six again," she replied, still looking in the mirror.

On the morning of her Birthday, he arose early, made her a nice big bowl of Lucky Charms, and then took her to Six Flags theme park. What a day! He put her on every ride in the park: the Death Slide, the Wall of Fear, the Screaming Monster Roller Coaster, everything there was. Five hours later they staggered out of the theme park. Her head was reeling and her stomach felt upside down.

He then took her to a McDonald's where he ordered her a Happy Meal with extra fries and a chocolate shake.

Then it was off to a movie, popcorn, a soda pop, and her favorite candy, M&M's. What a fabulous adventure! Finally she wobbled home with her husband and collapsed into bed exhausted. He leaned over his wife with a big smile and lovingly asked, "Well Dear, what was it like being six again??"

Her eyes slowly opened and her expression suddenly changed. "I meant my dress size, you dumb ass!"

On an airplane, I overheard a stewardess talking to an elderly couple in front of me. Learning that it was the couple's 50th wedding anniversary, the flight attendant congratulated them and asked how they had done it.

"It all felt like five minutes . . ." the gentleman said slowly. The stewardess had just begun to remark on what a sweet statement that was when he finished his sentence with a word that earned him a sharp smack on the head: ". . . underwater."

A man had 50 yard line tickets for the Super Bowl. As he sits down, another man comes down and asks if anyone is sitting in the seat next to him. "No," he says, "The seat is empty."

"This is incredible," said the man. "Who in their right mind would have a seat like this for the Super Bowl, the biggest sporting event in the world, and not use it?"

"Well, actually, the seat belongs to me. I was supposed to come with my wife, but she passed away. This is the first Super Bowl we haven't been to together since we got married in 1967."

"Oh, I'm sorry to hear that. That's terrible. But couldn't you find someone else—a friend or relative, or even a neighbor to take the seat?"

The man shakes his head. "Nope, they're all at the funeral."

Three members of a weekly bridge quartet were all impressed when the fourth arrived wearing a gorgeous new mink coat. "That's a lovely garment, Myrna," purred one woman. "It must have cost you a fortune!"

"But it didn't," said Dottie, "Just a single piece of ass."

"You mean," continued the admirer of the coat, "One that you gave your husband?"

"No," smiled the coat wearer, "One that he got from the maid."

A couple just started their Lamaze class and they were given an activity requiring the husband to wear a bag of sand- to give him an idea of what it feels like to be pregnant. The husband stood up and shrugged saying, "This doesn't feel so bad."

The Lamaze instructor then dropped a pen and asked the husband to pick it up.

"You want me to pick up the pen as if I were pregnant, the way my wife would do it?" the husband asked.

"Exactly," replied the instructor.

To the delight of the other husbands, he turned to his wife and said, "Honey, pick up that pen for me."

The man walked over to the perfume counter and told the clerk he'd like a bottle of Chanel No. 5 for his wife's birthday.

"A little surprise, eh?" smiled the clerk.

"You bet," answered the customer. "She's expecting a cruise."

A man was complaining to a friend, "I had it all—money, a magnificent house, a fast car, the love of a beautiful woman . . . then, poof! It was all gone!" "What happened?" asked the friend. "My wife found out . . ."

A man and his wife were driving home one very cold night when the wife asks her husband to stop the car. There was a baby skunk lying at the side of the road, and she got out to see if it was still alive. It was, and she said to her husband, "It's nearly frozen to death. Can we take it with us, get it warm, and let it go in the morning?"

He says, "Ok, Get in the car with it."
The wife says, "Where shall I put it to get it warm?"
He says, "Put it between your legs. It's nice and warm there."
"But what about the smell?" said the wife.
"Just hold its little nose."

My husband and I divorced over religious differences. He thought he was God, and I didn't.

Marriage is a three-ring circus: engagement ring, wedding ring, and suffering.

For Sale: Wedding dress, size 8. Worn once by mistake.

There are two times when a man doesn't understand a woman: Before marriage and after marriage.

Why were hurricanes usually named after women? Because when they arrive, they're wet and wild, but when they go, they take your house and car.

The woman applying for a job in a Florida lemon grove seemed way too qualified for the job. "Look Miss," said the foreman, "have you any actual experience in picking lemons?"

"Well, as a matter of fact, yes!" she replied? "I've been divorced three times."

Reason Why It's So Hard To Solve A Redneck Murder: All the DNA is the same.

Because they had no reservations at a busy restaurant, my elderly neighbor and his wife were told there would be a 45-minute wait for a table. "Young man, we're both 90 years old," the husband said. "We may not have 45 minutes." They were seated immediately.

All eyes were on the radiant bride as her father escorted her down the aisle. They reached the altar and the waiting groom; the bride kissed her father and placed something in his hand. The guests in the front pews responded with ripples of laughter. Even the priest smiled broadly. As her father gave her away in marriage, the bride gave him back his credit card.

A man and his wife were having some problems at home and were giving each other the silent treatment. Suddenly, the man realized that the next day, he would need his wife to wake him at 5:00 A.M. for an early morning business flight. Not wanting to be the first to break the silence (and LOSE), he wrote on a piece of paper, "Please wake me at 5:00 AM."

He left it where he knew she would find it.

The next morning, the man woke up, only to discover it was 9:00 AM and he had missed his flight. He was furious, he was about to go and see why his wife hadn't wakened him, when he noticed a piece of paper by the bed. The paper said, "It is 5:00 AM. Wake up." Men are not equipped for these kinds of contests.

UNDERSTANDING WOMEN
(A MAN'S PERSPECTIVE)

I know I'm not going to understand women. I'll never understand how you can take boiling hot wax, pour it onto your upper thigh, rip the hair out by the root, and still be afraid of a spider.

This man was sitting quietly reading his paper one morning, peacefully enjoying himself, when his wife sneaks up behind him and whacks him on the back of his head with a huge frying pan.

He asks, "What was that for?!"

She replies, "What was that piece of paper in your pants with the name 'Marylou' written on it?!"

He says, "Oh honey, remember two weeks ago when I went to the horse races? Marylou was the name of one of the horses I bet on." She is appeased and goes off to work around the house.

Three days later he is once again sitting in his chair reading and she repeats the frying pan swatting. He says, "What's that for?"

She answered "Your horse called!"

My wife and I were sitting at a table at my high school reunion, and I kept staring at a drunken lady swigging her drink as she sat alone at a nearby table.

My wife asked, "Do you know her?"

"Yes," I sighed, "she's my old girlfriend. I understand she took to drinking right after we split up those many years ago, and I hear she hasn't been sober since."

"My God!" says my wife, "Who would think a person could go on celebrating that long?"

KID JOKES

A 4-year-old boy was asked to say grace before Christmas dinner. The family members bowed their heads in expectation.

He began his prayer, thanking God for all his friends, naming them one by one. Then he thanked God for Mommy, Daddy, Brother, Sister, Grandma, Grandpa, and all his aunts and uncles. Then he began to thank God for the food.

He gave thanks for the turkey, the dressing, the fruit salad, the cranberry sauce, the pies, the cakes, even the Cool Whip. Then he paused, and everyone waited—and waited. After a long silence, the young fellow looked up at his mother and asked, "If I thank God for the broccoli, won't he know that I'm lying?"

A little boy goes to his dad and asks,

"What is Politics?"

Dad says,

"Well son, let me try to explain it this way.

I am the head of the family, so call me The President.

Your mother is the administrator of the money, so we call her The Government.

We are here to take care of your needs, so we will call you The People.

The nanny, we will consider her The Working Class.

And your baby brother, we will call him The Future.

Now think about that and see if it makes sense.

So the little boy goes off to bed thinking about what Dad has said.

Later that night, he hears his baby brother crying, so he gets up to check on him.

He finds that the baby has severely soiled his diaper.

So the little boy goes to his parent's room and finds his mother sound asleep.

Not wanting to wake her, he goes to the nanny's room.

Finding the door locked, he peeks in the keyhole and sees his father in bed with the nanny.

He gives up and goes back to bed.

The next morning, the little boy say's to his father,

"Dad, I think I understand the concept of politics now".

The father says, "Great son, tell me in your own words what you think politics is all about".

The little boy replies,

"The President is screwing The Working Class while The Government is sound asleep, the People are being ignored and The Future is in deep shit".

A 3-year old little boy was examining his testicles while taking a bath.

"Mama", he asked, "Are these my brains?"

She said, "Not Yet!"

For his birthday, little Patrick asked for a 10-speed bicycle. His father said, "Son, we'd give you one, but the mortgage on this house is $80,000 & your mother just lost her job. There's no way we can afford it." The next day the father saw little Patrick heading out the front door with a suitcase. So he asked, "Son, where are you going?" Little Patrick told him, "I was walking past your room last night heard you telling mom you were pulling out. Then I heard her tell you to wait because she was coming too. And I'll be damned if I'm staying here by myself with an $80,000 mortgage & no bike!"

A woman takes a lover home during the day while her husband is at work.

Her 9-year old son comes home unexpectedly, sees them and hides in the bedroom closet to watch.

The woman's husband also comes home.

She puts her lover in the closet, not realizing that the little boy is in there already.

The little boy says, "Dark in here."

The man says, "Yes, it is."

Boy: "I have a baseball."

Man: "That's nice"

Boy: "Want to buy it?"

Man: "No, thanks."

Boy: "My Dad's outside."

Man: "OK, how much?"

Boy: "$250"

In the next few weeks, it happens again that the boy and the lover are in the closet together.

Boy: "Dark in here."

Man: "Yes, it is."

Boy: "I have a baseball glove."

The lover, remembering the last time, asks the boy, How much?"

Boy: "$750"

Man: "Sold."

A few days later, the Dad says to the boy, "Grab your glove, let's go outside and have a game of catch."

The boy says, "I can't, I sold my baseball and my glove."

The Dad asks, "How much did you sell them for?"

Boy: "$1,000"

The Dad says, "That's terrible to over charge your friends like that . . . that is way more than those two things cost. I'm taking you to church, to confession."

They go to the church and the Dad makes the little boy sit in the confessional booth and closes the door.

The boy says, "Dark in here."

The priest says, "Don't start that shit again; you're in my closet now."

A lady was picking through the frozen turkeys at the grocery store, but couldn't find one big enough for her family.

She asked a stock boy, "Do these turkeys get any bigger?"

The stock boy replied, "No ma'am, they're dead."

A 5th grader asked her mother the age-old question, 'How did I get here?'

Her mother told her, 'God sent you.'

'Did God send you, too?' asked the chid.

'Yes, Dear,' the mother replied.

'What about Grandma and Grandpa?' the child persisted.

'He sent them also,' the mother said.

Did he send their parents, too?' asked the child.

'Yes, Dear, He did,' said the mother patiently.

'So you're telling me that there has been NO sex in this family for 200 years?

No wonder everyone's so damn grouchy around here.'

Having just finished reading a story to my sixth-grade class, I decided to check the student's knowledge of some of the vocabulary that had been used. "Who knows what the word 'adolescent' means?" I asked.

Out of the entire class of 35, not one child raised a hand.

After a few more silent moments, I decided to give them a hint: "Adolescent–it's something all of you are, and I am not."

Finally one boy tentatively raised his hand, and in a very soft voice said, "Virgins?"

A boss wondered why one of his most valued employees had not phoned in sick one day. Having an urgent problem with one of the main computers, he dialed the employee's home phone number and was greeted with a child's whisper.

"Hello."

"Is your daddy home?" he asked.

"Yes," whispered the small voice.

"May I talk with him?"

The child whispered, "No."

Surprised and wanting to talk with an adult, the boss asked, "Is your Mommy there?"

"Yes."

"May I talk with her?"

Again the small voice whispered, “No.”

Hoping there was somebody with whom he could leave a message, the Boss asked, “Is anybody else there?”

“Yes,” whispered the child, “a policeman.”

Wondering what a cop would be doing at his employee’s homes, the boss asked, “May I speak with the policeman?

No, he’s busy”, whispered the child.

“Busy doing what?”

“Talking to Daddy and Mommy and the Fireman,” said the whispered answer.

Growing more worried as he heard what sounded like a helicopter through the earpiece on the phone, the boss asked, “What is that noise?”

“A helicopter” answered the whispering voice.

“What is going on there?” demanded the boss, now truly apprehensive. Again, whispering, the child answered, “The search team just landed the helicopter.”

Alarmed, concerned, and a little frustrated the boss asked, “What are they searching for?”

Still whispering, the young voice replied with a muffled giggle: “ME.”

A kindergarten teacher was observing her classroom of children while they drew. She would occasionally walk around to see each child’s artwork. As she got to one little girl who was working diligently, she asked what the drawing was.

The girl replied. “I’m drawing God.”

The teacher paused and said, “But no one knows what God looks like.”

Without missing a beat, or looking up from her drawing the girl replied, “They will in a minute.”

Little Thelma comes home from first grade and tells her father that they learned about the history of Valentine’s Day. And, “Since Valentine’s Day is for a Christian saint and we’re Jewish,” she asks,

"Will God get mad at me for giving someone a valentine?

Thelma's father thinks a bit, then says "No, I don't think God would get mad. Who do you want to give a valentine to?"

"Osama Bin Laden," she says.

"Why Osama Bin Laden," her father asks in shock?

"Well," she says, "I thought that if a little American Jewish girl could have enough love to give Osama a valentine, he might start to think that maybe we're not all bad, and maybe start loving people a little bit.

And if other kids saw what I did and sent valentines to Osama, he'd love everyone a lot. And then . . . he'd start going all over the place to tell everyone how much he loved them and how he didn't hate anyone anymore."

Her father's heart swells and he looks at his daughter with newfound pride. "Thelma, that's the most wonderful thing I've ever heard."

"I know," Thelma says, "and once that gets him out in the open, the Marines could blow the shit out of him."

One evening after dinner, my five-year-old-son noticed that his mother had gone out and he asked, "Where did mommy go?"

In answer to his questions, I told him, "Mommy is at a Tupperware party." This explanation satisfied him for only a moment.

Puzzled, he asked, "What's a Tupperware party, Dad?"

I've always given my son honest answers, so I figured a simple explanation would be the best approach. "Well, son," I said, "at a Tupperware party, a bunch of ladies sit around and sell plastic bowls to each other."

He nodded, indicating that he understood this curious pastime. Then he burst into laughter.

"Come on, Dad," he said. "What is it really?"

Little Johnny's neighbors had a baby. Unfortunately, the baby was born without ears.

When the mother and new baby came home from the hospital, Johnny's family was invited over to see the baby. Before they left their house, Little Johnny's dad had a talk with him and explained that the baby had no ears. His dad also told him that if he so much as mentioned anything about the baby's missing ears or even said the word "ears" he would get the spanking of his life when they came back home. Little Johnny told his dad he understood completely.

When Johnny looked in the crib he said, "What a cute baby you have. The mother said, "Why, thank you, Little Johnny." Johnny said, "He has beautiful little feet and beautiful little hands, a cute little nose and really beautiful eyes. Can he see?" yes", the mother replied, "we are so thankful; the Doctor said he will have 20/20 vision."

"That's great," said Little Johnny, " 'cuz he'd be shit-outta-luck if he needed glasses"

A little girl was sitting on her grandfather's lap as he read her a bedtime story.

From time to time she would take her eyes off the book and reach up to touch his wrinkled cheek.

She was alternately stroking her own cheek and then his.

Finally she spoke up "Did God make you".

"Yes sweetheart" he answered, "God made me a long time ago".

There was a pause. Then the girl asked "Did God make me too".

"Yes indeed honey" he said, "God made you just a few years ago".

Feeling their respective face again, she observed "He's getting better at it, isn't he?"

Little Johnny came home from school to see the families pet rooster dead in the front yard. Rigor mortis had set in and it was flat on its back with its legs in the air. When his Dad came home Johnny said, "Dad our roosters dead and his legs are sticking in the air. Why are his legs sticking in the air?"

His father thinking quickly said, "Son, that's so God can reach down from the clouds and lift the rooster straight up to heaven."

"Gee Dad that's great," said little Johnny. A few days later, when Dad came home from work, Johnny rushed out to meet him yelling, "Dad, Dad we almost lost Mom today!"

"What do you mean?" said Dad.

"Well Dad, I got home from school early today and went up to your bedroom and there was Mom flat on her back with her legs in the air screaming, "Jesus I'm coming, I'm coming" If it hadn't of been for Uncle George holding her down we'd have lost her for sure!"

A teacher was giving a lesson on the circulation of blood. Trying to make the matter clearer, he said: "Now class, if I stood on my head, the blood as you know, would run into it and I should turn red in the face."

"Yes, sir," the class said.

"Then why is it that while I am standing upright in an ordinary position the blood doesn't run into my feet?"

A class member shouted, "Cause your feet ain't empty."

A tourist from New York was hiking through the mountains of North Georgia when he came upon the tiniest cabin he had ever seen in his life.

Intrigued, he went up and knocked on the door.

'Anybody home?' he asked.

'Yep,' came a kid's voice through the door.

'Is your father there?' asked the tourist.

'Pa? Nope, he left before Ma came in,' said the kid.

'Well, is your mother here?

No, she left before I got here,' said the kid.

'But,' protested the city slicker, 'are you never together as a family?'

'Sure, but not here,' said the kid through the door.

'This is the outhouse!'

Two young boys walked into a pharmacy, picked up a box of Tampax and proceeded to the checkout counter.

The man at the counter asked the older boy, 'Son, how old are you?'

'Eight,' said the boy.

The man continued, 'Do you know how these are used?'

The boy replied, 'Not exactly, but they aren't for me. They're for him. He's my brother. He's four. We saw on TV that if you use these you would be able to swim and ride a bike. He can't do either one.

A minister decided that a visual demonstration would add emphasis to his Sunday sermon.

Four worms were placed into four separate jars.

The first worm was put into a container of alcohol.

The second worm was put into a container of cigarette smoke.

The third worm was put into a container of chocolate syrup.

The fourth worm was put into a container of good clean soil.

At the conclusion of the sermon, the Minister reported the following results:

The first worm in alcohol—Dead.

The second worm in cigarette smoke—Dead.

Third worm in chocolate syrup—Dead.

Fourth worm in good clean soil—Alive.

So the Minister asked the congregation—

What can you learn from this demonstration?

Mary was setting in the back, quickly raised her hand and said, "As long as you drink, smoke and eat chocolate, you won't have worms!"

Two kids are arguing over whose father is the biggest scaredy-cat.

The first kid says, "My dad is so scared that when lightning strikes, he hides underneath the bed."

The second kid replies, "Yeah? Well, that's nothing. My dad is so scared that when my mom has to work the nightshift, he sleeps with the lady next door."

A little boy was lost at a large shopping mall. He approached a uniformed policeman and said, "I've lost my dad!"

The cop asked, "What's he like?"

The little boy replied, "Beer and women with big boobs."

A little girl asked her mother, "How did the human race come about?"

The Mother answered, "God made Adam and Eve; they had children and, so all mankind was made."

A few days later, the little girl asked her father the same question. The father answered, "Many year ago there were monkeys, and we developed from them."

The confused girl returns to her mother and says, "Mom, how is it possible that you told me that the human race was created by God, and Papa says we developed from monkeys?"

The Mother answers, "Well, dear, it is very simple. I told you about the origin of my side of the family, and your father told you about his side."

A firefighter is working on the engine outside the station when he notices a little girl next door in a little red wagon with little ladders hung off the sides and a garden hose tightly coiled in the middle

The girl is wearing a fire fighter's helmet.

The wagon is being pulled by her dog and her cat.

The fire fighter walked over to take a closer look.

"That sure is a nice fire truck," the fire fighter says with admiration.

"Thanks" the girl said.

The firefighter looks a little closer and notices the girl has tied the wagon to her dog's collar and to the cat's testicles.

"Little Partner," the fire fighter says, "I don't want to tell you how to run your rig, but if you were to tie that rope around the cat's collar too, I think you could go faster."

The little girl replies thoughtfully, "You're probably right, but then I wouldn't have a siren."

A 6 year old and his 4 year old brother are upstairs in their bedroom. "You know what?" says the 6 year old. "I think it's about time we started cussing."

The 4 year old nods his head in approval. The 6 year old continues, "When we go downstairs for breakfast, I'm gonna say something with hell and you say something with ass."

The 4 year old agrees with enthusiasm. When the mother walks into the kitchen and asks the 6 year old what he wants for breakfast, he replies, "Aw, hell, Mom, I guess I'll have some Cheerios."

WHACK! He flies out of his chair, tumbles across the kitchen floor, gets up, and runs upstairs crying his eyes out, with his mother in hot pursuit, slapping his rear with every step. His mom locks him in his room and shouts, "You can stay there until I let you out!"

She then comes back downstairs, looks at the 4 year old and asks with a stern voice, "And what do YOU want for breakfast, young man?"

I don't know, he blubbers, "but you can bet your ass it won't be Cheerios!"

A mother passing by her daughter's bedroom was astonished to see the bed was nicely made and everything was picked up. Then she saw an envelope propped up prominently on the center of the bed. It was addressed, "Mom."

With the worst premonition, she opened the envelope and read the letter with trembling hands:

Dear Mom,

It is with great regret and sorrow that I'm writing you. I had to elope with my new boyfriend because I wanted to avoid a scene with Dad and you.

I've been finding real passion with Ahmed and he is so nice-even with all his piercing, tattoos, beard, and his motorcycle clothes. But it's not only the passion mom, I'm pregnant and Ahmed said that we will be very happy. He already owns a trailer in the woods and has a stack of firewood for the whole winter. He wants to have many more children with me and that's now one of my dreams too.

Ahmed taught me that marihuana doesn't really hurt anyone and we'll be growing it for us and trading it with his friends for all the cocaine and ecstasy we want. In the meantime, we'll pray that science will find a cure for AIDS so Ahmed can get better; he sure deserves it!!

Don't worry Mom, I'm 15 years old now and I know how to take care of myself. Some day I'm sure we'll be back to visit so you can get to know your grandchildren.

Your daughter,

Judith

PS: Mom, none of the above is true. I'm over at the neighbor's house.

I just wanted to remind you that there are worse things in life than my report card that's in my desk center drawer. I love you! Call when it is safe for me to come home.

My grandson was visiting one day when he asked, 'Grandma, do you know how you and God are alike?' I mentally polished my halo while I asked, 'No, how are we alike?'

'You're both old,' he replied.

A little girl was diligently pounding away on her grandfather's word processor. She told him she was writing a story. 'What's it about?' he asked. 'I don't know,' she replied. 'I can't read.'

When my grandson Billy and I entered our vacation cabin, we kept the lights off until we were inside to keep from attracting pesky insects. Still, a few fireflies followed us in. Noticing them before I did, Billy whispered, 'It's no use, Grandpa. The mosquitoes are coming after us with flashlights.'

When my grandson asked me how old I was, I teasingly replied, 'I'm not sure.'

'Look in your underwear, Grandpa,' he advised. 'Mine says I'm four to six.'

A second grader came home from school and said to her grandmother, 'Grandma, guess what? We learned how to make babies today.'

The grandmother, more than a little surprised, tried to keep her cool.

'That's interesting,' she said, 'how do you make babies?'

'It's simple,' replied the girl. 'You just change 'y' to 'i' and add 'es'.'

'Give me a sentence about a public servant,' said a teacher.

The small boy wrote: 'The fireman came down the ladder pregnant.'

The teacher took the lad aside to correct him. 'Don't you know what pregnant means? she asked.

'Sure,' said the young boy confidently. 'It means carrying a child.'

She was in the bathroom, putting on her makeup, under the watchful eyes of her young granddaughter as she'd done many times before. After she applied her lipstick and started to leave, the little one said, 'But Gramma, you forgot to kiss the toilet paper good-bye!'

My young grandson called the other day to wish me Happy Birthday. He asked me how old I was, and I told him, '62.' He was quiet for a moment, and then he asked, 'Did you start at 1?'

A grandmother was telling her little granddaughter what her own childhood was like: 'We used to skate outside on a pond. I had a swing made from a tire; it hung from a tree in our front yard. We rode our pony. We picked wild raspberries in the woods.' The little girl was wide-eyed, taking this all in. At last she said, 'I sure wish I'd gotten to know you sooner!'

A nursery school teacher was delivering a station wagon full of kids home one day when a fire truck zoomed past. Sitting in the front seat of the truck was a Dalmatian dog. The children started discussing the dog's duties.

'They use him to keep crowds back,' said one child.

'No,' said another, 'he's just for good luck.'

A third child brought the argument to a close. 'They use the dogs,' she said firmly, 'to find the fire hydrants . . .

A new teacher was trying to make use of her psychology courses. She started her class by saying, "Everyone who thinks they're stupid, stand up!" After a few seconds, Little Johnny stood up. The teacher said, "Do you think you're stupid, Little Johnny?" "No, ma'am, but I hate to see you standing there all by yourself!"

Little Johnny watched, fascinated, as his mother smoothed cold cream on her face. "Why do you do that, mommy?" he asked. "To make myself beautiful," said his mother, who then began removing the cream with a tissue. "What's the matter?" asked Little Johnny. "Giving up?"

Little Johnny's kindergarten class was on a field trip to their local police station where they saw pictures tacked to a bulletin board of the 10 most wanted criminals. One of the youngsters pointed to a picture and asked if it really was the photo of a wanted person. "Yes," said the policeman. "The detectives want very badly to capture him." Little Johnny asked, "Why didn't you keep him when you took his picture?"

Little Johnny attended a horse auction with his father. He watched as his father moved from horse to horse, running his hands up and down the horse's legs and rump, and chest. After a few minutes, Johnny asked, "Dad, why are you doing that?" His father replied, "Because when I'm buying horses, I have to make sure that they are healthy and in good shape before I buy. Johnny, looking worried, said, "Dad, I think the UPS guy wants to buy Mom."

A kindergarten pupil told his teacher he'd found a cat, but it was dead. "How do you know that the cat was dead?" she asked him.

"Because I pissed in its ear and it didn't move," answered the child innocently. "You did WHAT?!!" the teacher exclaimed in surprise.

"You know," explained the boy, "I leaned over and went 'Pssst!' and it didn't move."

A little girl goes to the barber shop with her father. She stands next to the barber chair, while her dad gets his hair cut, eating a snack cake. The barber says to her, "Sweetheart, you're gonna get hair on your Twinkie." She says, "Yes, I know, and I'm gonna get boobs, too."

An exasperated mother, whose son was always getting into mischief, finally asked him, "How do you expect to get into Heaven?" The boy thought it over and said, "Well, I'll run in and out and in and out and keep slamming the door until St. Peter says, 'For Heaven's sake, John, come in or stay out!"

One summer evening during a violent thunderstorm a mother was tucking her son into bed. She was about to turn off the light when he asked with a tremor in his voice, "Mommy, will you sleep with me tonight?" The mother smiled and gave him a reassuring hug. "I can't dear," she said. "I have to sleep in Daddy's room." A long silence was broken at last by his shaky little voice: "The big sissy."

It was that time, during the Sunday morning service, for the children's sermon. All the children were invited to come forward. One little girl was wearing a particularly pretty dress and, as she sat down, the pastor leaned over and said, "That is a very pretty dress. Is it your Easter Dress?" The little girl replied, directly into the pastor's clip-on microphone, "Yes, and my Mom says it's a bitch to iron."

When I was six months pregnant with my third child, my three year-old came into the room as I was preparing to get into the shower. She said, "Mommy, you are getting fat!" I replied, "Yes, honey, remember Mommy has a baby growing in her tummy." "I know," she replied, "but what's growing in your butt?"

One day the first grade teacher was reading the story of Chicken Little to her class. She came to the part where Chicken Little warns the farmer. She read, ". . . and Chicken Little went up to the farmer and said, "The sky is falling!" She then asked the class, "And what do you think that farmer said?" One little girl raised her hand and said, "I think he said: 'Holy Shit! a talking chicken!'"

A woman was trying hard to get the ketchup out of the bottle. During her struggle the phone rang so she asked her 4-year-old daughter to answer the phone. "Mommy can't come to the phone to talk to you right now. She's hitting the bottle."

While taking a routine vandalism report at an elementary school, I was interrupted by a little girl about 6 years old Looking up and down at my uniform, she asked, "Are you a cop? "Yes," I answered and continued writing the report. "My mother said if I ever needed help I should ask the police. Is that right?" "Yes, that's right, "I told her. "Well, then," she said as she extended her foot toward me, "would you please tie my shoe?"

It was the end of the day when I parked my police van in front of the station As I gathered my equipment, my K-9 partner, Jake, was barking, and I saw a little boy staring in at me "Is that a dog you got back there?" he asked. "It sure is," I replied.

Puzzled, the boy looked at me and then towards the back of the van.

Finally he said, "What'd he do?"

While working for an organization that delivers lunches to elderly shut-ins, I used to take my 4-year-old daughter on my afternoon rounds. She was unfailingly intrigued by the various appliances of old age, particularly the canes, walkers and wheelchairs.

One day I found her staring at a pair of false teeth soaking in a glass. As I braced myself for the inevitable barrage of questions, she merely turned and whispered, "The tooth fairy will never believe this!"

A little girl was watching her parents dress for a party. When she saw her dad donning his tuxedo, she warned, "Daddy, you shouldn't wear that suit." "And why not, darling?" She answered "You know that it always gives you a headache the next morning."

A little girl had just finished her first week of school. "I'm just wasting my time," she aid to her mother." I can't read, I can't write and they won't let me talk!"

A little boy opened the big family Bible. He was fascinated as he fingered through the old pages. Suddenly, something fell out of the Bible. He picked up the object and looked at it. What he saw was an old leaf that had been pressed in between the pages.

"Mama, look what I found," the boy called out. "What have you got there, dear?" the mom said.

With astonishment in the young boy's voice, he answered, "I think it's Adam's underwear!"

"Little Tim was in the garden filling in a hole when his neighbor peered over the fence. Interested in what the cheeky-faced youngster was up to, he politely asked, "What are you up to there, Tim?"

"My goldfish died," replied Tim tearfully, without looking up, "and I've just buried him."

The neighbor was concerned, "That's an awfully big hole for a goldfish, isn't it?"

Tim patted down the last heap of earth then replied, "That's because he's inside your damn cat."

A ten-year-old Jewish boy was failing math. His parents tried everything from tutors to hypnosis; but to no avail. Finally, at the insistence of a family friend, they decided to enrol their son in a private Catholic school.

After the first day, the boy's parents were surprised when he walked in after school with a stern, focused and very determined expression on his face.

He went straight past them, right to his room and quietly closed the door. For nearly two hours he toiled away in his room—with math books strewn about his desk and the surrounding floor. He emerged long enough to eat, and after quickly cleaning his plate, went straight back to his room, closed the door and worked feverishly at his studies until bedtime.

This pattern of behavior continued until it was time for the first quarter's report card. The boy walked in with it unopened, laid it on the dinner table and went straight to his room.

Cautiously, his mother opened it and, to her amazement, she saw a large red 'A' under the subject of Math. Overjoyed, she and her husband rushed into their son's room, thrilled at his remarkable progress.

"Was it the nuns that did it?" the father asked.

The boy shook his head and said "No."

"Was it the one-to-one tutoring? The peer-mentoring?"

"No."

"The textbooks? The teachers? The curriculum?"

"No", said the son. "On that first day, when I walked in the front and saw that guy nailed to the plus sign, I KNEW they meant business!"

I was testing the children in my Sunday school class to see if they understood the concept of getting to Heaven.

I asked them, "If I sold my house and my car, had a big garage sale and gave all my money to the church, would that get me into Heaven?"

"No!" the children answered.

"If I cleaned the church every day, mowed the yard, and kept everything neat and tidy, would that get me into Heaven?"

Again, the answer was, "NO!" By now I was starting to smile. Hey, this was fun! "Well, then, if I was kind to animals and gave candy to all the children, and loved my husband, would that get me into Heaven?" I asked them again.

Again, they all answered, "NO!" I was just bursting with pride for them.

Well, I continued, "then how can I get into Heaven?"

A six-year-old boy shouted out, "YOU GOTTA BE DEAD!

Two little kids are in a hospital, lying side-by-side on stretchers outside the operating room. The first kid leans over and asks, "What are you in here for?'

The second kid says, "I'm here to get my tonsils out, and I'm a little nervous."

The first kid says, "You've got nothing to worry about. I had that done when I was four. They put you to sleep and when you wake up, they give you lots of ice cream. It's a breeze!"

The second kid then asks, "What are you here for?"

The first kid says, "A circumcision."

The second kid says, "Whoa ! I had that done when I was born, I couldn't walk for a year!"

Kids were asked questions about the Old and New Testaments. The following statements about the Bible were written by these children. They have not been retouched or corrected i.e., incorrect spelling has been left in.

In the first book of the bible, Guinessis, God got tired of creating the world, so he took the Sabbath off.

Adam and Eve were created from an apple tree. Noah's wife was called Joan of Ark. Noah built an ark, which the animals come on to in pears.

Lot's wife was a pillar of salt by day, but a ball of fire by night.

The Jews were a proud people and throughout history they had trouble with the unsympathetic Genitals.

Samson was a strongman who let himself be led astray by a Jezebel like Delilah.

Samson slayed the Philistines with the axe of the Apostles.

Moses led the Hebrews to the Red Sea, where they made unleavened bread which is bread without any ingredients.

The Egyptians were all drowned in the dessert.

Afterwards, Moses went up on Mount Cyanide to get the ten ammendments.

The first commandment was when Eve told Adam to eat the apple.

The seventh commandment is thou shalt not admit adultery.

Moses died before he ever reached Canada. Then Joshua led the Hebrews in the battle of Geritol.

The greatest miracle in the Bible is when Joshua told his son to stand still and he obeyed him.

David was a Hebrew king skilled at playing the liar, he fought with the Finklesteins, a race of people who lived in Biblical times.

Solomon, one of David's sons, had 300 wives and 700 porcupines.

When Mary heard that she was the mother of Jesus, she sang the Magna Carta.

Three wise guys from the east side arrived, they found Jesus in the manager.

Jesus was born because Mary had an immaculate contraption.

John the blacksmith dumped water on his head.

Jesus enunciated the Golden Rule, which says to do one to

others before they do one to you. He also explained, "a man doth not live by sweat alone."

It was a miracle when Jesus rose from the dead and managed to get the tombstone off the entrance.

The people who followed the lord were called the 12 decibels.

The epistles were the wives of the apostles.

One of the opossums was St. Matthew who was also a taximan.

St. Paul cavorted to Christianity. He preached holy acrimony, which is another name for marriage.

Christians have only one spouse. This is called monotony.

ANIMAL JOKES

A cat died and went to Heaven. God met her at the gates and said, 'You have been a good cat all these years. Anything you want is yours for the asking.'

The cat thought for a minute and then said, 'All my life I lived on a farm and slept on hard wooden floors. I would like a real fluffy pillow to sleep on.'

God said, 'Say no more.' Instantly the cat had a huge fluffy pillow.

A few days later, six mice were killed in an accident and they all went to Heaven together. God met the mice at the gates with the same offer that He made to the cat.

The mice said, 'Well, we have had to run all of our lives: from cats, dogs, and even people with brooms! If we could just have some little roller skates, we would not have to run again.'

God answered, 'It is done.' All the mice had beautiful little roller skates.

About a week later, God decided to check on the cat. He found her sound asleep on her fluffy pillow. God gently awakened the cat and asked, 'Is everything okay? How have you been doing? Are you happy?'

The cat replied, 'Oh, it is WONDERFUL. I have never been so happy in my life. The pillow is so fluffy, and those little Meals on Wheels you have been sending over are delicious!'

A guy named David received a parrot for his birthday. The parrot was fully grown, with a bad attitude and worse vocabulary. Every other word was an expletive. Those that weren't expletives were, to say the least, rude.

David tried hard to change the bird's attitude and was constantly saying polite words, playing soft music, anything he could think of to try and set a good example. Nothing worked. He yelled at the bird and the bird yelled back. He shook the bird and the bird just got more angry and more rude. Finally, in a moment of desperation, David put the parrot in the freezer.

For a few moments he heard the bird squawk and kick and scream. Then suddenly there was quiet. Not a sound for a half a minute. David was frightened that he might have hurt the bird and quickly opened the freezer door. The parrot calmly stepped out onto David's extended arm and said, "I believe I may have offended you with my rude language and actions. I will endeavor at once to correct my behavior. I really am truly sorry and beg your forgiveness."

David was astonished at the bird's change in attitude and was about to ask what had made such a dramatic change when the parrot continued, "May I ask what the chicken did?"

A young woman goes to the veterinarian with her German Shepherd dog and explains a problem.

"Every time I bend over, he jumps on my back and, well, you know, does the business. If I'm getting something out of the fridge, making the bed, tying my shoe, every time I bend over, he starts humping away."

"I see" says the vet "I suppose you want him put down?"

"No, just clip his nails, please"

Three handsome male dogs are walking down the street when they see a beautiful, enticing, female Poodle. The three male dogs fall all over themselves in an effort to be the one to reach her first, but end up arriving in front of her at the same time. The males are speechless before her beauty, slobbering on themselves and hoping for just a glance from her in return. Aware of her charms and her obvious effect on the three suitors, she decides to be kind and tells them "The first one who can use the words "liver" and "cheese" together in an imaginative, intelligent sentence can go out with me." The sturdy, muscular black Lab speaks up quickly and says "I love liver and cheese." "Oh, how childish," said the Poodle. "That shows no imagination or intelligence whatsoever." She turned to the tall, shiny Golden Retriever and said "How well can you do?" "Ummmm . . . I HATE liver and cheese," blurts the Golden Retriever. "My, my," said the Poodle. "I guess it's hopeless. That's just as dumb as the Lab's sentence." She then turns to the last of the three dogs and says, "How about you, little guy?" The last of the three, is tiny in stature but big in charm and finesse, gives her a smile, a sly wink, turns to the other males & says . . .

"Liver alone. Cheese mine."

Four men were bragging about how smart their dogs are. The first man was an Engineer, the second was an Accountant, the third was a Chemist, and the fourth man was a Government Worker. To show off, the Engineer called to his dog. "T-Square, do your stuff." T-Square trotted over to a desk, took out some paper and a pen and promptly drew a circle, a square, and a triangle. Everyone agreed that was pretty smart.

The Accountant said his dog could do better, and said, "Slide Rule, do your stuff." Slide Rule went out into the kitchen and returned with a dozen cookies. He divided them into 4 equal piles of 3 cookies each. Everyone agreed that was good.

The Chemist said his dog could do better still, so he called his dog and said, "Measure, do your stuff." Measure got up, walked over to the fridge, took out a quart of milk, got a 10 ounce glass from the cupboard and poured exactly 8 ounces without spilling a drop. Everyone agreed that was great.

The Government Worker called to his dog and said, "Coffee Break, do your stuff!" Coffee Break jumped to his feet, ate the cookies, drank the milk, dumped on the paper, sexually assaulted the other three dogs, claimed he injured his back while doing so, filed a grievance for unsafe working conditions, put in for Workers Compensation and went home on sick leave.

A circus owner walked into a bar to see everyone crowded about a table watching a little show. On the table was an upside down pot and a duck tap dancing on it. The circus owner was so impressed that he offered to buy the duck from its owner. After some wheeling and dealing, they settled for $10,000 for the duck and the pot.

Three days later the circus owner runs back to the bar in anger, "Your duck is a ripoff! I put him on the pot before a large audience, and he didn't dance a single step!"

"So?" asked the ducks former owner, "did you remember to light the candle under the pot?"

In 1986, Dan was on vacation in Kenya after graduating from the University. On a hike through the bush, he came across a young bull elephant standing with one leg raised in the air. The elephant seemed distressed, so Dan approached it very carefully. He got down on one knee and inspected the elephant's foot and found a large piece of wood deeply embedded in it.

As carefully and as gently as he could, Dan worked the wood out with his hunting knife, after which the elephant gingerly put down its foot.

The elephant turned to face the man, and with a rather curious look on its face, stared at him for several tense moments.

Dan stood frozen, thinking of nothing else but being trampled. Eventually the elephant trumpeted loudly, turned, and walked away.

Dan never forgot that elephant or the events of that day.

Twenty years later, Dan was walking through the Chicago Zoo with his teenaged son.

As they approached the elephant enclosure, one of the creatures turned and walked over to near where Dan and his son were standing.

The large bull elephant stared at Dan, lifted its front foot off the ground, and then put it down. The elephant did that several times then trumpeted loudly, all the while staring at the man.

Remembering the encounter in 1986, Dan couldn't help wondering if this was the same elephant.

Dan summoned up his courage, climbed over the railing and made his way into the enclosure. He walked right up to the elephant and stared back in wonder. The elephant trumpeted again, wrapped its trunk around one of Dan's legs and slammed him against the railing, killing him instantly.

Probably wasn't the same elephant.

A man had just settled into his seat next to the window on the plane when another man sat down in the aisle seat and put his black Labrador retriever in the middle seat next to the man.

The first man looks very quizzically at the dog and asks why the dog is allowed on the plane.

The second man explained that he is a Drug Enforcement Agent and that the dog is a “Sniffing dog”

“His name is Sniffer and he’s the best there is. I’ll show you once we get airborne, when I put him to work.”

The plane takes off, and once it has leveled out, the agent says: “Watch this.”

He tells Sniffer to “search.” Sniffer jumps down, walks along the aisle, and finally sits very purposefully next to a woman for several seconds.

Sniffer returns to its seat and puts one paw on the Agent’s arm.

The agent says, “Good boy”, and he turns to the man and says: “That woman is in possession of marijuana, so I’m making a note of her seat number and the authorities will apprehend her when we land.”

“That’s brilliant” replies the first man.

Once again, the agent sends Sniffer to search the aisles.

The Lab sniffs about, sits down beside a man for a few seconds, returns to its seat, and this time, he places TWO paws on the agent’s arm.

The agent says, “That man is carrying cocaine, so again, I’m making a note of his seat number for the police.”

“I like it!” says his seat mate.

The agent then told Sniffer to “search” again.

Sniffer walked up and down the aisles for a little while, sat down for a moment, and then came racing back to the agent, jumped into the middle seat and proceeded to defecate all over the place.

The first man is really upset by this foul behavior and can’t work out why a well-trained dog would act like that, so he asks the agent

“What’s going on?”

The agent nervously replied, “He just found a bomb!”

A farmer had five female pigs. Times were hard, so he decided to take them to the county fair and sell them. At the fair, he met another farmer who owned five male pigs.

After talking a bit, they decided to mate the pigs and split everything 50/50. The farmers lived sixty miles apart. So they agreed to drive thirty miles each, and find a field in which to let the pigs mate.

The first morning, the farmer with the female pigs got up at 5 a.m., loaded the pigs into the family station wagon, which was the only vehicle he had, and drove the thirty miles.

While the pigs were mating, he asked the other farmer, "How will I know if they are pregnant?" The other farmer replied, "If they're in the grass in the morning, they're pregnant, if they're in the mud, they're not."

The next morning the pigs were rolling in the mud. So he hosed them off, loaded them into the family station wagon again and proceeded to try again. This continued each morning for more than a week.

One morning the farmer was so tired, he couldn't get out of bed. He called to his wife, "Honey, please look outside and tell me whether the pigs are in the mud or in the grass."

"Neither," yelled his wife, "they're in the station wagon and one of them is honking the horn."

A woman brought a very limp duck into a veterinary surgeon.

As she lay her pet on the table, the vet pulled out his stethoscope and listened to the bird's chest. After a moment or two, the vet shook his head sadly and said, "I'm so sorry, your pet has passed away."

The distressed owner wailed, "Are you sure?"

"Yes, I'm sure. The duck is dead," he replied.

"How can you be so sure", she protested. "I mean, you haven't done any testing on him or anything. He might just be in a coma or something."

The vet rolled his eyes, turned around and left the room. He returned a few moments later with a black Labrador Retriever.

As the duck's owner looked on in amazement, the dog stood on his hind legs, put his front paws on the examination table and sniffed the duck from top to bottom. He then looked at the vet with sad eyes and shook his head.

The vet patted the dog and took it out and returned a few moments later with a beautiful cat.

The cat jumped up on the table and also sniffed the bird from its beak to its tail and back again. The cat sat back on its haunches, shook its head, meowed softly, jumped down and strolled out of the room.

The vet looked at the woman and said, "I'm sorry, but as I said, this is most definitely, 100% certifiably, a dead duck."

Then the vet turned to his computer terminal, hit a few keys, and produced a bill, which he handed to the woman.

The duck's owner, still in shock, took the bill. "$150!" she cried.

. . . .$150 just to tell me my duck is dead?!!"

The vet shrugged. "I'm sorry. If you'd taken my word for it, the bill would have been $20. But with the Lab Report and the Cat Scan, it all adds up."

A man was on a walking holiday in Ireland. He became thirsty so decided to stop at a little cottage and ask for something to drink. The lady of the house invited him in and served him a bowl of soup by the fire. There was a wee pig running around the kitchen, running up to the visitor and giving him a great deal of attention.

The visitor commented that he had never seen a pig this friendly. The housewife replied: "Ah, he's not that friendly. That's his bowl you're using."

After a lady's car had leaked motor oil on her cement driveway, she bought a large bag of cat litter to soak it up. It worked so well, that she went back to the convenience store to get another bag to finish the job.

The clerk remembered her. Looking thoughtfully at her purchase, he said, "Lady, if that were my cat, I'd put him outside!"

While sitting in the classroom waiting to take an exam, one veterinary student suddenly turned to another. "Good Lord," he declared. "I've just realized I haven't the faintest notion why dogs lick their balls!"

His colleague looked up at him and said, "Because they can."

This guy sees a sign in front of a house: "Talking Dog for Sale." He rings the bell and the owner tells him the dog is in the backyard. The guy goes into the backyard and sees a black mutt just sitting there.

"You talk?" he asks.

"Yep," the mutt replies.

"So, what's your story?"

The mutt looks up and says, "Well, I discovered this gift pretty young and I wanted to help the government, so I told the CIA about my gift, and in no time they had me jetting from country to country, sitting in rooms with spies and world leaders, because no one figured a dog would be eavesdropping. I was one of their most valuable spies eight years running. The jetting around really tired me out, and I knew I wasn't getting any younger and I wanted to settle down. So I signed up for a job at the airport to do some undercover security work, mostly wandering near suspicious characters and listening in. I uncovered some incredible dealings there and was awarded a batch of medals. Had a wife, a mess of puppies, and now I'm just retired."

The guy is amazed. He goes back in and asks the owner what he wants for the dog.

The owner says, "Ten dollars."

The guy says, "This dog is amazing. Why on earth are you selling him, so cheap?"

The owner replies, "He's such a liar. He didn't do any of that stuff.

A burglar broke into a house one night. He shined his flashlight around, looking for valuables, and when he picked up a CD player to place in his sack, a strange, disembodied voice echoed from the dark saying, "Jesus is watching you."

He nearly jumped out of his skin, clicked his flashlight out, and froze.

When he heard nothing more after a bit, he shook his head, promised himself a vacation after the next big score, then clicked the light on and began searching for more valuables.

Just as he pulled the stereo out so he could disconnect the wires, clear as a bell he head, “Jesus is watching you.” Freaked out, he shone his light around frantically, looking for the source of the voice. Finally, in the corner of the room, his flashlight beam came to rest on a parrot.

“Did you say that?” he hissed at the parrot.

“Yep,” the parrot confessed, then squawked, “I’m just trying to warn you.”

The burglar relaxed. “Warn me, huh? Who in the world are you?”

“Moses,” replied the bird.

“Moses?” the burglar laughed. “What kind of people would name a bird Moses.”

“The kind of people that would name a Rottweiler Jesus.”

Two bees met in a field. One said to the other, “How are things going?”

“Really bad,” said the second bee. “The weather has been cold, wet and damp, and there aren’t any flowers, so I can’t make honey.” “No problem,” said the first bee. “Just fly down five blocks and turn left. Keep going until you see all the cars.

There’s a Bar Mitzvah going on and there are all kinds of fresh flowers and fresh fruit.”

“Thanks for the tip,” said the second bee, and flew away.

A few hours later the two bees ran into each other again. The first bee asked, “How’d it go?”

“Great!” said the second bee. “It was everything you said it would be. There was plenty of fruit and, oh, such huge floral arrangements on every table.”

“Uh, what’s that thing on your head?” asked the first bee.

“That’s my yarmulke,” said the second bee. “I didn’t want them to think I was a wasp.”

An atheist was taking a walk through the woods, admiring all that the "accident of evolution" had created. "What majestic trees! What powerful rivers! What beautiful animals!" he said to himself. As he was walking alongside the river he heard a rustling in the bushes behind him. He turned to look. He saw a 7-foot grizzly charge towards him. He ran as fast as he could up the path. He looked over his shoulder and saw that the bear was closing. He ran even faster, so scared that tears were coming to his eyes. He looked over his shoulder again, and the bear was even closer. His heart was pumping frantically and he tried to run even faster. He tripped and fell to the ground. He rolled over to pick himself up but saw the bear, right on top of him: reaching for him with his left paw and raising his right paw to strike him.

At that instant the atheist cried out "Oh my God! . . . ."

Time stopped.

The bear froze.

The forest was silent.

Even the river stopped moving.

As a bright light shone upon the man, a voice came out of the sky: "You deny my existence for all of these years; teach others I don't exist; and, even credit creation to a cosmic accident. Do you expect me to help you out of this predicament? Am I to count you as a believer?" The atheist looked directly into the light: "It would be hypocritical of me to suddenly ask You to treat me as a Christian now, but perhaps could you make the bear a Christian?"

"Very well," the voice said.

The light went out.

The river ran again.

And the sounds of the forest resumed.

And then the bear dropped its right paw . . . . brought both paws together. . . . bowed its head and spoke: "Lord, for this food which I am about to receive I am truly thankful."

This guy was lonely, and decided life would be more fun if he had a pet. So he went to the pet store and told the owner that he wanted to buy an unusual pet. After some discussion, he finally bought a centipede, which came in a little white box to use for his house. He took the box back home, found a good location for it, and decided he would start off by taking his new pet to the bar to have a drink. So he asked the centipede in the box, "Would you like to go to Frank's with me and have a beer?" But there was no answer from his new pet. This bothered him a bit, but he waited a few minutes and then asked him again, "How about going to the bar and having a drink with me?" But again there was no answer from his new pet.

So he waited a few minutes more, thinking about the situation.

He decided to ask him one more time; this time putting his face up against the centipede's house and shouting, "Hey, in there! Would you like to go to Frank's place and have a drink with me?"

A little voice came out on the box: "I heard you the first time!

I'm putting on my darn shoes."

Solly goes to visit Abe and sees he has a new dog.

"So what kind of dog is this?", asks Solly.

"He's a Jewish dog", says Abe. "His name is Irving. Watch."

"Irving", says Abe. "Fetch!"

Irving walks slowly to the door, then turns around, and out of his mouth comes the following.

"So why are you talking to me like that? You always order me around like I'm nothing. And then you make me sleep on the floor, with my arthritis. Then you give me this ferkakta food with all the salt and fat and you tell me it's a special diet and it tastes like dreck! YOU should eat it yourself! And do you ever take me for a decent walk? NO, it's out of the house, give a pisch, and right back home. Maybe if I could stretch out a little the sciatica wouldn't kill me so much!"

Solly is amazed and he says to Abe how remarkable this is, to which Abe answers, "I don't know, I think this dog isn't so smart.

His hearing is no good. I said fetch, and he thought I said kvetch

A guy hears a knocking on his door. He opens it up, and no one is there. He looks all around and he finally sees a little snail sitting on the doormat. He picks it up and throws it across the street into a field.

Ten years later, he hears a knocking on his door. He opens it up and no one is there. He looks all around, and he finally sees the same little snail sitting on the doormat.

The snail says, "What the hell was that all about?"

A wealthy man decided to go on a safari in Africa. He took his faithful pet dachshund along for company. One day, the dachshund starts chasing butterflies and before long the dachshund discovers that he is lost.

So, wandering about, he notices a leopard heading rapidly in his direction with the obvious intention of having lunch. The dachshund thinks, "OK, I'm in deep trouble now!"

Then he noticed some bones on the ground close by, and immediately settles down to chew on the bones with his back to the approaching cat. Just as the leopard is about to leap, the dachshund exclaims loudly, "Boy, that was one delicious leopard. I wonder if there are any more around here?"

Hearing this, the leopard halts his attack in mid-stride, as a look of terror comes over him, and slinks away into the trees. "Whew," says the leopard. "That was close. That dachshund nearly had me."

Meanwhile, a monkey who had been watching the whole scene from a nearby tree figures he can put this knowledge to good use and trade it for protection from the leopard. So, off he goes.

But the dachshund saw him heading after the leopard with great speed, and figured that something must be up. The monkey soon catches up with the leopard, spills the beans and strikes a deal for himself with the leopard.

The leopard is furious at being made a fool of and says, "Here monkey, hop on my back and see what's going to happen to that conniving canine." Now the dachshund sees the leopard coming with the monkey on his back, and thinks, "What am I going to do now?"

But instead of running, the dog sits down with his back to his attackers, pretending he hasn't seen them yet . . . and just when they get close enough to hear, the dachshund says, "Where's that monkey? I sent him off half an hour ago to bring me another leopard."

THE MORAL TO THIS STORY IS:

SOMETIMES IF YOU CAN'T DAZZLE THEM WITH BRILLIANCE, THEN BAFFLE THEM WITH YOUR BULLSHIT!!

MAN/WOMAN JOKES

A man wanted to get married. He was having trouble choosing among three likely candidates. He gives each woman a present of $5,000 and watches to see what they do with the money.

The first does a total make over. She goes to a fancy beauty salon gets her hair done, new make up and buys several new outfits and dresses up very nicely for the man. She tells him that she has done this to be more attractive for him because she loves him so much.

The man was impressed.

The second goes shopping to buy the man gifts. She gets him a new set of golf clubs, some new gizmos for his computer, and some expensive clothes. As she presents these gifts, she tells him that she has spent all the money on him because she loves him so much.

Again, the man is impressed.

The third invests the money in the stock market. She earns several times the $5,000. She gives him back his $5000 and reinvests the remainder in a joint account. She tells him that she wants to save for their future because she loves him so much.

Obviously, the man was impressed.

The man thought for a long time about what each woman had done with the money he'd given her . . .

Then, he married the one with the biggest boobs.

On our last vacation, my wife and I saved some money by staying in a cheap hotel.

Just as we were falling asleep, we heard the sounds of mattress springs and a banging headboard from the next room.

At first we were amused by the amorous couple.

After five minutes it had lost its charm.

After ten minutes we were a little annoyed.

After fifteen minutes, we were just plain ticked off, as it was keeping us awake.

After half an hour we were incensed!

After an hour we were pretty damned impressed.

After being with her all evening, the man couldn't stand another minute with his blind date. Earlier, he had secretly arranged to have a friend call him on the phone so he would have an excuse to leave if something like this happened.

When he returned to the table, he lowered his eyes, put on a grim face and said, "I have some bad news. My grandfather has just died."

"Thank God," his date said. "If yours hadn't, mine would've had to."

A man is dining in a fancy restaurant and there is a gorgeous redhead sitting at the next table. He has been checking her out since he sat down, but lacks the nerve to start a conversation.

Suddenly she sneezes, and her glass eye comes flying out of its socket towards the man.

He reflexively reaches out, grabs it out of the air, and hands it back.

"Oh my, I am so sorry," the woman says as she pops her eye back in place. "Let me buy your dinner to make it up to you," she says.

They enjoy a wonderful dinner together, and afterwards they go to the theater followed by drinks. They talk, they laugh, she shares her deepest dreams and he shares his. She listens.

After paying for everything, she asks him if he would like to come to her place for a nightcap. . . . . . . and stay for breakfast. They have a wonderful, wonderful time.

The next morning, she cooks a gourmet meal with all the trimmings. The guy is amazed!! Everything has been SO incredible!!!! "You know," he said, "you are the perfect woman. Are you this nice to every guy you meet?"

"No," she replies . . . ." She says: "You just happened to catch my eye."

Dan was a single guy living at home with his father and working in the family business.

When he found out he was going to inherit a fortune when his sickly father died, he decided he needed a wife with whom to share his fortune.

One evening at an investment meeting he spotted the most beautiful woman he had ever seen.

Her natural beauty took his breath away. "I may look like just an ordinary man," he said to her, "but in just a few years, my father will die, and I'll inherit 20 million dollars."

Impressed, the woman obtained his business card and three months later, she became his stepmother.

Women are so much better at estate planning than men

The Smiths were unable to conceive children and decided to use a surrogate father to start their family. On the day the proxy father was to arrive, Mr. Smith kissed his wife goodbye and said, "Well, I'm off now. The man should be here soon."

Half an hour later, just by chance, a door-to-door baby photographer happened to ring the doorbell, hoping to make a sale. "Good morning, Ma'am", he said, "I've come to . . ."

"Oh, no need to explain," Mrs. Smith cut in, embarrassed, "I've been expecting you."

"Have you really?" said the photographer. "Well, that's good. Did you know babies are my specialty?"

"Well that's what my husband and I had hoped. Please come in and have a seat".

After a moment she asked, blushing, "Well, where do we start?"

"Leave everything to me. I usually try two in the bathtub, one on the couch, and perhaps a couple on the bed. And sometimes the living room floor is fun. You can really spread out there."

"Bathtub, living room floor? No wonder it didn't work out for Harry and me!"

"Well, Ma'am, none of us can guarantee a good one every time. But if we try several different positions and I shoot from six or seven angles, I'm sure you'll be pleased with the results."

"My, that's a lot!", gasped Mrs. Smith.

"Ma'am, in my line of work a man has to take his time. I'd love to be in and out in five minutes, but I'm sure you'd be disappointed with that."

"Don't I know it," said Mrs. Smith quietly.

The photographer opened his briefcase and pulled out a portfolio of his baby pictures. "This was done on the top of a bus," he said.

"Oh, my God!" Mrs. Smith exclaimed, grasping at her throat.

"'And these twins turned out exceptionally well—when you consider their mother was so difficult to work with."

"She was difficult?" asked Mrs. Smith.

"Yes, I'm afraid so. I finally had to take her to the park to get the job done right. People were crowding around four and five deep to get a good look"

"Four and five deep?" said Mrs. Smith, her eyes wide with amazement.

"Yes", the photographer replied. "And for more than three hours, too.

The mother was constantly squealing and yelling—I could hardly concentrate, and when darkness approached I had to rush my shots.

Finally, when the squirrels began nibbling on my equipment, I just had to pack it all in."

Mrs. Smith leaned forward. "Do you mean they actually chewed on your, uh . . . equipment?"

"It's true, Ma'am, yes. . Well, if you're ready, I'll set-up my tripod and we can get to work right away."

"Tripod?"

"Oh yes, Ma'am. I need to use a tripod to rest my Canon on. It's much too big to be held in the hand very long."

Mrs. Smith fainted!

Emerging from the chiropractor's treatment room, a young man said aloud in the crowded waiting room, "I feel like a new man!"

"I do, too," a middle-aged woman responded, "but I'll probably go home with the same old one,"

At a country-club party a young man was introduced to an attractive girl. Right away he began flattering her outrageously. The girl liked the young man, but she was taken a bit aback by his fast and ardent pitch. She was amazed when after 30 minutes he seriously proposed marriage.

"Look," she said. "We only met a half hour ago. There is no way you could be so sure. We don't know a thing about each other."

"You're wrong," the young man declared. "For the past 5 years I've been working in the bank where your father has his account.

Bourdreaux dun got old and his children put him in the old folk home near Beaux Bridge, Louisiana where he dun met a lovely lady dat were from Texas. Now Boudreaux being a fine upstanding religious man, he didn't want to do nutin dat were aganst his religion, no. So he dun propose marriage. Now both Boudreaux and Mable were in their 80's.

Mable went and told everyone at the Senior Citizens Home the good news. Renee, Mable's best friend told her that since she was very wealthy and the person she was about to wed was, well, to say the least, not worth much and she should insist on a prenuptial agreement.

Mable was sitting on the porch swing with Boudreaux and she told him she would marry him providing he would sign a prenuptial agreement.

Boudreaux dun told Mable "Mais cher, I'll sign agreement, you bet, 'cause I luv you so much."

Mable got out her pen and paper and started:

She said: "I want to keep my house down in Texas with all the oil wells."

He said: “Mais dat’s fine wit me. I’ll keeps my shack on da bayou.”

She said: “I want to keep my Cadillac, BMW and Lexus.”

He said: “Dat’s fine wit me too. I’ll keeps my pick ’em up truck.”

She said: “I want to keep my yacht that is moored near my summer home in Padre Island, Texas.”

He said: “Dat’s agan fine wit me. I’ll keep my pirogue down on da bayou.”

She said: “I want to keep all my jewelry.”

He said: “Dat’s fine ’cause me, I don’t wear dat stuff.”

She said: “I want to have sex 6 times a week.”

He said: “Mais cher, put me down for Fridays.”

A husband was with his wife when she decided to buy something for their daughter-in-law at an exclusive lingerie shop.

Inside, the husband was feeling very out of place when a beautiful clerk asked if she could help him.

In a cocky manner, he asked, “Where are all the men’s clothes?”

In a demure voice the clerk replied, “All of these clothes ARE for men, sir.”

A Doctor was addressing a large audience in Miami:

“The material we put into our stomachs is enough to have killed most of us sitting here, years ago. Red meat is awful. Soft drinks corrode your stomach lining. Chinese food is loaded with MSG. High fat diets can be disastrous, and none of us realizes the long-term harm caused by the germs in our drinking water. But there is one thing that is the most dangerous of all, and we all have, or will, eat it. Would anyone care to guess what food causes the most grief and suffering for years after eating it?”

After several seconds of quiet, a small 75-year-old man in the front row, raised his hand and said, “Wedding Cake?”

TRANSLATION OF WOMEN'S PERSONAL ADS

40-ish.............................49
Adventurous...................Slept with all your friends
Athletic............................No boobs
Average looking.............Ugly
Beautiful..........................Pathological liar
Contagious Smile...........Does a lot of pills
Emotionally secure.........On medication
Feminist..........................Fat
Free spirit........................Junkie
Friendship first................Former slut
Fun.................................Annoying
Gentle.............................Dull
New Age.........................Body hair in strange places
Open-minded..................Desperate
Outgoing.........................Loud and Embarrassing
Jovial..............................Sloppy drunk
Poet................................Depressed
Professional....................Bitch
Romantic........................Frigid
Voluptuous......................Very Fat
Large frame....................Hugely Fat
Wants Soul mate............Stalker
Widow............................Murderer

WOMEN'S ENGLISH

1. Yes = No
2. No = Yes
3. Maybe = No
4. We need = I want
5. I am sorry = you'll be sorry
6. We need to talk = you're in trouble
7. Sure, go ahead = you better not
8. Do what you want = you will pay for this later
9. I am not upset = of course I am upset, you moron!
10. You're very attentive tonight = is sex all you ever think about?

MEN'S TRANSLATION

1. I am hungry = I am hungry
2. I am sleepy = I am sleepy

3. I am tired = I am tired
4. Nice dress = Nice cleavage!
5. I love you = let's have sex now
6. I am bored = Do you want to have sex?
7. May I have this dance? = I'd like to have sex with you right after the dance
8. Can I call you sometime? = I'd like to have sex with you.
9. Do you want to go to a movie? = I'd like to have sex with you.
10. Can I take you out to dinner? = I'd like to have sex with you.
11. Those shoes don't go with that outfit= I'm gay.

And finally. . . . .

A recent scientific study found that women have different perceptions of men depending on where they are in their menstrual cycle.

For example, when a woman is ovulating she will prefer a man with rugged, masculine features.

However when she is menstruating, she prefers a man doused in gasoline and set on fire, with scissors stuck in his eyes and a baseball bat shoved up his ass.

Men Are Just Happier People—

What do you expect from such simple creatures?

Your last name stays put.

The garage is all yours

Wedding plans take care of themselves. Chocolate is just another snack.

You can never be pregnant.

You can wear a white T-shirt to a water park.

You can wear NO shirt to a water park.

Car mechanics tell you the truth.

The world is your urinal.

You never have to drive to another gas station restroom because this one is just too icky.

You don't have to stop and think of which way to turn a nut on a bolt.

Same work, more pay.

Wrinkles add character
Wedding dress $5000. Tux rental-$100.
People never stare at your chest when you're talking to them.
New shoes don't cut, blister, or mangle your feet.
One mood all the time.
Phone conversations are over in 30 seconds flat.
You know stuff about tanks.
A five-day vacation requires only one suitcase.
You can open all your own jars. .
You get extra credit for the slightest act of thoughtfulness.
If someone forgets to invite you, he or she can still be your friend.
Your underwear is $8.95 for a three-pack.
Three pairs of shoes are more than enough.
You almost never have strap problems in public.
You are unable to see wrinkles in your clothes.
Everything on your face stays its original color.
The same hairstyle lasts for years, maybe decades.
You only have to shave your face and neck.
You can play with toys all your life.
One wallet and one color for all seasons.
You can wear shorts no matter how your legs look.
You can 'do' your nails with a pocket knife.
You have freedom of choice concerning growing a mustache.

A man boarded an airplane in New Orleans, with a box of crabs. A female crew member took the box and promised to put it in the crew's refrigerator, which she did. The man firmly advised her that he was holding her personally responsible for the crabs staying frozen, and proceeded to rant and rave about what would happen if she let the crabs thaw out.

Shortly before landing in New York, she announced over the intercom to the entire cabin, 'Would the gentleman who gave me the crabs in New Orleans, please raise your hand?'

Not one hand went up . . . so she took them home and ate them herself.

Men never learn.

1. It's important to have a man who helps at home, who cooks from time to time, cleans up and has a job.

2. It's important to have a man who can make you laugh.

3. It's important to have a man who you can trust and who doesn't lie to you

4. It's important to have a man who is good in bed and who likes to be with you.

5. It's very, very, very important that these four men do not know each other.

Two women met for the first time since graduating from high school.

One asked the other, "You were always so organized in school, Did you manage to live a well planned life?"

"Yes," said her friend.

"My first marriage was to a millionaire; my second marriage was to an actor; my third marriage was to a preacher; and now I'm married to an undertaker."

Her friend asked, "What do those marriages have to do with a well planned life?"

"One for the money, two for the show, three to get ready, and four to go

A guy sticks his head into a barber shop and asks, "How long before I can get a haircut?" The barber looks around the shop and says, "About 2 hours." The guy leaves.

A few days later the same guy sticks his head in the door and asks, "How long before I can get a haircut?" The barber looks around the shop and says, "About an hour and a half." The guy leaves.

A week later the same guy sticks his head in the shop and asks, "How long before I can get a haircut?" The barber looks around the shop and says, "About an hour and half." The guy leaves.

The barber looks over at a friend in the shop and says, "Hey,

Bill. Follow that guy and see where he goes." In a little while, Bill comes back into the shop laughing hysterically. The barber asks, "Bill, where did he go when he left here?"

Bill looks up and says, "Your house."

A Marine stationed in Afghanistan recently received a "Dear John" letter from his girlfriend back home. It read as follows:

Dear Ricky:

I can no longer continue our relationship. The distance between us is just too great. I must admit that I have cheated on you twice, since you've been gone, and it's not fair to either of us. I'm sorry.

Love, Becky

P.S. Please return the picture of me that I sent to you.

The Marine, with hurt feelings, asked his fellow Marines for any snapshots they could spare of their girlfriends, sisters, ex-girlfriends, aunts, cousins etc. In addition to the picture of Becky, Ricky included all the other pictures of the gals he had collected from his buddies. There were 57 photos in that envelope. . . . along with this note:

Dear Becky,

I'm so sorry, but I can't quite remember who you are. Please take your picture form the pile, and send the rest back to me.

Take Care, Ricky

A woman was having a daytime affair while her husband was at work. One rainy day she was in bed with her boyfriend when, to her horror, she heard her husband's car pull into the driveway.

"Oh my God—Hurry! Grab your clothes and jump out the window. My husband's home early!"

"I can't jump out the window. It's raining out there!"

"If my husband catches us in here, he'll kill us both!" she replied. "He's got a hot temper and a gun, so the rain is the least of your problems!"

So the boyfriend scoots out of bed, grabs his clothes & jumps out the window. Running down the street in the rain, he quickly discovered he had run right into the middle of the town's annual marathon, so he started running along beside the others, about 300 of them.

Being naked, with his clothes tucked under his arm, he tried to blend in as best he could.

After a little while a small group of runners who had been watching him with some curiosity, jogged closer.

"Do you always run in the nude?" one asked. "Oh yes!" he replied, gasping for air. "I feel so wonderfully free!"

Another runner moved along side. "Do you always run carrying your clothes with you under your arm?"

"Oh, yes" our friend answered breathlessly. "That way I can get dressed at the end of the run and get in my car to go home!

Then a third runner cast his eyes a little lower and asked, "Do you always wear a condom when you run?"

"Nope. . . . . just when it's raining."

A woman was having a passionate affair with an inspector from a pest-control company. One afternoon they were carrying on in the bedroom together when her husband arrived home unexpectedly.

"Quick," said the woman to the lover, "into the closet!" and she pushed him in the closet, stark naked.

The husband, however, became suspicious and after a search of the bedroom discovered the man in the closet.

"Who are you?" he asked him.

"I'm an inspector from Bugs-B-Gone," said the exterminator.

"What are you doing in there?" the husband asked.

"I'm investigating a complaint about an infestation of moths," the man replied.

"And where are your clothes?" asked the husband.

The man looked down at himself and said, "Those little bastards!"

A WOMAN'S POEM:

Before I lay me down to sleep,
I pray for a man, who's not a creep,

One who's handsome, smart and strong.
One who loves to listen long,
One who thinks before he speaks,
One who'll call, not wait for weeks.
I pray he's gainfully employed,
When I spend his cash, won't be annoyed.
Pulls out my chair and opens my door.
Massages my back and begs to do more.
Oh! Send me a man who'll make love to my mind,
Knows what to answer to "how big is my behind?"
I pray that this man will love me to no end,
And always be my very best friend.

A MAN'S POEM:

I pray for a deaf-mute gymnast nymphomaniac with huge boobs who owns a bar on a golf course, and loves to send me fishing and drinking.

This doesn't rhyme and I don't give a damn.

The only cow in a small town in Arkansas stopped giving milk. The people did some research and found they could buy a cow in Oklahoma, for $200.00.

They bought the cow from Oklahoma and the cow was wonderful. It produced lots of milk all of the time, and the people were pleased and very happy.

They decided to acquire a bull to mate with the cow and produce more cows like it.

They would never have to worry about their milk supply again.

They bought a bull and put it in the pasture with their beloved cow.

However whenever the bull came close to the cow, the cow would move away.

No matter what approach the bull tried, the cow would move away from the bull and he could not succeed in his quest.

The people were very upset and decided to ask the Vet, who was very wise, what to do.

They told the Vet what was happening.

'Whenever the bull approaches our cow, she moves away. If he approaches from the back, she moves forward. When he approaches her from the front, she backs off. An approach from the side and she walks away to the other side.'

The Vet thinks about this for a minute and asked, 'Did you buy this cow in Oklahoma?'

The people were dumbfounded, since they had never mentioned where they bought the cow.

'You are truly a wise Vet,' they said.

'How did you know we got the cow in Oklahoma?'

The Vet replied with a distant look in his eye,

'My wife is from Oklahoma.'

A man was walking down the street when he was accosted by a particularly dirty and shabby-looking homeless man who asked him for a couple of dollars for dinner.

The man took out his wallet, extracted ten dollars and asked, "If I give you this money, will you buy some beer with it instead?"

"No, I had to stop drinking years ago," the homeless man replied.

"Will you use it to gamble instead of buying food?" the man asked.

"No, I don't gamble," the homeless man said. "I need everything I can get just to stay alive."

"Will you spend this on greens fees at a golf course instead of food?" the man asked.

"Are you NUTS!" replied the homeless man. "I haven't played golf in 20 years!"

"Will you spend the money on a woman in the red light district instead of food?" the man asked.

"What disease would I get for ten lousy bucks?" exclaimed the homeless man.

"Well," said the man, "I'm not going to give you the money. Instead, I'm going to take you home for a terrific dinner cooked by my wife."

The homeless man was astounded. "Won't your wife be furious with you for doing that? I know I'm dirty, and I probably smell pretty disgusting."

The man replied, "That's okay. I just want her to see what a man looks like who has given up beer, gambling, golf, and sex."

Recently a "Husband Super Store" opened where women could go to choose a husband from among many men. It was laid out in five floors, with the men increasing in positive attributes as you ascended.

The only rule was, once you opened the door to any floor, you HAD to choose a man from that floor; if you went up a floor, you couldn't go back down except to leave the place, never to return.

A couple of girlfriends went to the shopping center to find some husbands —

First Floor, the door had a sign saying, "These men have jobs and love kids." The women read the sign and said, "Well, that's better than not having a job or not loving kids, but I wonder what's further up?" So up they went.

Second Floor, the sign read, "These men have high paying jobs, love kids, and are extremely good looking." "Hmmm," said the ladies, "But, I wonder what's further up?"

Third Floor, this sign read, "These men have high paying jobs, are extremely good looking, love kids and help with the housework." "Wow," said the women, "Very tempting." But there was another floor, so further up they went. .

Fourth Floor, this door had a sign saying "These men have high paying jobs, love kids, are extremely good looking, help with the housework and have a strong romantic streak." "Oh, mercy me," they cried, "Just think what must be awaiting us further on!

So up to the fifth floor they went.

Fifth Floor, the sign on that door said, "This floor is empty and exists only to prove that women are impossible to please. The exit is to your left, we hope you fall down the stairs."

In a crowded city at a busy bus stop, a beautiful young woman who was waiting for a bus was wearing a tight mini skirt. As the bus stopped and it was her turn to get on, she became aware that her skirt was too tight to allow her leg to come up to the height of the first step of the bus.

Slightly embarrassed and with a quick smile to the bus driver, she reached behind her to unzip her skirt a little, thinking that this would give her enough slack to raise her leg. Again, she tried to make the step only to discover she still couldn't. So, a little more embarrassed, she once again reached behind her to unzip her skirt a little more, and for the second time attempted the step, and, once again, much to her chagrin, she could not raise her leg. With a little smile to the driver, she again reached behind to unzip a little more and again was unable to make the step.

About this time, a large man who was standing behind her picked her up easily by the waist and placed her gently on the step of the bus. She went ballistic and turned to the would-be Samaritan and yelled, "How dare you touch my body! I don't even know who you are!"

The man smiled and drawled, "Well, ma'am, normally I would agree with you, but after you unzipped my fly three times, I kinda figured we was friends.

1. THINGY

Female . . . . . . Any part under a car's hood.

Male . . . . The strap fastener on a woman's bra.

2. VULNERABLE

Female . . . . . . Fully opening up one's self emotionally to another.

Male . . . . Playing football without a cup.

3. COMMUNICATION

Female . . . . . . The open sharing of thoughts and feelings with one's partner.

Male . . . . Leaving a note before taking off on a fishing trip with the boys.

4. COMMITMENT

Female . . . . . . A desire to get married and raise a family.

Male . . . . Trying not to hit on other women while out with this one.

5. ENTERTAINMENT
Female . . . . . . A good movie, concert, play or book.
Male . . . . Anything that can be done while drinking beer.

6. FLATULENCE
Female . . . . . . An embarrassing by product of indigestion.
Male . . . . A source of entertainment, self-expression, male bonding.

7. MAKING LOVE
Female . . . . . . The greatest expression of intimacy a couple can achieve.
Male . . . . Call it whatever you want just as long as we do it.

8. REMOTE CONTROL
Female . . . . . . A device for changing from one TV channel to another.
Male . . . . A device for scanning through all 375 channels every 5 minutes.

For all those men who say, "Why buy the cow when you can get the milk for free."

Here's an update for you. . . .

Nowadays 80% of women are against marriage.

Why?

Because women realize its not worth buying an entire Pig, . . . Just to get a little sausage.

A man is getting into the shower just as his wife is finishing up her shower, when the doorbell rings. The wife quickly wraps herself in a towel and runs downstairs. When she opens the door, there stands Bob, the next-door neighbor. Before she says a word, Bob says, "I'll give you $800 to drop that towel."

After thinking for a moment, the woman drops her towel and stands naked in front of Bob. After a few seconds, Bob hands her

$800 and leaves. The woman wraps back up in the towel and goes back upstairs.

When she gets to the bathroom, her husband asks, "Who was that?"

"It was Bob the next door neighbor," she replies.

"Great!" the husband says, "Did he say anything about the $800 he owes me?"

In a recent Harris On-line poll 38,562 men across the US were asked to identify woman's ultimate fantasy. 97.8% of the respondents said that a woman's ultimate fantasy is to have two men at once.

While this has been verified by a recent sociological study, it appears that most men do not realize that in this fantasy, one man is cooking and the other is cleaning.

A man boarded a plane at Sydney airport and, taking his seat as he settled in, he noticed a very beautiful woman boarding the aircraft. He realized she was heading straight towards his seat, and bingo! She took the seat right beside him.

Eager to strike up a conversation, he blurted out: "Business trip or holiday?"

She turned, smiled enchantingly and said, "Business. I'm going to the Annual Nymphomaniac Convention in the United States."

The man swallowed hard. Here was the most gorgeous woman he had ever seen sitting next to him, and she was going to a meeting for nymphomaniacs!

Struggling to maintain his composure, he calmly asked, "What's your business role at this convention?" "Lecturer", she responded. "I use my experience to debunk some of the popular myths about sexuality."

"Really?" he smiled, "What myths are those?" "Well", she explained, one popular myth is that African-American men are the most well-endowed when, in fact, it's the Native American Indian who is most likely to possess that trait.

Another popular myth is that French men are the best lovers, when actually it is the men of Greek descent. We have also found that the best potential lovers in all categories are the Irish."

Suddenly the woman became uncomfortable and blushed. "I'm sorry", she said. I really shouldn't be discussing this with you, I don't even know your name!"

Tonto", said the man. "Tonto Poppoudopoulos . . . But all my friends call me Paddy."

How to take a shower—Woman vs. Man

How To Shower Like a Woman

1. Take off clothing and place it in sectioned laundry hamper according to lights and darks.

2. Walk to bathroom wearing long dressing gown. If you see husband along the way, cover up any exposed areas.

3. Look at your womanly physique in the mirror—make mental note to do more sit-ups

4. Get in the shower. Use face cloth, arm cloth, leg cloth, long loofah, wide loofah, and pumice stone.

5. Wash your hair once with cucumber and sage shampoo with 43 added vitamins.

6. Wash your hair again to make sure it's clean.

7. Condition your hair with grapefruit mint conditioner enhanced with natural avocado oil. Leave on hair for 15 minutes . . .

8. Wash your face with crushed apricot facial scrub for 10 minutes until red.

9. Wash entire rest of body with ginger nut and jaffa cake body wash.

10. Rinse conditioner off hair.

11. Shave armpits and legs.

12. Turn off shower.

13. Squeegee off all wet surfaces in shower. Spray mold spots with Tilex.

14. Get out of shower. Dry with towel the size of a small country. Wrap hair in super absorbent towel.

15. Check entire body for zits, tweeze hairs.

16. Return to bedroom wearing long dressing gown and towel on head.

17. If you see husband along the way, cover up any exposed areas.

How To Shower Like a Man

1. Take off clothes while sitting on the edge of the bed and leave them in a pile.
2. Walk naked to the bathroom. If you see wife along the way, shake weiner at her making the 'woo-woo' sound.
3. Look at your manly physique in the mirror. Admire the size of your weiner and scratch your ass.
4. Get in the shower.
5. Wash your face
6. Wash your armpits.
7. Blow your nose in your hands and let the water rinse them off.
8. Make fart noises (real or artificial) and laugh at how loud they sound in the shower.
9. Spend majority of time washing privates and surrounding area.
10. Wash your butt, leaving those coarse butt hairs stuck on the soap.
11. Shampoo your hair.
12. Make a Shampoo Mohawk.
13. Pee.
14. Rinse off and get out of shower.
15. Partially dry off. Fail to notice water on floor because curtain was hanging out of tub the whole time.
16. Admire weiner size in mirror again.
17. Leave shower curtain open, wet mat on floor, light and fan on.
18. Return to bedroom with towel around your waist. If you pass wife, pull off towel, shake weiner at her and make the 'woo-woo' sound again.
19. Throw wet towel on bed.

WHITE WOMEN:

First date: You get to kiss her goodnight.

Second Date: You get to grope all over and make out.

Third date: You get to have sex but only in the missionary position.

IRISH WOMEN:

First date: You both get blind drunk and have sex.

Second Date: You both get blind drunk and have sex.

20th Anniversary: You both get blind drunk and have sex.

ITALIAN WOMEN:

First Date: You take her to a play and an expensive restaurant.

Second Date: You meet her parents and her Mom makes spaghetti & meatballs.

Third Date: You have sex, she wants to marry you & insists on a 3 carat ring.

5th Anniversary: You already have 5 kids together & hate the thought of having sex.

6th Anniversary: You find yourself a girlfriend.

JEWISH WOMEN:

First Date: You get dynamite head.

Second Date: You get more great head.

Third Date: You tell her you'll marry her and never get head again.

POLISH WOMEN:

First Date: You pick her up, she isn't home. She gave you the wrong address.

Second Date: You decide to meet at a restaurant. She gets lost getting to the restaurant and then again going home.

Third Date: She's pregnant. She's not sure if its hers.

CHINESE WOMEN:

First date: You get to buy her an expensive dinner but nothing happens.

Second date: You buy her an even more expensive dinner. Nothing happens again.

Third date: You don't even get to the third date and you already realized nothing is going to happen.

INDIAN WOMEN:

First date: Meet her parents.

Second date: Set the date of the wedding.

Third date: Wedding night.

BLACK WOMEN:

First Date: You get to buy her a real expensive dinner.

Second Date: You get to buy her and her girlfriends a real expensive dinner.

Third Date: She's pregnant by someone other than you.

LATIN WOMEN:

First Date: You buy her an expensive dinner, get drunk on Riunite, have sex in the back of her car.

Second Date: She's pregnant.

Third Date: Move in with her, her two cousins, her sister's boyfriend and live happily ever after eating rice and beans in the Bronx

There were two nuns . . .

One of them was known as Sister Mathematical (SM), and the other one was known as Sister Logical (SL.)

It is getting dark and they are still far away from the convent.

SM: Have you noticed that a man has been following us for the past thirty-eight and a half minutes? I wonder what he wants.

SL: It's logical. He wants to rape us.

SM: Oh, no! At this rate he will reach us in 15 minutes at the most! What can we do?

SL: The only logical thing to do of course is to walk faster.

SM: It's not working.

SL: Of course it's not working. The man did the only logical thing. He started to walk faster, too.

SM: So, what shall we do? At this rate he will reach us in one minute.

SL: The only logical thing we can do is split. You go that way and I'll go this way. He cannot follow us both.

So the man decided to follow Sister Logical.

Sister Mathematical arrives at the convent and is worried about what has happened to Sister Logical.

Then Sister Logical arrives.

SM: Thank God you are here! Tell me what happened!

SL: The only logical thing happened.

The man couldn't follow us both, so he followed me

SM: Yes, yes! But what happened then?

SL: The only logical thing happened. I started to run as fast as I could and he started to run as fast as he could.

SM: And?

SL: The only logical thing happened. He reached me.

SM: Oh, dear! What did you do?

SL: The only logical thing to do. I lifted my dress up.

SM: Oh, Sister! What did the man do?

SL: The only logical thing to do.

He pulled down his pants.

SM: Oh, no! What happened then?

SL: Isn't it logical, Sister?

A nun with her dress up can run faster than man with his pants down.

On the day of their 50th anniversary, the reminiscing wife finds the negligee she wore on her wedding night and puts it on. She goes to her Husband and says, "Honey, do you remember this?"

He looks up from his newspaper and says, "Yes, dear, I do. You wore the same negligee the night we were married."

She says, "Yes, that's right. Do you remember what you said to me that night?"

He nods and says, "Yes, dear, I still remember". "Well, what was it?" she asks.

He's not much in the mood for this, but he sighs and responds, "Well, honey, as I remember, I said, 'Oh, baby, I'm going to suck the life out of those Boobs and screw your brains out.'"

She giggles and says, "Yes, dear, that's it. That's exactly what you said. So now, it's fifty years later and I'm in the same negligee. What do you have to say tonight?"

He looked her up and down, and replied, "Mission accomplished"

Men are like Floor Tiles:
If you lay them right the first time, you can walk all over them for years!

Men are like Bank Accounts:
Without a lot of money, they don't generate much interest.

Men are like Blenders:
You need one, but you're not quite sure why.

Men are like Chocolate Bars:
Sweet, smooth, and they usually head right for your hips.

Men are like Coffee:
The best ones are rich, warm, and can keep you up all night.

Men are like Commercials:
You can't believe a word they say.

Men are like Computers:
Hard to figure out and never have enough memory.

Men are like Coolers:
Load them with beer and you can take them anywhere.

Men are like Copiers:
You need them for reproduction, but that's about it.

Men are like Curling irons:
They're always hot, and they're always in your hair.

Men are like Government bonds:
They take so long to mature.

Men are like High heels:
They're easy to walk on once you get the hang of it.

Men are like Horoscopes:
They always tell you what to do and are usually wrong.

Men are like Lava lamps:
Fun to look at, but not all that bright.

Men are like Mascara:
They usually run at the first sign of emotion.

Men are like Parking spots:
The good ones are already taken and the ones that are left are handicapped or extremely small.

Men are like Popcorn:
They satisfy you, but only for a little while.

Men are like place mats:
They only show up when there's food on the table.

Men are like snow storms:
You never know when they're coming, how many inches you'll get or how long they will last.

Men are like Used Cars:
Both are easy-to-get, cheap, and unreliable.

Men are like Bank Machines:
Once they withdraw they lose interest.

Men are like bananas:
The older they get, the less firm they are.

Men are like newborn babies:
They're cute at first, but you get tired of cleaning up their crap.

Men are like Crystal:
Some look real good, but you can still see right through them.

Men are like Laxatives:
They irritate the shit out of you

Because I'm a man, when I lock my keys in the car, I will fiddle with a coat hanger long after hypothermia has set in. Calling the AAA is not an option. I will win.

Because I'm a man, when the car isn't running very well, I will pop the hood and stare at the engine as if I know what I'm looking at. If another man shows up, one of us will say to the other, "I used to be able to fix these things, but now with all these computers and everything, I wouldn't know where to start." We will then drink a couple of beers and break wind, as a form of holy communion.

Because I'm a man, when I catch a cold, I need someone to bring me soup and take care of me while I lie in bed and moan. You're a woman. You never get as sick as I do, so for you, this is no problem.

Because I'm a man, I can be relied upon to purchase basic groceries at the store, like milk or bread. I cannot be expected to find exotic items like "cumin" or "tofu." For all I know, these are the same thing.

Because I'm a man, when one of our appliances stops working, I will insist on taking it apart, despite evidence that this will just cost me twice as much once the repair person gets here and has to put it back together.

Because I'm a man, I must hold the television remote control in my hand while I watch TV. If the thing has been misplaced, I may miss a whole show looking for it, though one time I was able to survive by holding a calculator instead.

Because I'm a man, there is no need to ask me what I'm thinking about. The true answer is always either sex, cars, sex, sports or sex. I have to make up something else when you ask, so just don't ask.

Because I'm a man, you don't have to ask me if I liked the movie. Chances are, if you're crying at the end of it, I didn't . . . and if you are feeling amorous afterwards . . . then I will certainly at least remember the name and recommend it to others.

Because I'm a man, I think what you're wearing is fine. I thought what you were wearing five minutes ago was fine, too. Either pair of shoes is fine. With the belt or without it, looks fine. It does not make your rear look too big. It was the pasta and potatoes and chocolates and cakes that did that. Your hair is fine. You look fine. Can we just go now?

Because I'm a man, I will share equally in the housework. You just do the laundry, the cooking, the cleaning, the vacuuming, and the dishes, and I'll do the rest. Like wandering around in the garden with a beer, wondering what to do.

This has been a public service message to help women to better understand men.

Everything has a gender

You know how they say a boat is referred to as “She” and classified as female?

Well, I believe everything in this world actually does have a gender.

And here are some of them:

ZIPLOC BAGS are male, because they hold everything in, but you can always see right through them.

SHOES are male, because they are usually unpolished, with their tongues hanging out.

PHOTOCOPIERS are female, because once turned off, they take a while to warm up.

TIRES are male, because they go bald and are often over-inflated.

HOT AIR BALLOONS are male, because to get them to go anywhere you have to light a fire under them and, of course, there’s the hot air part.

SPONGES are female, because they are soft, squeezable and retain water.

THE SUBWAY is male, because it uses the same old lines to pick people up.

AN HOURGLASS is female, because over time, the weight shifts to the bottom.

HAMMERS are male, because they haven’t evolved much over the last 5,000 years, but they are handy to have around.

A REMOTE CONTROL is female . . . Ha! You thought it would be “male”. But consider this: it gives men pleasure, they’d be lost without it, and while they don’t always know the right buttons to push, they keep on trying

A guy out on the golf course takes a high speed ball right in the crotch.

Screaming in agony, he falls to the ground. As soon as he could manage, he took himself to the doctor.

He said “How bad is it doc? I’m going on my honeymoon next week and my fiancé is still a virgin in every way.”

The doctor told him, “Your testicles are fine, but I’ll have to put your penis in a splint to let it heal and keep it straight. It should be okay next week."

So he took four tongue depressors and formed a neat little 4-sided splint, and wired it altogether in an impressive work of art. The guy mentions none of this to his girl, marries her and goes on their honeymoon.

That night in the hotel room she rips open her blouse to reveal a gorgeous set of breasts. This was the first time he saw them.

"She said, You're the first, no one has ever touched these breasts."

Next she! takes off! her panties and says, "you're the first, no one has ever touched me here."

Barely able to contain himself, he immediately drops his pants and replies . . . .

"Look at this, it's still in the CRATE."

'Whatever you give a woman, she will make greater. If you give her sperm, she'll give you a baby. If you give her a house, she'll give you a home.

If you give her groceries, she'll give you a meal.

If you give her a smile, she'll give you her heart.

She multiplies and enlarges what is given to her.

So, if you give her any crap, be ready to receive a ton of shit.'

A man walks out to the street and catches a taxi just going by.

He gets into the taxi, and the cabbie says, "Perfect timing. You're just like Frank."

Passenger: 'Who?'

Cabbie: "Frank Feldman. He's a guy who did everything right all the time. Like my coming along when you needed a cab, things happened like that to Frank Feldman every single time."

Passenger: "There are always a few clouds over everybody."

Cabbie: "Not Frank Feldman He was a terrific athlete. He could have won the Grand-Slam at tennis. He could golf with the pros. He sang like an opera baritone and danced like a Broadway star and you should have heard him play the piano. He was an amazing guy."

Passenger: "Sounds like he was something really special."

Cabbie: "There's more . . . He had a memory like a computer. He remembered everybody's birthday. He knew all about wine, which foods to order and which fork to eat them with. He could fix anything. Not like me. I change a fuse, and the whole street blacks out. But Frank Feldman, he could do everything right."

Passenger: "Wow, some guy then."

Cabbie: "He always knew the quickest way to go in traffic and avoid traffic jams. Not like me, I always seem to get stuck in them. But Frank, he never made a mistake. He would never answer his wife back even if she was in the wrong; and his clothing, always immaculate, shoes highly polished too. He was the perfect man! No one could ever measure up to Frank Feldman."

Passenger: "An amazing fellow. How did you meet him?"

Cabbie: "Well, I never actually met Frank. He died. I'm married to his widow."

Guy, naked in front of the mirror: "Two inches more, and I would be a king." Wife: "Two inches less, and you'd be a queen."

DRUNK JOKES

A man drinks a shot of whiskey every night before bed. After years of this, the wife wants him to quit; she gets two shot glasses, filling one with water and the other with whiskey.

After getting him to the table that had the glasses, she brings his bait box. She says "I want you to see this." She puts a worm in the water, and it swims around.

She puts a worm in the whiskey, and the worm dies immediately. She then says, feeling that she has made her point clear, "what do you have to say about this experiment?"

He responds by saying: "If I drink whiskey, I won't get worms!"

A man walks into a bar and has a couple of beers. Once he is done the bartender tells him he owes $9.00.

"But I paid, don't you remember?" says the customer.

"Okay," says the bartender. "If you said you paid, you did."

The man then goes outside and tells the first person he sees that the bartender can't keep track of whether his customers have paid.

The second man then rushes in, orders a beer and later pulls the same stunt.

The barkeep replies, "If you say you paid, I'll take your word for it."

Soon the customer goes into the street, sees an old friend, and tells him how to get free drinks.

The man hurries into the bar and begins to drink high-balls when, suddenly, the bartender leans over and says, "You know, a funny thing happened in here tonight. Two men were drinking beer, neither paid and both claimed that they did. The next guy who tries that is going to get punched right in the nose."

"Don't bother me with your troubles," the final patron responds. "Just give me my change and I'll be on my way."

One night, this guy came into a bar and asks the bartender for a drink. Then he asks for another. After a couple more drinks, the bartender gets worried.

"What's the matter?" the bartender asks.

"My wife and I got into a fight," explained the guy "and now she isn't talking to me for a whole 31 days."

The bartender thought about this for a while. "But, isn't it a good thing that she isn't talking to you?" asked the bartender.

"Yeah, except today is the last night."

John Smith lived in Staten Island, New York and worked in Manhattan. He had to take the ferry home every night. One evening, he got down to the ferry and found there was a wait for the next boat, so John decided to stop at a nearby tavern. Before long he was feeling no pain.

When he got back to the ferry slip, the ferryboat was just eight feet from the dock. Smith, afraid of missing this one and being late for dinner, took a running leap and landed right on the deck of the boat.

"How did you like that jump, buddy?" said a proud John to a deck hand.

"It was great," said the sailor. "But why didn't you wait? We were just pulling in!"

A man walks into a pub and sits down next to a man with a dog at his feet. "Does your dog bite?"

"No."

A few minutes later the dog takes a huge chunk out of his leg.

"I thought you said your dog didn't bite!" the man says indignantly.

"That's not my dog."

A man goes to a bar with his dog. He goes up to the bar and asks for a drink. The bartender says "You can't bring that dog in here!" The guy, without missing a beat, says "This is my seeing-eye dog." "Oh man," the bartender says, "I'm sorry, here, the first one's on me." The man takes his drink and goes to a table near the door.

Another guy walks in the bar with a Chihuahua. The first guy sees him, stops him and says, "You can't bring that dog in here unless you tell him it's a seeing-eye dog." The second man graciously thanks the first man and continues to the bar. He asks for a drink. The bartender says "Hey, you can't bring that dog in here!"

The second man replies, "This is my seeing-eye dog." The bartender says, "No, I don't think so. They do not have Chihuahuas as seeing-eye dogs." The man pauses for a half-second and replies, "What?! They gave me a Chihuahua?!"

A man goes into a bar and seats himself on a stool. The bartender looks at him and says, "What'll it be buddy?"

The man says, "Set me up with seven whiskey shots and make them doubles." The bartender does this and watches the man slug one down, then the next, then the next, and so on until all seven are gone almost as quickly as they were served. Staring in disbelief, the bartender asks why he's doing all this drinking.

"You'd drink them this fast too if you had what I have."

The bartender hastily asks, "What do you have pal?"

The man quickly replies, "I have a dollar."

Two guys were in a bar, and they were both watching the television when the news came on. It showed a guy on a bridge who was about to jump, obviously suicidal. "I'll bet you $10 he'll jump," said the first guy. "Bet you $10 he won't," said the second guy.

Then, the guy on the television closed his eyes and threw himself off the bridge. The second guy hands the first guy the money.

"I can't take your money," said the first guy. "I cheated you. The same story was on the five o'clock news." "No, no. Take it," said the second guy. "I saw the five o'clock news too. I just didn't think the guy was dumb enough to jump again!"

John was sitting outside his local pub one day, enjoying a quiet pint and generally feeling good about himself, when a nun suddenly appears at his table and starts decrying the evils of drink.

"You should be ashamed of yourself young man! Drinking is a sin! Alcohol is the blood of the devil!"

Now John gets pretty annoyed about this, and goes on the offensive.

"How do you know this, Sister?"

"My Mother Superior told me so."

"But have you ever had a drink yourself? How can you be sure that what you are saying is right?"

"Don't be ridiculous of course I have never taken alcohol myself."

"Then let me buy you a drink-if you still believe afterwards that it is evil I will give up drink for life."

"How could I, a Nun, sit outside this public house drinking?"

"I'll get the barman to put it in a teacup for you, then no one will ever know."

The Nun reluctantly agrees, so John goes inside to the bar.

"Another pint for me, and a triple vodka on the rocks," then he lowers his voice and says to the barman, "and could you put the vodka in a teacup?"

"Oh no! It's not that Nun again is it?"

A serious drunk walked into a bar and, after staring for some time at the only woman seated at the bar, walked over to her and kissed her. She jumped up and slapped him silly. He immediately apologized and explained, "I'm sorry. I thought you were my wife. You look exactly like her."

"Why you worthless, insufferable, wretched, no good drunk!" she screamed.

"Funny," he muttered, "you even sound exactly like her."

A man in a bar sees a friend at a table, drinking by himself.

Approaching the friend he comments, "You look terrible. What's the problem?"

"My mother died in August," he said, "and left me $25,000."

"Gee, that's tough," he replied.

"Then in September," the friend continued, "My father died, leaving me $90,000."

"Wow. Two parents gone in two months. No wonder you're depressed."

"And last month my aunt died, and left me $15,000."

"Three close family members lost in three months? How sad."

"Then this month," continued, the friend, "absolutely nothing!"

A seaman meets a pirate in a bar, and talk turns to their adventures on the sea. The seaman notes that the pirate has a peg-leg, a hook, and an eye patch.

The seaman asks, "So, how did you end up with the peg-leg?" The pirate replies, "We were in a storm at sea, and I was swept overboard into a school of sharks. Just as my men were pulling me out, a shark bit my leg off."

"Wow!" said the seaman. "What about your hook?" "Well,'" replied the pirate, "We were boarding en enemy ship and were battling the other sailors with swords. One of the enemy cut my hand off."

"Incredible!" remarked the seaman. "How did you get the eye patch?" "A seagull dropping fell into my eye," replied the pirate.

"You lost your eye to a seagull dropping?," the sailor asked incredulously. "Well," said the pirate, "it was my first day with my hook"

A man walks into the front door of a bar. He is obviously drunk. He staggers up to the bar, seats himself on a stool, and with a belch, asks the bartender for a drink.

The bartender politely informs the man that it appears that he has already had plenty to drink-he could not be served additional liquor at this bar but could get a cab called for him.

The drunk is briefly surprised then softly scoffs, grumbles, climbs down off the bar stool, and staggers out the front door.

A few minutes later, the same drunk stumbles in the side door of the bar. He wobbles up to the bar and hollers for a drink. The bartender comes over, and still politely—but more firmly refuses service to the man due to his inebriation. Again, the bartender offers to call a cab for him.

The drunk looks at the bartender for a moment angrily, curses, and shows himself out the side door, all the while grumbling and shaking his head.

A few minutes later, the same drunk bursts in through the back door of the bar. He plops himself up on a bar stool, gathers his wits, and belligerently orders a drink.

The bartender comes over and emphatically reminds the man that he is clearly drunk, will be served no drinks, and either a cab or the police will be called immediately.

The surprised drunk looks at the bartender and in hopeless anguish, cries "Man! How many bars do you work at?"

A drunk phoned the police to report that thieves had been in his car. "They've stolen the dashboard, the steering wheel, the brake pedal, the radio, and even the accelerator," he cried out.

However, before the police investigation could start, the phone rang a second time and the same voice came over the line. "Never mind," he said with a hiccup, "I got in the back seat by mistake."

A man walks into a bar and asks the bartender, "If I show you a really good trick, will you give me a free drink?" The bartender considers it, then agrees. The man reaches into his pocket and pulls out a tiny rat. He reaches into his other pocket and pulls out a tiny piano. The rat stretches, cracks his knuckles, and proceeds to play the blues.

After the man finished his drink, he asked the bartender, "If I show you an even better trick, will you give me free drinks for the rest of the evening?" The bartender agrees, thinking that no trick could possibly be better than the first. The man reaches into his pocket and pulls out a tiny rat. He reaches into his other pocket and pulls out a tiny piano. The rat stretches, cracks his knuckles, and proceeds to play the blues. The man reaches into another pocket and pulls out a small bullfrog, who begins to sing along with the rat's music.

While the man is enjoying his beverages, a stranger confronts him and offers him $100,000.00 for the bullfrog. "Sorry," the man replies, "he's not for sale." The stranger increases the offer to $250,000.00 cash up front. "No," he insists, "he's not for sale." The stranger again increases the offer, this time to $500,000.00 cash. The man finally agrees, and turns the frog over to the stranger in exchange for the money.

"Are you insane?" the bartender demanded. "That frog could have been worth millions to you, and you let him go for a mere $500,000!" "Don't worry about it," the man answered. "The frog was really nothing special. You see, the rat's a ventriloquist."

An Irishman's been at a pub all night drinking beer. The bartender finally says that the bar is closed. So he stands up to leave and falls flat on his face. He figures he'll crawl outside and get some fresh air and maybe that will sober him up.

Once outside he stands up and falls flat on his face. So he crawls home and at the door stands up and falls flat on his face. He crawls through the door and up the stairs. When he reaches his bed he tries one more time to stand up. This time he falls right into bed and is sound asleep.

He awakens the next morning to his wife standing over him shouting at him. "So, you've been out drinking again!"

"How did you know?" he asks.

"The pub called, you left your wheelchair there again."

A drunk was proudly showing off his new apartment to a couple of his friends late one night. He led the way to his bedroom where there was a big brass gong and a mallet.

"What's with that big brass gong?" one of the guests asked.

"It's not a gong. It's a talking clock", the drunk replied.

"A talking clock? Seriously?" asked his astonished friend.

"Yup", replied the drunk.

"How's it work?" the friend asked, squinting at it.

"Watch", the drunk replied. He picked up the mallet, gave the gong an ear-shattering pound. The three stood looking at one another for a moment. Suddenly, someone on the other side of the wall screamed, "You idiot! It's one-fifteen in the morning!"

Seven signs that you may be drinking too much:

#1 You lose arguments with inanimate objects.

#2 Your job interferes with your drinking.

#3 You believe that a drinking problem is having two hands and just one mouth.

#4 The world comes into focus when you use one eye.

#5 Your car mysteriously moves every time you leave a bar.

#6 You believe it is no coincidence that there are twenty four hours in a day and twenty four beers in a case.

#7 You have to hang on to the floor to keep from falling off the planet.

Three Irishmen, Paddy, Sean and Seamus, were stumbling home from the pub late one night and found themselves on the road which led past the old graveyard. "Come have a look over here," says Paddy. "It's Michael O'Grady's grave, God bless his soul. He lived to the ripe old age of 87."

"That's nothing," says Sean, "here's one named Patrick O'Toole, it says here that he was 95 when he died.!"

Just then, Seamus yelled out, "Good God, here's a fella that got to be 145!"

"What was his name?" asks Paddy.

Seamus stumbles around a bit, awkwardly lights a match to see what else is written on the stone marker, and exclaims, "Miles, from Dublin."

Two men were sitting next to each other at a bar. After a while, one guy looks at the other and says, "I can't help but think, from listening to you, that you're from Ireland."

The other guy responds proudly, "Yes, that I am!"

The first guy says, "So am I! And where about from Ireland might you be?"

The other guy answers, "I'm from Dublin, I am."

The first guy responds, "Sure and begora, and so am I! And what street did you live on in Dublin?"

The other guy says, "A lovely little area it was, I lived on McCleary Street in the old central part of town."

The first guy says, "Faith and it's a small world, so did I! And to what school would you have been going?"

The other guy answers, "Well now, I went to St. Mary's of course."

The first guy gets really excited, and says, "And so did I. Tell me, what year did you graduate?"

The other guy answers, "Well, now, I graduated in 1964."

The first guy exclaims, "The Good Lord must be smiling down upon us! I can hardly believe our good luck at winding up in the same bar on this very night. Can you believe it, I graduated from St. Mary's in 1964 my own self."

About this time, another guy walks into the bar, sits down, and orders a beer. The bartender walks over shaking his head and mutters, "It's going to be a long night tonight, the Murphy twins are drunk again."

A man and his wife are awakened at 3 o'clock in the morning by a loud pounding on the door. The man gets up and goes to the door where a drunken stranger, standing in the pouring rain, is asking for a push.

"Not a chance," says the husband, "it is three o'clock in the morning!" He slams the door and returns to bed.

"Who was that?" asked his wife.

"Just some drunk guy asking for a push," he answers.

"Did you help him?" she asks.

"No, I did not; it is three in the morning, and it is pouring outside!"

"Well, you have a short memory," says the wife. "Can't you remember about three months ago when we broke down and those two guys helped us? I think you should help him, and you should be ashamed of yourself!"

The man does as he's told, gets dressed, and goes out into the pouring rain.

He calls out into the dark, "Hello, are you still there?"

"Yes," comes back the answer.

"Do you still need a push?" calls out the husband.

"Yes, please!" comes the reply from the dark.

"Where are you?" asks the husband.

"Over here on the swing!" replies the drunk.

POLITICAL JOKES

Are You Liberal, Conservative or Southerner?

How do you tell the difference between Liberals, Conservatives and Southerners? Pose the following question:

You're walking down a deserted street with your wife and two small children. Suddenly, a dangerous looking man with a huge knife comes around the corner, locks eyes with you, screams obscenities, raises the knife, and charges. You are carrying a Glock .40 — and you are an expert shot. You have mere seconds before he reaches you. What do you do?

Liberal Answer:

Well, that's not enough information to answer the question! Does the man look poor or oppressed? Have I ever done anything to him that would inspire him to attack? Could we run away? What does my wife think? What about the kids? Could I possibly swing the gun like a club and knock the knife out of his hand? What does the law say about this situation? Does the Glock have an appropriate safety built into it? Why am I carrying a loaded gun anyway—and what kind of message does this send to society and to my children? Is it possible he'd be happy with killing just me? Does he definitely want to kill me, or would he be content just to wound me? If I were to grab his knees and hold on, could my family get away while he was stabbing me? Should I call 9-1-1? Would the ACLU be able to advise? Why is this street so deserted? We need to raise taxes, have a paint and weed day, and make this a happier, healthier street that would discourage such behavior. This is all so confusing! I need to debate this with some friends for a few days and try to come to a consensus.

Conservative Answer: BANG!

Southerner's Answer:

BANG! BANG! BANG! BANG! BANG! BANG! BANG! BANG! BANG!

rackety-click . . . (sounds of reloading).

Wife: 'Hon, he looks like he's still moving, whadda y'all kids think?"

Son: "Mama's right Daddy, I saw it, too."

BANG! BANG! BANG! BANG! BANG! BANG! BANG! BANG! BANG! . . . . click.

Daughter: "Nice group, Daddy! Were those the Winchester Silver Tips?"

Four ex-U.S. Presidents are caught in a tornado, and off they whirled to OZ.

They finally make it to the Emerald City and come before the Great Wizard.

"What brings you before the great wizard of Oz?"

Jimmy Carter stepped forward timidly: "I've come for some courage."

"No problem!" says the Wizard. "Who is next?"

Ronald Reagan steps forward, "Well, ... I . . . . I think I need a brain."

"Done," says the Wizard. "Who comes next before the great and powerful Oz?"

Up stepped George Bush sadly and said, "I'm told by the American people that I need a heart."

"I've heard it's true!" says the Wizard. "Consider it done."

There is a great silence in the hall. Bill Clinton is just standing there, looking around, but doesn't say a word. Irritated, the Wizard finally asks, "What do you want?"

He says "Is Dorothy here?"

Dear Friends,

This chain letter was started in hopes of bringing relief to other tired and discouraged woman.

Unlike most chain letters, this one does not cost anything. Just send a copy of this letter to five of your friends who are equally tired and discontented.

Then bundle up your husband or boyfriend and send him to the woman whose name appears at the top of the following list, and add your name to the bottom of the list.

When your turn comes, you will receive 15,625 men. One of them is bound to be better than the one you already have.

At the writing of this letter, a friend of mine had already received 184 men, of whom 4 were worth keeping.

REMEMBER this chain letter brings luck.

One woman's cat died, and the next day she received a hunk.

A woman living with her mother was able to choose between a Chippendale dancer and an Olympic swimmer.

You can be lucky, too, but DO NOT BREAK THE CHAIN! One woman broke the chain and got her own husband again!

Keep it going, ladies! Just add your name to the list below!

Hillary Clinton
Chappaqua, NY

A cowboy was herding his cows in a remote pasture when suddenly a brand-new BMW advanced out of a dust cloud towards him. The driver, a young man in a Brioni suit, Gucci shoes, Ray Ban sunglasses and YSL tie, leans out the window and asks the cowboy,

"If I tell you exactly how many cows and calves you have in your herd, will you give me a calf?"

The cowboy looks at the man, obviously a yuppie, then looks at his peacefully grazing herd and calmly answers,

"Sure, Why not?"

The yuppie parks his car, whips out his Dell notebook computer, connects it to his Cingular RAZR V3 cell phone, and surfs to a NASA page on the Internet, where he calls up a GPS satellite navigation system to get an exact fix on his location which he then feeds to another NASA satellite that scans the area in an ultra-high-resolution photo. The young man then opens the digital photo in Adobe Photoshop and exports it to an image processing facility in Hamburg, Germany.

Within seconds, he receives an email on his Palm Pilot that the image has been processed and the data stored.

He then accesses a MS-SQL database through an ODBC

connected Excel spreadsheet with email on his Blackberry and, after a few minutes, receives a response.

Finally, he prints out a full-color, 150-page report on his hi-tech, miniaturized HP LaserJet printer and turns to the cowboy and says,

"You have exactly 1,586 cows and calves."

"That's right. Well, I guess you can take one of my calves," says the cowboy.

He watches the young man select one of the animals and looks on amused as the young man stuffs it into the trunk of his car.

Then the cowboy says to the young man,

"Hey, if I can tell you exactly what your business is, will you give me back my calf?"

The young man thinks about it for a second and then says,

"Okay, why not?"

You're a Congressman for the U.S. Government", says the cowboy.

"Wow! That's correct," says the yuppie, "but how did you guess that?"

"No guessing required." answered the cowboy.

"You showed up here even though nobody called you; you want to get paid for an answer I already knew, to a question I never asked. You tried to show me how much smarter than me you are; and you don't know a thing about cows . . .

Now give me back my dog."

Students were assigned to read 2 books, "Titanic" & "My Life" by Bill Clinton. One smart ass student turned in the following book report, with the proposition that they were nearly identical stories! His cool professor gave him an A+ for this report:

Titanic: Cost $29.99

Clinton: Cost $29.99

Titanic: Over 3 hours to read

Clinton: Over 3 hours to read

Titanic: The story of Jack and Rose, their forbidden love, and subsequent catastrophe.

Clinton: The story of Bill and Monica, their forbidden love, and subsequent catastrophe.

Titanic: Jack is a starving artist.

Clinton: Bill is a bullshit artist.
Titanic: In one scene, Jack enjoys a good cigar.
Clinton: Ditto for Bill.
Titanic: During ordeal, Rose's dress gets ruined.
Clinton: Ditto for Monica.
Titanic: Jack teaches Rose to spit.
Clinton: Let's not go there.
Titanic: Rose gets to keep her jewelry.
Clinton: Monica's forced to return her gifts.
Titanic: Rose remembers Jack for the rest of her life.
Clinton: Clinton doesn't remember Jack.
Titanic: Rose goes down on a vessel full of seamen.
Clinton: Monica . . . ooh, let's not go there, either.
Titanic: Jack surrenders to an icy death.
Clinton: Bill goes home to Hillary . . . basically the same thing.

A driver is stuck in a traffic jam on the highway. Nothing is moving. Suddenly a man knocks on the window.

The driver rolls down his window and asks, "What happened?"

"Terrorists have kidnapped Hillary Clinton, Jesse Jackson, and Al Sharpton. They are asking for a $10 million ransom. Otherwise they are going to douse them with gasoline and set them on fire. We are going from car to car, taking up a collection."

The driver asks, "How much is everyone giving, on average?"

"About a gallon"

John the farmer was in the fertilized egg business. He had several hundred young layers (hens), called "pullets", and ten roosters, whose job it was to fertilize the eggs.

The farmer kept records and any rooster that didn't perform went into the soup pot and was replaced. That took an awful lot of his time, so he bought a set of tiny bells and attached them to his roosters. Each bell had a different tone so John could tell from a distance, which rooster was performing. Now he could sit on the porch and fill out an efficiency report simply by listening to the bells.

The farmer's favorite rooster was old Butch, a very fine

specimen he was, too. But on this particular morning John noticed old Butch's bell hadn't rung at all John went to investigate. The other roosters were chasing pullets, bells- a-ringing. The pullets, hearing the roosters coming, would run for cover.

But to Farmer John's amazement, old Butch had his bell in his beak, so it couldn't ring. He'd sneak up on a pullet, do his job and walk on to the next one. John was so proud of old Butch, he entered him in the County Fair and he became an overnight sensation among the judges. The result . . . The judges not only awarded old Butch the No Bell Piece Prize but they also awarded him the Pulletsurprise as well. Clearly old Butch was a politician in the making: who else but a politician could figure out how to win two of the most highly coveted awards on our planet by being he best at sneaking up on the populace and screwing them when they weren't paying attention.

Al Gore and Bill and Hillary Clinton go to heaven, and God addresses Al first. "Al, what do you believe in?"

Al replies: "Well, I believe that I won that election, but that it was your will that I did not serve. And I've come to understand that now."

God thinks for a second and says: "Very good. Come and sit at my left."

Got then addresses Bill. "Bill, what do you believe in?"

Bill Replies: "I believe in forgiveness. I've sinned, but I've never held a grudge against my fellow man,;

And I hope no grudges are held against me."

God thinks for a second and says: "You are forgiven, my son. Come and sit at my right."

Then God addresses Hillary. "Hillary, what do you believe in?"

She replies: "I believe you're in my chair."

Hillary Clinton goes to her doctor for a physical, only to find out that she's pregnant.

She is furious . . . Here she's in the middle of her new job as Secretary of State and this has happened to her.

She calls home, gets Bill on the phone and immediately starts screaming; "How could you have let this happen? With all that's going on right now, you go and get me pregnant!

How could you? I can't believe this! I just found out I am five weeks pregnant and it is all your fault! Your fault!

Well, what have you got to say?"

There is nothing but dead silence on the phone.

She screams again, "Did you hear me?"

Finally she hears Bill's very, very quiet voice. In a barely audible whisper, he says, "Who is this?."

One morning a blind bunny was hopping down the bunny trail, tripped over a large snake and fell, kerplop right on his twitchy little nose.

"Oh please, excuse me!" said the bunny. "I didn't mean to trip over you, but I'm blind & can't see."

"That's perfectly all right," replied the snake. "To be sure, it was my fault. I didn't mean to trip you, but I'm blind too, and I didn't see you coming. By the way, what kind of animal are you?"

"Well, I really don't know," replied the bunny. "I'm blind and I've never seen myself. Maybe you could examine me and find out."

So the snake felt the bunny all over, and said, "Well, you're soft and cuddly, and you have long silky ears and a little fluffy tail and a dear twitchy little nose. You must be a bunny rabbit!"

The bunny replied, "I can't thank you enough! But by the way, what kind of animal are you?" The snake replied that he didn't know, and the bunny agreed to examine him.

When the bunny was finished, the snake asked, "Well, what kind of an animal am I?"

The bunny had felt the snake all over, and replied, "You're soft, you're cold, you're slippery and you haven't got any balls. You must be a politician."

I just got a letter from the IRS indicating that I still owed $3,405 from my last years taxes. I have packaged up my payment along with this letter:

Dear IRS:

Enclosed is my last years Tax Deficiency Notice & payment. Please take note of the attached article from the USA Today newspaper. In the article, you will see that the Pentagon is paying $171.50 for hammers and NASA has paid $600.00 for a toilet seat. Please find enclosed four toilet seats (value $2400) and six hammers (value $1029). This brings my total payment to $3429.00. Please note the overpayment of $24.00 and apply it to the "Presidential Election Fund," as noted on my return. Might I suggest you send the above mentioned fund a "1.5 inch screw." (See attached article . . . HUD paid $22.00 for a 1.5 inch Phillips Head Screw.) It has been a pleasure to pay my tax bill this year, and I look forward to paying it again next year.

Sincerely, Joe Six-pack

One afternoon, the US President is sitting in his office when his phone rings.

"Hello Mr. President," a heavily accented voice says. "This is Yankel down in Tel-Aviv Israel. I am ringing to inform you that I am officially declaring war on you!"

"Well, Yankel," he replies, "This indeed is important news! Tell me, how big is your army?"

"At this moment in time," says Yankel, after a moments calculation, "There is myself, my cousin Berl, my next door neighbor Gerry and the entire Lubavitch team from the schul. That makes 8!"

The President sighs and says, "I must tell you Yankel, that I have 1 million men in my army waiting to move on my word".

"OK," says Yankel. "I'll have to ring you back!"

Sure enough, the next day Yankel calls back.

"Right Mr. President, the war is still on! We have managed to acquire some equipment!"

What equipment would that be, Yankel?" he asks.

"Well, we have 2 combine harvesters, a bulldozer and Berl's tractor from the kibbutz".

Once more the President sighs and says, "I must tell you Yankel, that I have 50,000 tanks, 2000 mine layers, 10,000 armored cars and my army has increased 1 and a half million since we last spoke".

"A Choleria!!" says Yankel. "I'll have to ring you back!"

Sure enough, Yankel calls again the next day.

"Right Mr. President, the war is still on! We have managed to get ourselves airborne! We've gotten out old Chiam's crop duster with a couple of rifles in the cockpit and the Torah Group has joined us as well!"

Once more the President sighs and says "I must tell you Yankel, that I have 4000 bombers and 8000 high maneuverability attack planes and my military installations are surrounded by laser guided surface to air missiles and since we last spoke, my army has increased to 2 million."

"Oi Vaiy!," says Yankel. "I'll have to ring you back"

Sure enough, Yankel calls again the next day.

"Right Mr. President, I am sorry to tell you that we have had to call off the war"

"I'm very sorry to hear that," says the President. "Why the sudden change of heart?"

"Well," says Yankel, "We've all had a talk, and to be sure there's no way we can cope with 2 million prisoners"

Cheney gets a call from his "boss", W.

"I've got a problem," says W.

"What's the matter?" asks Cheney.

"Well, you told me to keep busy in the Oval Office, so, I got a jigsaw puzzle, but it's too hard. None of the pieces fit together and I can't find any edges."

"What's it a picture of?" asks Cheney.

"A big rooster," replies W.

"All right," sighs Cheney, "I'll come over and have a look."

So he leaves his office and heads over to the Oval Office. W points at the jigsaw on his desk. Cheney looks at the desk and then turns to W and says, "For crying out loud, Georgie—put the corn flakes back in the box."

A lot of folks can't understand how we came to have an oil shortage here in America. Well, there's a very simple answer. Nobody bothered to check the oil. We just didn't know we were getting low. The reason for that is purely geographical.

Our OIL is located in Alaska, California, Oklahoma and TEXAS.

Our DIPSTICKS are ALL located in Washington DC.

A woman went to her doctor for advice. She told him that her husband had developed a penchant for anal sex, and she was not sure that it was such a good idea

"Do you enjoy it?" The doctor asked.

"Actually, yes, I do."

"Does it hurt you?" he asked.

"No. I rather like it."

"Well, then,' the doctor continued, 'there's no reason that you shouldn't practice anal sex, if that's what you like, so long as you take care not to get pregnant."

The woman was mystified. 'What? You can get pregnant from anal sex?'

"Of course," the doctor replied. 'Where do you think politicians come from?

An Indian walks into a cafe with a shotgun in one hand and pulling a male buffalo with the other.

He says to the waiter:

"Want coffee."

The waiter says, "Sure, Chief. Coming right up."

He gets the Indian a tall mug of coffee.

The Indian drinks the coffee down in one gulp,

Turns and blasts the buffalo with the shotgun,

Causing parts of the animal to splatter everywhere

And then just walks out.

The next morning the Indian returns.

He has his shotgun in one hand, pulling

Another male buffalo with the other.

He walks up to the counter and says to the waiter

"Want coffee."

The waiter says "Whoa, Tonto!

We're still cleaning up your mess from yesterday. What was all that about, anyway?"

The Indian smiles and proudly says

"Training for position in United States Congress:

Come in, drink coffee, shoot the bull,

Leave mess for others to clean up,

Disappear for rest of day."

Jose & Carlos are panhandling on the street.

Jose drives a Mercedes, lives in a mortgage free house and has a lot of money to spend.

Carlos only brings in 2 to 3 dollars a day.

Carlos asks Jose how he can bring home a suitcase full of $10 bills every day.

Jose says "Look at your sign. It says: I have no work, a wife and 6 kids to support".

Then Carlos looks at Jose's sign. It reads:

"I only need another $10.00 to move back to Mexico."

I was traveling between Phoenix and Ajo the other day south of Gila Bend when a tire blew out. Checking my spare, I found that it too was flat. My only option was to flag down a passing motorist and get a ride to the next town.

The first vehicle to stop was an old man in a van. He yelled out the window, "Need a lift?"

"Yes, I sure do," I replied.

"You a Republican or Democrat," asked the old man.

"Republican," I replied.

"Well, you can just go to Heck," yelled the old man as he sped off.

Another guy stopped, rolled down the window, and asked me the same question. Again, I gave the same answer, "Republican"

The driver gave me the finger and drove off.

I thought it over and decided that maybe I should change my

strategy, since this area seemed to be overly political and there appeared to be few Republicans.

The next car to stop was a red convertible driven by a beautiful blonde. She smiled seductively and asked if I was a Republican or Democrat.

"Democrat," I shouted

"Hop in!" replied the blonde.

Driving down the road, I couldn't help but stare at the gorgeous woman in the seat next to me, the wind blowing through her hair, perfect breasts, and a short skirt that continued to ride higher and higher up her thighs.

Finally, I yelled, "Please stop the car." She immediately slammed on the brakes and as soon as the car stopped, I jumped out.

"What's the matter", she asked.

"I can't take it anymore," I replied. "I've only been a Democrat for five minutes and already I want to screw somebody."

Three contractors were bidding to fix the White House fence. One was from New York, another was from Kentucky and the third was from Florida. Along with a White House official, they examined the fence.

The Florida contractor took out a tape measure, did some measuring, then worked on some figures with a pencil. "Well," he said, "I figure the job will run about $900. That would be $400 for materials, $400 for my crew, and a $100 profit for me."

The Kentucky contractor also did some measuring and figuring, then said, "I can do this job for $700. That would be $300 for materials, $300 for my crew, and a $100 profit for me."

The New York contractor didn't do any measuring or figuring, but leaned over to the White House official and whispered, "$2,700."

The official was incredulous and said, "You didn't even measure like the other guys! How did you come up with such a high figure?"

"Easy," the New Yorker explained; "$1,000 for you, $1,000 for me, and we hire the guy from Kentucky."

THE WORST FOURSOME IN GOLF:
1. MONICA LEWINSKI
2. O. J. SIMPSON
3. TED KENNEDY
4. BILL CLINTON
WHY YOU ASK: Well, , , , , , ,
1. MONICA IS A HOOKER
2. O. J. IS A SLICER
3. TED CAN'T DRIVE OVER WATER, and. .
4. BILL CAN'T REMEMBER WHICH HOLE HE PLAYED

One night, George W. Bush is tossing restlessly in his White House bed.

He awakens to see George Washington standing by him. Bush asks him, "George, what's the best thing I can do to help the country?"

"Set an honest and honorable example, just as I did," Washington advises, then fades away.

The next night, Bush is astir again, and sees the ghost of Thomas Jefferson moving through the darkened bedroom.

Bush calls out, "Tom, please! What is the best thing I could do to help the country?"

"Respect the Constitution, as I did," Jefferson advises, and dims from sight.

The third night sleep is still not in the cards for Bush. He awakes to see the ghost of F. D. R. hovering over his bed. Bush whispers, "Franklin, What is the best thing I could do to help the country?"

"Help the less fortunate, just as I did," FDR replies and fades into the mists.

Bush isn't sleeping well the fourth night when he sees another figure moving in the shadows. It is Abraham Lincoln's ghost.

"Abe, what is the best thing I can do right now, to help the country?" Bush pleads.

Abe replies, "Go see a play."

Al Gore and George Bush were in New Hampshire campaigning. In the spirit of bipartisanship, they shared a tiny "puddle jumper" airplane between the smaller campaign stops. After one stop, they were joined by a Catholic priest and an Orthodox Rabbi, who were on their way to an ecumenical retreat deep in the New Hampshire woods.

As they crossed the White Mountains, the plane lost power and the pilot bailed out. They quickly found out the reason for the pilot's haste—the plane had only four parachutes.

Gore shouted, "I'm the Vice President. I have to survive!", grabbed one of the remaining three 'chutes, and jumped.

Bush shouted, "I'm the only hope for the Republican party and I have to survive!", grabbed another 'chute, and jumped.

The priest turned to the rabbi and said, "Rabbi, I am an old man. I have never married and have no family. You, on the other hand, have a wife, children, and even grandchildren. They will feel your loss terribly. Take the last parachute and save yourself."

The Rabbi calmly replied, "Don't worry, Father, there are still two 'chutes left. I fear I should have warned him, but George W jumped with my tallis and tefillin."

President Bush was invited to address a major gathering of the American Indian Nation in upper New York State. He spoke for almost an hour on his future plans for increasing every Native American's present standard of living. He referred to his career as a Texas Governor and then as President, how he had signed "YES" for every Indian issue that came to his desk for approval. Although the President was vague on the details of his plan, he seemed most enthusiastic about his future ideas for helping his "red brothers and sisters".

At the conclusion of his speech, the Tribes presented the President with a plaque inscribed with his new Indian name—Walking Eagle. The proud President then departed in his motorcade, waving to the crowds. A news reporter later inquired of the group of chiefs of how they came to select the new name given to the President. They explained that Walking Eagle is the name given to a bird so full of shit it can no longer fly.

The government today announced that it is changing its national symbol to a CONDOM because it more accurately reflects the government's political stance. A condom allows for inflation, halts production, destroys the next generation, and gives you a sense of security while you're actually being screwed.

Damn, it just doesn't get more accurate than that.

RELIGION JOKES

Back in the old west, a westbound wagon train was lost and low on food. No other humans had been seen for days and then the pioneers saw an old Jew sitting beneath a tree.

"Is there some place ahead where we can get food?"

"Vell, I tink so," the old man said, "but I wouldn't go up dat hill und down de udder side. Somevun tole me you'd run into a big bacon tree."

"A bacon tree?" asked the wagon train leader.

"Yah, a bacon tree. Vould I lie? Trust me. I vouldn't go dere."

The leader goes back and tells his people what the old Jew said.

"So why did he say not to go there?" a person asked. Other pioneers said, "Oh, you know those Jews—they have a thing about pork."

So the wagon train goes up the hill and down the other side.

Suddenly, Indians attack them from everywhere and massacre all except the leader who manages to escape and get back to the old Jew.

Near dead, the man shouts, "You fool! You sent us to our deaths! We followed your route, but there was no bacon tree, just hundreds of Indians who killed everyone but me."

The old man holds up his hand and says, "Vait a minute."

He quickly picks up an English-Yiddish dictionary and begins thumbing through it.

Oy, I made such ah big mishtake! It vuzn't a bacon tree . . .

"It vuz a ham bush."

A kindergarten teacher gave her class a 'show and tell' assignment. Each student was instructed to bring in an object to share with the class that represented their religion. The first student got up in front of the class and said, 'My name is Benjamin and I am Jewish and this is a Star of David.'

The second student got up in front of the class and said, 'My name is Mary. I'm a Catholic and this is a Rosary.'

The third student got in up front of the class and said, 'My name is Tommy. I am a Baptist, and this is a casserole.'

A priest, a minister and a guru sat discussing the best positions for prayer, while a telephone repairman worked nearby.

'Kneeling is definitely the best way to pray,' the priest said.

'No,' said the minister. 'I get the best results standing with my hands outstretched to Heaven.'

'You're both wrong,' the guru said. 'The most effective prayer position is lying down on the floor.'

The repairman couldn't contain himself any longer. 'Hey, fellas,' he interrupted. 'The best prayin' I ever did was when I was hangin' upside down from a telephone pole.'

The LOST CHAPTER IN GENESIS: Adam was walking around the garden of Eden feeling very lonely, so God asked him, "What is wrong with you?" Adam said he I didn't have anyone to talk to. God said that He was going to make Adam a companion and that it would be a woman. He said, "This person will gather food for you, cook for you, and when you discover clothing she'll wash it for you. She will always agree with every decision you make. She will bear your children and never ask you to get up in the middle of the night to take care of them. She will not nag you and will always be the first to admit she was wrong when you've had a disagreement. She will never have a headache and will freely give you love and passion whenever you need it.

Adam asked God, "What will a woman like this cost?"

God replied, "An arm and a leg."

Then Adam asked, "What can I get for a rib?"

The rest is history!

A crusty old man walks into the local First Baptist Church and says to the secretary, “I would like to join this damn church.”

The astonished woman replies, “I beg your pardon, sir. I must have misunderstood you. What did you say?”

“Listen up, damn it. I said I want to join this damn church!”

“I’m very sorry sir, but that kind of language is not tolerated in this church.”

The secretary leaves her desk and goes into the pastor’s study to inform him of her situation. The pastor agrees that the secretary does not have to listen to that foul language. They both return to her office and the pastor asks the old geezer, “Sir, what seems to be the problem here?”

“There is no damn problem,” the man says. “I just won $200 million bucks in the damn lottery and I want to join this damn church to get rid of some of this damn money.”

“I see,” said the pastor. “And is this bitch giving you a hard time?”

A lawyer and an elderly Jewish man are sitting next to each other on a long flight. The lawyer is thinking that Jews are so dumb that he could get over on them easy . . . so the lawyer asks if the Jew would he like to play a fun game.

The old Jewish man is tired and just wants to take a nap, so he politely declines and tries to catch a few winks. The lawyer persists, and says that the game is a lot of fun. I ask you a question, and if you don’t know the answer, you pay me only $5; you ask me one, and if I don’t know the answer, I will pay you $500, he says. This catches the Jew’s attention and to keep the lawyer quiet, he agrees to play the game.

The lawyer asks the first question. ‘What’s the distance from The Earth to the Moon?’ The elderly Jew doesn’t say a word, reaches in his pocket pulls out a five-dollar bill, and hands it to the lawyer.

Now, it’s the Jew’s turn. He asks the lawyer, ‘What goes up a hill with three legs, and comes down with four?’ The lawyer uses his laptop and searches all references he could find on the Net. He sends e-mails to all the smart friends he knows, all to no avail. After one hour of searching he finally gives up. He wakes up the Jewish man and hands him $500. The old Jew pockets the $500 and goes right back to sleep.

The lawyer is going nuts not knowing the answer. He wakes the elderly Jew up and asks, 'Well, so what goes up a hill with three legs and comes down with four?'

The Jew shrugs, reaches in his pocket, hands the lawyer $5 and goes back to sleep.

Bill Gates has advertised for a new chairman of Microsoft Europe.

Five thousand candidates assemble in a large room. One of them is Maurice Cohen, a little Jewish man who was born in Tunisia.

Bill Gates thanks the candidates for coming, but asks all those who are not familiar with the JAVA program language to leave.

Two thousand people rise and leave the room. Maurice Cohen says to himself, 'I do not know this language but what have I got to lose if I stay? I'll give it a try!"

Bill Gates then asks all those who have no experience in managing teams of more than one hundred people to leave.

Another two thousand people go. Maurice Cohen says to himself, 'I have never managed anybody, but myself but what have I got to lose if I stay? What can happen to me?"

Then Bill Gates asks all candidates who do not have outstanding academic qualifications to rise and leave.

Five hundred more people remove themselves.

Maurice Cohen says to himself, 'I left school at 15, but what have I got to lose if I stay? So he stays in the room.

Lastly, Bill Gates asks all of the candidates who do not speak the Serbo-Croatian language to rise and leave. Four hundred and ninety-eight people get up and lave the room.

Maurice Cohen says himself, 'I do not speak Serbo-Croatian, but what the hell! Have I got anything to lose?"

He finds himself alone with one other candidate. Everyone else has gone. Bill Gats joins them and says, 'Apparently you are the only two candidates who speak Serbo-Croatian. I'd like to hear you converse with one another in Serbo-Coratian.'

Calmly, Maurice turns to the other candidate and says to him:

'Baroukh ata Adonai.'
The other candidate answers:
'Elohinou melekh holam

One very windy day, a rabbi was on his way to the temple. Suddenly a strong gust of wind blew his streimel (hat) off his head. The rabbi ran after it, but the wind was so strong that it kept blowing his hat farther and farther away. He could not catch up with it.

A young man, a gentile, witnessing this event and being fitter than the rabbi, ran after the hat, caught it and handed it over to him. The rabbi was so happy and grateful that he gave the man five dollars and put his hand on the man's head and blessed him. The young man was very excited about the tip and the blessing and decided to go to the racetrack to bet his five unexpected dollars.

After the races the young man returned home and recounted his very exciting day at the races to his father. "I arrived at the fifth race," said the young man, "looked at the program and saw a horse by the name of Top Hat running. The odds on the horse were 100 to 1, the longest shot in the field. Having received the rabbi's blessing and the five dollars and thinking of the rabbi's hat and the horse's name being Top Hat, I thought this was a message from God, so I bet the five dollars on this horse. An amazing thing happened; the horse that was the longest shot in the field and who did not have the slightest chance to even show came in first by five lengths."

"You must have made a fortune," said the father.

"Yes, $500, but wait, it gets better," replied the son. "On the following race, I looked at the program. A horse by the name of Stetson was running. The odds on the horse were 30 to 1. Stetson being some kind of hat and again thinking of the rabbi's blessing and his hat, I decided to bet all my winnings on this horse."

"What happened?" asked the excited father.

"The horse Stetson won and I collected big money."

"You mean you brought home all this money?" asked his excited father.

"No," said the son, "I lost it all on the next race. There was a horse in this race named Chateau, so I bet all the money on it, because the horse was the heavy favorite, and the name also means hat in French, and it all started with the rabbi's hat. But the horse broke down and came in last."

"Hat in French is chapeau not chateau, said the father. You lost all that money because of your ignorance. Tell me who won the race anyway?"

"A long-shot Japanese horse named Yamaka.

In the winter of 1926, Thelma Goldstein from Brooklyn treated herself to her first real vacation in Florida. Being unfamiliar with the area, she wandered into a restricted hotel in North Miami.

"Excuse me," she said to the manager. "My name is Mrs. Goldstein, and I'd like a small room for two weeks."

I'm awfully sorry, he replied, "but all our rooms are occupied." Just as he said that, a man came down and checked out.

"What luck," said Mrs. Goldstein. "Now there's a room."

"Not so fast, Madam. I'm sorry, but this hotel is restricted. No Jews allowed."

"Jewish? Who's Jewish? I happen to be Catholic."

"I find that hard to believe. Let me ask you, who was the Son of God?"

"Jesus, Son of Mary."

"Where was he born?"

"In a stable."

"And why was he born in a stable?"

"Because a schmuck like you wouldn't let a Jew rent a room in his hotel!"

While in Israel I found a great buy on a computer. It is a kosher computer called a DELLSHALOM.

If you or a friend are considering a kosher computer, you should know that there were some important upgrades and changes from the typical computer you are used to, such as:

1. The cursor moves from right to left.

2. It comes with two hard drives, one for fleishig business software and one for milchig games.

3. Instead of getting a "General Protection Fault" error, my PC now gets "Ferklempt."

4. The Chanukah screen savers include "Flying Dreidels."

5. The PC shuts down automatically at sundown on Friday evenings.

6. After my computer dies, I have to dispose of it within 24 hours.

7. The "Start" button has been replaced with a "Let's go! I'm not getting any younger!" button.

8. When disconnecting external devices from the back of my PC, I am instructed to "Remove the cable from the PC's tuchus."

9. The multimedia player has been renamed to "Nu, so play my music already!"

10. Internet Explorer has a spinning "Star of David" in the upper right

A Hassidic family is most concerned that their 30 year old son is unmarried. So, they call a marriage broker and ask him to find their son a good wife. The broker comes over to their house and spends a long time asking question of the son and his parents as to what they want in a wife/daughter-in-law. They give him a long shopping list of requirements.

The marriage broker takes a long time looking and finally asks to visit the family again. He then tells them of a wonderful woman he has found. He says she's just the right age for the son . . . she keeps a Glat Kosher home . . . she regularly attends synagogue and knows the prayers by heart . . . she is a wonderful cook . . . she loves children and wants a large family. And, to crown it all, she's gorgeous.

After hearing all this, the family is very impressed and begins to get excited about the prospects of a wedding in the near future. But the son pauses and asks inappropriately: "Is she also good in bed?" The marriage broker answers, "some say yes . . . some say no."

FOUR RELIGIOUS TRUTHS

1. Muslims do not recognize Jews as God's chosen people.
2. Jews do not recognize Jesus as the Messiah.
3. Protestants do not recognize the Pope as the leader of the Christian World.
4. Baptists do not recognize each other at Hooters.

God populated the earth with broccoli and cauliflower and spinach and green and yellow vegetables of all kinds so Man and Woman would live long and healthy lives.

And Satan created McDonald's. And McDonald's brought forth the 99 cent double cheeseburger. And Satan said to Man, "You want fries with that?"

And Man said, "Super size it!"

And Man gained pounds.

And God created the healthful yogurt that woman might keep her figure that man found so fair.

And Satan froze the yogurt and brought forth chocolate, nuts and brightly colored sprinkle candy to put on the yogurt.

And woman gained pounds.

And God said, "Try my crispy fresh salad."

And Satan brought forth creamy dressings, bacon bits and shredded cheese. And then for dessert, ice cream.

And woman gained pounds.

And God said, "I have sent you heart healthy vegetables and olive oil with which to cook them."

And Satan brought forth chicken fried steak from Cracker Barrel so big that it needed its own platter. And Man gained pounds and his bad cholesterol went through the roof.

And God brought forth running shoes and Man resolved to lose those extra pounds.

And Satan brought forth cable TV with remote control so Man would not have to toil to change channels between ESPN and ESPN2.

And Man gained pounds.

And God said, "You're running up the score, Devil."

And God brought forth the potato, a vegetable naturally low in fat and brimming with nutrition.

And Satan peeled off the healthful skin and sliced the starchy center into chips and deep fat fried them.

And he did also create sour cream dip.

And Man clutched his remote control and ate the potato chips swaddled in cholesterol. And Satan saw and said, “It is good.”

And Man went into cardiac arrest.

And God sighed and created quadruple bypass surgery.

And Satan created HMO’s. . . . .

A new priest at his first mass was so nervous he could hardly speak.

After mass he asked the monsignor how he had done. The monsignor replied, “When I am worried about getting nervous on the pulpit, I put a glass of vodka next to the water glass. If I start to get nervous, I take a sip.” So next Sunday he took the monsignor’s advice. At the beginning of the sermon, he got nervous and took a drink. He proceeded to talk up a storm. Upon his return to his office after mass, he found the following note on the door:

1. Sip the Vodka, don’t gulp.
2. There are 10 commandments, not 12.
3. There are 12 disciples, not 10.
4. Jesus was consecrated, not constipated.
5. Jacob wagered his donkey, he did not bet his ass.
6. We do not refer to Jesus Christ as the late J.C.
7. The Father, Son, and Holy Ghost are not referred to as daddy, junior and the spook.
8. David slew Goliath, he did not kick the shit out of him.
9. When David was hit by a rock and knocked off his donkey, don’t say he was stoned off his ass.
10. We do not refer to the cross as the “Big T”.

One particular Christmas season a long time ago, Santa was getting ready for his annual trip, but there were problems everywhere.

Four of his elves got sick, and the trainee elves did not produce the toys as fast as the regular ones, so Santa was beginning to feel the pressure of being behind schedule.

Then Mrs. Claus told Santa that her mom was coming to visit. This stressed Santa even more.

When he went to harness the reindeer, he found that three of them were about to give birth, and two had jumped the fence and were out, heaven knows where.

More stress.

Then when he began to load the sleigh, one of the boards cracked and the toy bag fell to the ground and scattered the toys.

So, frustrated, Santa went into the house for a cup of coffee and a shot of whiskey. When he went to the cupboard, he discovered that the elves had hid the liquor and there was nothing to drink.

In his frustration, he accidentally dropped the coffee pot, and it broke into hundreds of little pieces all over the kitchen floor.

He went to get the broom and found that mice had eaten the straw it was made from.

Just then, the doorbell rang and Santa cussed on his way to the door.

He opened the door, and there was a little angel with a great big Christmas tree. The angel said, very cheerfully, "Merry Christmas Santa. Isn't it just a lovely day? I have a beautiful tree for you. Isn't it just a lovely tree? Where would you like me to stick it?"

Thus began the tradition of the little angel on top of the Christmas tree.

One day Mrs. Jones went to have a talk with the minister at the local church. "Reverend," she said, "I have a problem, my husband keeps falling asleep during your sermons. It's very embarrassing. What should I do?"

"I have an idea," said the minister. "Take this hatpin with you. I will be able to tell when Mr. Jones is sleeping, and I will motion to you at specific times. When I motion, you give him a good poke in the leg."

In church the following Sunday, Mr. Jones dozed off. Noticing this, the preacher put his plan to work. "And who made the ultimate sacrifice for you?" he said, nodding to Mrs. Jones.

"Jesus!", Jones cried as his wife jabbed him the leg with the hatpin.

"Yes, you are right, Mr. Jones," said the minister. Soon, Mr. Jones nodded off again. Again, the minister noticed. "Who is your redeemer?" he asked the congregation, motioning towards Mrs. Jones.

"God!" Mr. Jones cried out as he was stuck again with the hatpin.

"Right again," said the minister, smiling. Before long, Mr. Jones again dozed off. However, this time the minister did not notice. As he picked up the tempo of his sermon, he made a few motions that Mrs. Jones mistook as signals to bayonet her husband with the hatpin again.

The minister asked, "And what did Eve say to Adam after she bore him his 99th son?"

Mrs. Jones poked her husband, who yelled, "You stick that damned thing in me one more time and I'll break it in half and shove it up your ass!"

"Amen," replied the women of the congregation.

A hardworking Jew finally makes it in business, and he treats himself to a new Lamborghini. After buying it, he feels guilty that he spent so much money on a car, so he goes to the Orthodox Rabbi in his neighborhood and asks for a mezuzah to put on the door of the Lamborghini to make himself feel better.

"You want a mezuzah for what?" the Rabbi asks.

"For my Lamborghini."

"What's a Lamborghini?" asks the Rabbi.

"A sports car,' he replies

"What? That's blasphemy!" the Rabbi shouts. "You want a mezuzah for a sports car? Go to a Conservative Rabbi!"

The fellow goes to the Conservative Rabbi and asks him for a mezuzah.

"You want a mezuzah for what?" the Rabbi asks.

"For my Lamborghini", the man replies.

"What's a Lamborghini?" asks the Rabbi.

"A car, a sports car."

'What kind of sports car?" asks the Rabbi.

"Italian."

What? That is ridiculous!" the Rabbi shouts. "You want a mezuzah for a Goyishe car? Go to a Reform Rabbi!"

Now the man feels even more guilty and more disappointed, but he goes to the Reform Rabbi in his neighborhood and asks him, "Can you give me a mezuzah for my Lamborghini?"

"You have a Lamborghini?" asks the Rabbi.

"You know what it is?" says the man.

"Of course! It's a fantastic Italian sports car. But, what's a mezuzah?"

Sister Mary Katherine entered the Monastery of Silence. The Priest said, "Sister, this is a silent monastery. You are welcome here as long as you like, but you may not speak until I direct you to do so".

Sister Mary Katherine lived in the monastery for 5 years before the Priest said to her, "Sister Mary Katherine, you have been here for 5 years. You may speak two words."

Sister Mary Katherine said, "Hard bed."

"I'm sorry to hear that," the Priest said, "We will get you a better bed."

After another 5 years, Sister Mary Katherine was called by the Priest. "You may say another two words, Sister Mary Katherine.

"Cold food," said Sister Mary Katherine, and the Priest assured her that the food would be better in the future.

On her 15th anniversary at the monastery, the Priest again called Sister Mary Katherine into his office. "You may say two words today."

"I quit," said Sister Mary Katherine.

"It's probably best", said the Priest, "You've done nothing but bitch since you got here."

A nun, badly needing to use the restroom, walked into a local Hooters.

The place was hopping with music and loud conversation and every once in a while, the lights would turn off. Each time the lights went out, the place would erupt into cheers. However, when the revelers saw the nun, the room went dead quiet. She walked up to the bartender and asked, “May I please use the restroom?”

The bartender replied, “OK, but I should warn you that there is a statue of a naked man in there wearing only a fig leaf.”

“Well, in that case, I’ll just look the other way,” said the nun. So the bartender showed the nun to the back of the restaurant.

After a few minutes, she came back out, and the whole place stopped just long enough to give the nun a loud round of applause. She went to the bartender and said, “Sir, I don’t understand. Why did they applaud me just because I went to the restroom?”

“Well, now they know you’re one of us,” said the bartender. “Would you like a drink?”

“But I still don’t understand,” said the puzzled nun.

“You see,” laughed the bartender, “every time someone lifts the fig leaf on that statue, the lights go out. Now, how about that drink?”

The Wednesday-night church service coincided with the last day of hunting season. So the pastor asked who had bagged a deer. No one raised a hand. Puzzled, the pastor said, “I don’t get it. Last Sunday many of you said you were missing because of hunting season. I had the whole congregation pray for your deer.”

On hunter groaned, “Well, it worked. They’re all safe.”

One Sunday our priest announced he was passing out miniature crosses made of palm leaves. “Put this cross in the room where your family argues most,” he advised. “When you look at it, the cross will remind you that God is watching.”

As I was leaving church, the woman in front of me walked up to the priest, shook his hand and said, “I’ll take five.”

The wise old Mother Superior was dying. The nuns gathered around her bed, trying to make her comfortable. They gave her some warm milk to drink, but she refused it.

Then one nun took the glass back to the kitchen. Remembering a bottle of whiskey received as a gift the previous Christmas, she opened it and poured a generous amount into the warm milk.

Back at Mother Superior's bed, she held the glass to her lips. Mother drank a little, then a little more, then before they knew it, it was all gone. "Mother, Mother" the nuns cried, "Give us some wisdom before you die!" She raised herself up in bed with a pious look on her face and pointing out the window, she said "Don't sell that cow.

There were 3 good arguments that Jesus was Black:

1. He called everyone brother.
2. He liked Gospel.
3. He couldn't get a fair trial.

But then there were 3 equally good arguments that Jesus was Jewish:

1. He went into His Father's business.
2. He lived at home until he was 33.
3. He was sure his Mother was a virgin and his Mother was sure He was God.

But then there were 3 equally good arguments that Jesus was Italian:

1. He talked with His hands.
2. He had wine with His meals.
3. He used olive oil.

But then there were 3 equally good arguments that Jesus was a Californian hippy:

1. He never cut His hair.
2. He walked around barefoot all the time.
3. He started a new religion.

But then there were 3 equally good arguments that Jesus was a Native American:

1. He was at peace with nature.

2. He ate a lot of fish.
3. He talked about the Great Spirit.

But then there were 3 equally good arguments that Jesus was Irish:

1. He never got married.
2. He was always telling stories.
3. He loved green pastures.

And there are three good reasons to think that Jesus was Gay: (Which is compatible, simultaneously, with any of the above).

1. He lived with his mother until he was middle aged.
2. He never married, but hung out with some interesting women.. . . .
3. He had at least twelve boy-friends, one of whom was a lout . . .

But the most compelling evidence of all—3 proofs that Jesus was a WOMAN:

1. He fed a crowd at a moment's notice—when there was no food.
2. He kept trying to get a message across to a bunch of men who just didn't get it.
3. And even when He was dead, He had to get up because there was work to do.

Mrs. Donovan was walking down O'Connell Street in Dublin when she met up with Father Flaherty. The Father said, 'Top o' the mornin' to ye! Aren't ye Mrs. Donovan, and didn't I marry ye and yer hoosband 2 years ago?' She replied, 'Aye, that ye did, Father.'

The Father asked, 'And be there any wee little ones yet?' She replied 'No, not yet, Father.' The Father said, 'Well now, I'm going to Rome next week and I'll light a candle for ye and yer hoosband.' She replied, 'Oh, thank ye, Father.' They then parted ways.

Some years later they met again. The Father asked, 'Well now, Mrs. Donovan, how are ye these days?' She replied, 'Oh, very well, Father!' The Father asked, 'And tell me, have ye any wee ones yet?' She replied, 'Oh yes, Father! Three sets of twins and 4 singles, 10 in all!'

The Father said, 'That's wonderful! How is yer loving hoosband doing?' She replied, 'E's gone to Rome to blow out yer damn candle.'

A drunk man who smelled like beer sat down on a subway seat next to a priest. The man's tie was stained, his face was plastered with red lipstick, and a half empty bottle of gin was sticking out of his torn coat pocket. He opened his newspaper and began reading.

After a few minutes the man turned to the priest and asked, "Say, Father, what causes arthritis?"

The priest replied, "My Son, it's caused by loose living, being with cheap, wicked women, too much alcohol and a contempt for your fellow man, sleeping around with prostitutes and lack of a bath."

The drunk muttered in response, "Well, I'll be damned," then returned to his paper.

The priest, thinking about what he had said, nudged the man and apologized. "I'm very sorry. I didn't mean to come on so strong. How long have you had arthritis?"

The drunk answered, "I don't have it, Father. I was just reading here that the Pope does."

"Bless me Father, for I have sinned. I have been with a loose girl".

The priest asks, "Is that you, little Tommy Iello?"

"Yes, Father, it is."

"And who was the girl you were with?"

"I can't tell you, Father, I don't want to ruin her reputation."

"Well, Tommy, I'm sure to find out her name sooner or later, so you may as well tell me now. Was it Tina Minetti?"

"I cannot say.

"Was it Teresa Volpe?"

"I'll never tell."

"Was it Nina Capelli?"

"I'm sorry, but I cannot name her."

"Was it Maria Piriano?"

"My lips are sealed."

"Was it Rosa Di Angelo, then?"

"Please, Father, I cannot tell you."

The priest sighs in frustration. "You're very tight lipped, Tommy, and I admire that. But you've sinned and have to atone. You cannot be an altar boy for 4 months. Now you go and behave yourself."

Tommy walks back to his pew, and his friend Nino slides over and whispers,

"What'd you get?"

"4 months vacation and five good leads. . . . . . ."

Moses and Jesus were in a threesome playing golf one day. Moses pulled up to the tee and drove a long one.

The ball landed in the fairway, but rolled directly toward a water hazard.

Quickly Moses raised his club, the water parted and it rolled to the other side, safe and sound.

Next, Jesus strolled up to the tee and hit a nice long one directly toward the same water hazard. It landed right in the center of the pond and kind of hovered over the water. Jesus casually walked out on the pond and chipped the ball onto the green.

The third guy got up and randomly whacked the ball.

It headed out over the fence and into oncoming traffic on a nearby street. It bounced off a truck and hit a nearby tree. From there, it bounced onto the roof of a shack close by and rolled down into the gutter, down the drain spout, out onto the fairway and straight toward the aforementioned pond. On the way to the pond, the ball hit a stone and bounced out over the water onto a lily pad, where it rested quietly. Suddenly a very large bullfrog jumped up on a lily pad and snatched the ball into his mouth. Just then, an eagle swooped down and grabbed the frog and flew away. As they passed over the green, the frog squealed with fright and dropped the ball, which bounced right into the cup for a hole in one.

Moses turned to Jesus and said, "I hate playing with your Dad."

A Catholic priest and a nun were taking a rare afternoon off and enjoying a round of golf. The priest stepped up to the first tee and took a mighty swing. He missed the ball entirely and said "Shit, I missed."

The good Sister told him to watch his language.

On his next swing, he missed again. "Shit, I missed."

"Father, I'm not going to play with you if you keep swearing," the nun said tartly.

The priest promised to do better and the round continued. On the 4th tee, he misses again. The usual comment followed.

Sister is really mad now and says, "Father John, God is going to strike you dead if you keep swearing like that."

On the next tee, Father John swings and misses again. "Shit, I missed."

A terrible rumble is heard and a gigantic bolt of lightning comes out of the sky and strikes Sister Marie dead in her tracks.

And from the sky comes a booming voice. . . . . . .

"Shit, I missed."

Three women die together in an accident and go to heaven.

When they get there, St. Peter says, "We only have one rule here in heaven: don't step on the ducks!"

So they enter heaven, and sure enough, there are ducks all over the place. It is almost impossible not to step on a duck, and although they try their best to avoid them, the first woman accidentally steps on one.

Along comes St. Peter with the ugliest man she ever saw.

St. Peter chains them together and says, "Your punishment for stepping on a duck is to spend eternity chained to this ugly man!"

The next day, the second woman accidentally steps on a duck and along comes St. Peter, who doesn't miss a thing. With him is another extremely ugly man. He chains them together with the same admonishment as for the first woman.

The third woman has observed all this and, not wanting to be chained for all eternity to an ugly man, is very, VERY careful where she steps.

She manages to go months without stepping on any ducks, but

one day St. Peter comes up to her with the most handsome man she has ever laid eyes on . . . very tall, long eyelashes, muscular, and thin.

St. Peter chains them together without saying a word.

The happy woman says, "I wonder what I did to deserve being chained to you for all of eternity?"

The guy says, "I don't know about you, but I stepped on a duck!"

A Jewish mother walks her son to school on his first day in kindergarten.

"Behave, my Bubelah" she says to him. "Take good care of yourself, my Tataleh". "Come right back home on the bus, Sheyneleh. Your Mommy loves you a lot, my Ketsaleh."

At the end of the school day the bus comes back and she runs to her son and hugs him. "So what did, my Pupelah, learn?"

The boy answers, "I learned my name is Marvin!!"

Sitting behind a couple of nuns at a baseball game (whose head gear partially blocked the view, three men decided to badger the nuns in an effort to get them to move.

In a very loud voice, the first guy said, "I think I'm going to move to Utah, there are only 100 nuns living there."

The second guy spoke up and said, "I want to go to Montana, there are only 50 nuns living there."

The third guy said, "I want to go to Idaho, there are only 25 nuns living there."

*One of the nuns turned around, looked at the men and in a very sweet, calm voice said, "Why don't you go to hell. . . . there aren't any nuns there".

A married Irishman went into the confessional and said to his priest, "I almost had an affair with another woman."

The priest said, "What do you mean, almost?"

The Irishman said, "Well, we got undressed and rubbed together, but then I stopped."

The priest said, "Rubbing together is the same as putting it in. You're not to see that woman again. For your penance, say five Hail Mary's and put $50 in the poor box."

The Irishman left the confessional, said his prayers, and then walked over to the poor box.

He paused for a moment and then started to leave.

The priest, who was watching, quickly ran over to him saying, "I saw that. You didn't put any money in the poor box!"

The Irishman replied, "Yeah, but I rubbed the $50 on the box, and according to you, that's the same as putting it in!"

There once was a religious young Irishwoman who went to Confession. Upon entering the confessional, she said, "Forgive me, Father, for I have sinned."

The priest said, "Confess your sins and be forgiven."

The young woman said, "Last night my boyfriend made mad, passionate love to me seven times."

The priest thought long and hard and then said, "Squeeze seven lemons into a glass and then drink the juice."

The young woman asked, "Will this cleanse me of my sins?"

The priest said, "No, but it will wipe that smile off of your face."

Muldoon lived alone in the Irish countryside with only a pet dog for company. One day the dog died, and Muldoon went to the parish priest and asked, "Father, my dog is dead. Could ya' be saying' a mass for the poor creature?"

Father Patrick replied, "I'm afraid not; we cannot have services for an animal in the church. But there are some Baptists down the lane, and there's no tellin' what they believe. Maybe they'll do something for the creature."

Muldoon said, "I'll go right away Father. Do ya' think $5,000 is enough to donate to them for the service?"

Father Patrick exclaimed, "Sweet Mary, Mother of Jesus! Why didn't ya tell me the dog was Catholic?

Father O'Malley answers the phone. "Hello, is this Father O'Malley?"

"It is!"

"This is the IRS. Can you help us?"

"I can!"

"Do you know a Ted Houlihan?"

"I do!"

"Is he a member of your congregation?"

"He is!"

"Did he donate $10,000 to the church?"

"He will."

An elderly man walks into a confessional. The following conversation ensues:

Man: "I am 92 years old, have a wonderful wife of 70 years, many children, grandchildren, and great grandchildren. Yesterday, I picked up two college girls, hitchhiking. We went to a motel, where I had sex with each of them three times."

Priest: "Are you sorry for your sins?"

Man: "What sins?"

Priest: "What kind of a Catholic are you?"

Man: "I'm Jewish."

Priest: "Why are you telling me all this?"

Man: "I'm telling everyone."

Smith climbs to the top of Mt. Sinai to get close enough to talk to God.

Looking up, he asks the Lord . . . "God, what does a million years mean to you?"

The Lord replies, "A minute."

Smith asks, "And what does a million dollars mean to you?"
The Lord replies, "A penny."
Smith asks, "Can I have a penny?"
The Lord replies, "In a minute."

A man goes to see the Rabbi. "Rabbi, something terrible is happening and I have to talk to you about it."

The Rabbi asked, "What's wrong?"

The man replied, "My wife is poisoning me."

The Rabbi, very surprised by this, asks, "How can that be?"

The man then pleads, "I'm telling you, I'm certain she's poisoning me, what should I do?"

The Rabbi then offers, "Tell you what. Let me talk to her, I'll see what I can find out and I'll let you know."

A week later the Rabbi calls the man and says, "Well, I spoke to your wife. I spoke to her on the phone for three hours.

You want my advice?"

The man said yes and the Rabbi replied,

"Take the poison."

Mother Superior called all the nuns together and said to them, "I must tell you all something. We have a case of gonorrhea in the convent."

"Thank God," said an elderly nun at the back. "I'm so tired of chardonnay."

A man in Topeka, Kansas, decided to write a book about churches around the country. He started by flying to San Francisco and started working east from there. Going to a very large church, he began taking photographs and making notes.

He spotted a golden telephone on the vestibule wall and was intrigued with a sign, which read "Calls: $10,000 a minute." Seeking out the pastor, he asked about the phone and the sign. The pastor answered that this golden phone is, in fact, a direct line to heaven and if he pays the price he can talk directly to GOD.

The man thanked the pastor and continued on his way.

As he continued to visit churches in Seattle, Denver, St. Louis, Chicago, Milwaukee, and around the United States, he found more phones, with the same sign, and the same answer from each pastor.

Finally, he arrived in Mississippi. Upon entering a church in Oxford, Ms., behold—he saw the usual golden telephone. But THIS time, the sign read "Calls: 35 cents."

Fascinated, he asked to talk to the pastor, "Reverend, I have been in cities all across the country, and in each church I have found this golden telephone and have been told it is a direct line to Heaven and that I could talk to GOD but in the other churches the cost was $10,000 a minute.

Your sign reads only 35 cents a call. Why?"

The pastor, smiling benignly, replied, "Son, you're in the South now

. . . . . . You're in God's Country. It's a local call."

There were two Catholic boys, Timothy Murphy and Antonio Secola, whose lives parallel each other in amazing ways.

In the same year Timothy was born in Ireland, Antonio was born in Italy. Faithfully they attended parochial School from Kindergarten through their senior year in high school. They took their vows to enter the priesthood early in college, and upon graduation, became priests.

Their careers had come to amaze the world, but it was generally acknowledged that Antonio Secola was just a cut above Timothy Murphy in all respects.

Their rise through the ranks of Bishop, Archbishop and finally Cardinal was swift to say the least, and the Catholic world knew that when the present Pope died, it would be one of the two who would become the next Pope.

In time the Pope did die, and the College of Cardinals went to work.

In less time than anyone had expected, white smoke rose

from the chimney and the world waited to see whom they had chosen.

The world, Catholic, Protestant and secular, was surprised to learn that Timothy Murphy had been elected Pope!

Antonio Secola was beyond surprise. He was devastated, because even with all of Timothy's gifts, Antonio knew he was the better qualified. With gall that shocked the Cardinals, Antonio Secola asked for a private Session with them in which he candidly asked, "Why Timothy?"

After a long silence, an old Cardinal took pity on the bewildered man and rose to reply. "We knew you were the better of the two, but we just could not bear the thought of the leader of the Roman Catholic Church being called Pope Secola."

An Irish priest is driving down to New York and gets stopped for speeding in Connecticut.

The state trooper smells alcohol on the priest's breath and then sees an empty wine bottle on the floor of the car. He says, "Sir, have you been drinking?"

"Just water," says the priest.

The trooper says, "Then why do I smell wine?"

The priest looks at the bottle and says, "Good Lord! He's done it again!"

Mary Clancy goes up to Father O'Grady after his Sunday morning service, and she's in tears.

He says, "So what's bothering you, Mary my dear?"

She says, "Oh, Father, I've got terrible news. My husband passed away last night."

The priest says, "Oh, Mary, that's terrible. Tell me, did he have any last requests?"

She says, "That he did, Father . . ."

The priest says, "What did he ask, Mary?"

She says, "He said, 'Please Mary, put down the gun!'

Drunk Ole Mulvihill (From the Northern Irish Clan) staggers into a Catholic Church, enters a confessional box, sits down but says nothing.

The Priest coughs a few times to get his attention but Ole just sits there.

Finally, the Priest pounds three times on the wall.

The drunk mumbles, "ain't no use knockin, there's no paper on this side either."

Two Irishmen were sitting at a pub having beer and watching the brothel across the street.

They saw a Baptist minister walk into the brothel, and one of them said, "Aye, 'tis a shame to see a man of the cloth goin' bad."

Then they saw a rabbi enter the brothel, and the other Irishman said, "Aye, 'tis a shame to see that the Jews are fallin' victim to temptation as well."

Then they see a catholic priest enter the brothel, and one of the Irishmen said, "What a terrible pity . . . one of the girls must be dying.

Yeshiva University decided to field a rowing team. Unfortunately, they lose race after race. Even though they practice and practice for hours everyday, they never manage to come in any better than dead last. Finally, the team decides to send Morris Goldberg, its captain, to spy on Harvard, the perennial championship team.

So Morris schleps off to Cambridge and hides in the bushes next to the Charles River, where he carefully watches the Harvard team at its daily practices. After a week, Morris returns to Yeshiva.

"Well, I figured out their secret", he announces.

"What? Tell us! Tell us!" his teammates shout.

"We should have only one guy yelling. The other eight should row."

A visitor to Israel attended a recital and concert at the Moscovitz Auditorium. He was quite impressed with the architecture and the acoustics. He inquired of the tour guide, "Is this magnificent auditorium named after Chaim Moscovitz, the famous Talmudic scholar?"

"No," replied the guide. "It is named after Sam Moscovitz, the writer.

Never heard of him. What did he write?"

"A check", replied the guide.

The Italian says, "I'm tired and thirsty. I must have wine."

The Frenchman says, "I'm tired and thirsty. I must have cognac."

The Russian says, "I'm tired and thirsty. I must have vodka."

The German says, "I'm tired and thirsty. I must have beer."

The Mexican says, "I'm tired and thirsty. I must have tequila."

The Jew says, "I'm tired and thirsty. I must have diabetes

I saw a billboard the other day that said:

NEED HELP?, CALL JESUS 1-800-555-3787

Out of curiosity, I called.

A Mexican showed up with a lawnmower.

Three very pious Jews dressed in long black coats with beards were playing golf.

A guy named Murphy wanted to play golf and this was the only threesome in which he could play.

So, he joins the Rabbis and plays 18 holes. At the end of the 18 holes, his score was 104.

The Rabbis had shot 69, 70 and 72.

So, he says to the Rabbis "How come you guys shoot such good golf?"

The lead Rabbi says, "When you lead a religious life, join and attend the right synagogue, you are rewarded."

Murphy, a true lover of golf, thinks, "what have I got to lose?" He finds a synagogue near his home, converts to Judaism, joins the synagogue, regularly attends services and leads a holy life.

About a year later, he again plays golf with the three Rabbis. He shoots a 104 and they shoot a 69, 70 and 71.

He says to them: "OK, I converted, joined a synagogue, live a religious life and I still shoot a 104.

What's the deal?"

"What synagogue did you join?" asks the lead Rabbi.

"Beth El," is the reply.

The Rabbi retorted, "Schmuck, Beth El is for tennis!"

Two Jewish sisters-in-law meet at their weekly session at the beauty shop. Ruth says to Golda, "Such news I got for you, Golda! My Irving is finally getting married. He tells me he is engaged to this wonderful Jewish girl, but he thinks the poor darling may have some strange illness called herpes." After offering congratulations, Golda says to Ruth, "So, Ruthie, do you have any idea what is this herpes, and can our Irving catch it?" Ruth answers, "God forbid! But his Papa and I are just so happy to hear about his engagement. You know how we've all worried about him. It's past time he's settled with a nice girl. As far as the herpes goes, who knows?" "Well," Golda says, "I have a very fine medical dictionary, you know, Ruthie. I'll just run home right now and look it up and call you." So, Golda goes home, looks it up, and calls Ruth excitedly, "Ruth! Ruth! Thank goodness, I found it. Not to worry! It says herpes is a disease affecting the gentiles.

An elderly woman walked into the local country church. The friendly usher greeted her at the door and helped her up the flight of steps, 'Where would you like to sit?' he asked politely.

'The front row please,' she answered.

'You really don't want to do that,' the usher said 'The pastor is really boring.'

'Do you happen to know who I am?' the woman inquired. 'No.' he said. 'I'm the pastor's mother,' she replied indignantly.

'Do you know who I am?' he asked. 'No.' she said. 'Good,' he answered.

One Sunday morning, a mother went in to wake her son and tell him it was time to get ready for church, to which he replied, 'I'm not going.'

'Why not?' she asked.

I'll give you two good reasons,' he said, '(1), they don't like me, and (2), I don't like them.'

His mother replied, 'I'll give YOU two good reasons why YOU SHOULD go to church.

(1) You're 59 years old, and (2) you're the pastor!'

A Jewish Rabbi and a Catholic Priest met at the town's annual 4th of July picnic. Old friends, they began their usual banter.

'This baked ham is really delicious,' the priest teased the rabbi. 'You really ought to try it. I know it's against your religion, but I can't understand why such a wonderful food should be forbidden! You don't know what you're missing. You just haven't lived until you've tried Mrs. Hall's prized Virginia Baked Ham. Tell me, Rabbi, when are you going to break down and try it?'

The rabbi looked at the priest with a big grin, and said, 'At your wedding.'

The young couple invited their elderly pastor for Sunday dinner. While they were in the kitchen preparing the meal, the minister asked their son what they were having. 'Goat,' the little boy replied.

'Goat?' replied the startled man of the cloth, 'Are you sure about that?'

'Yep,' said the youngster. 'I heard Dad say to Mom, 'Today is just as good as any to have the old goat for dinner.'

On a flight from Atlanta, GA., a middle-aged, well to do woman found herself sitting next to a man wearing a kipa ("yarmulka" in Yiddish).

She called the attendant over to complain about her seating. "What seems to be the problem Madam?" asked the attendant. "You've sat me next to a Jew!! I can't possibly sit next to this disgusting person. Find me another seat!"

"Please calm down Madam." the attendant replied. "The flight is very full today, but I'll tell you what I'll do. I'll go and check to see if we have any seats available in club or first class."

The woman shoots a snooty look at the snubbed Jewish man beside her (not to mention many of the surrounding passengers). A few minutes later the attendant returns. The woman cannot help but look at the people around her with a smug and self satisfied grin.

The flight attendant then says . . . "Madam, unfortunately, as I suspected, economy is full. I've spoken to the cabin services director, and club is also full. However, we do have one seat in first class. "Before the lady has a chance to respond, the attendant continues . . . "It is most extraordinary to make this kind of upgrade, however, and I have had to get special permission from the captain. But, given the circumstances, the captain felt that it was outrageous that someone should be forced to sit next to such a person." . . .

With which, the attendant turned to the Jewish man sitting next to her, and said; "So if you'd like to get your things, sir, I have your seat in first class ready for you. . . ."

At this point, the surrounding passengers stood and gave a standing ovation, while the Jewish man walked up to the front of the plane. "Shabbat Shalom".

. . . When the attendant tells the lady the Captain's arrangement the lady says indignantly "I think that The Captain must have made some kind of mistake." To which the attendant replied, "No M'am. Captain Cohen never makes any mistakes."

A priest and a rabbi were sitting next to each other on an airplane.

After a while, the priest turned to the rabbi and asked, 'Is it still a requirement of your faith that you not eat pork?'

The rabbi responded, "Yes, that is still one of our beliefs.'

The priest then asked, 'Have you ever eaten pork?'

To which the rabbi replied, 'Yes, on one occasion I did succumb to temptation and tasted a ham sandwich.'

The priest nodded in understanding and went on with his reading.

A while later, the rabbi spoke up and asked the priest, 'Father, is it still a requirement of your church that you remain celibate?'

The priest replied, 'Yes, that is still very much a part of our faith.'

The rabbi then asked him, 'Father, have you ever fallen to the temptations of the flesh?

The priest replied, 'Yes, rabbi, on one occasion I was weak and broke with my faith.'

The rabbi nodded understandingly and remained silent, thinking, for about five minutes.

Finally, the rabbi said, 'Beats a ham sandwich, doesn't it?

A fleeing Taliban, desperate for water, was trudging through the Afghanistan desert when he saw something far off in the distance. Hoping to find water, he hurried towards it, only to find a little old Jewish man at a small stand selling ties.

The Taliban asked, "Do you have water?"

The Jewish man replied, "I have no water. Would you like to buy a tie? They are only $5."

The Taliban shouted, "Infidel! I do not need an over-priced tie! I need water! I should kill you, but I must find water first!"

"OK, OK" said the old Jewish man, "It does not matter that you do not want to buy a tie and that you hate me. I will show you that I am bigger than that. If you continue over that hill to the east for about two miles, you will find a lovely restaurant. It has all the ice cold water you need. Shalom."

Muttering, the Taliban staggered away over the hill. Several hours later he staggered back, almost dead . . . "Your lousy brother won't let me in without a tie!"

The Israelis and Arabs finally realized that if they continued fighting, they would someday end up destroying the world. So they sat down and decided to settle the whole dispute with a dogfight. The negotiators agreed that each country would take five years to develop the best fighting dog they could. The dog that won the fight would earn its country the right to rule the disputed areas. The losing side would have to lay down its arms.

The Arabs found the biggest, meanest Dobermans and Rottweilers in the world. They bred them together and then crossed their offspring with the meanest Siberian wolves. They selected only the biggest, strongest puppy from each litter, and fed them the best food. They used steroids and trainers in their quest for the perfect killing machine.

After the five years were up, they had a dog that needed iron prison bars on its cage. Only the trainers could handle this beast. When the day of the big fight arrived, the Israelis showed up with a strange animal. It was a nine-foot-long Dachshund.

Everyone felt sorry for the Israelis. No one thought this weird animal stood a chance against the growling beast in the Arab camp. The bookies predicted the Arabs would win in less than a minute. The cages were opened. The Dachshund waddled toward the center of the ring.

The Arab dog leapt from his cage and charged the giant wiener-dog. As he got to within an inch of the Israeli dog, the Dachshund opened its jaws and swallowed the Arab beast in one bite. There was nothing left but a small bit of fur from the killer dog's tail.

The Arabs approached the Israelis, shaking their heads in disbelief. 'We do not understand,' said their leader. 'Our top scientists and breeders worked for five years with the meanest, biggest Dobermans and Rottweilers. They developed a killing machine.'

'Really?' the Israeli General replied. 'For five years, we've had a team of Jewish plastic surgeons in Beverly Hills working to make an alligator look like a Dachshund.'

Rosh Hashanah is quickly approaching. Meyer, a lonely widower, was walking home along Delancy Street one day wishing something wonderful would happen into his life, when he passed a pet store and heard a squawking voice shouting out in Yiddish: "Quawwwwk . . . vus macht du. . Yeah, du . . . outside, standing like a putzel . . . eh?"

Meyer rubbed his eyes and ears. Couldn't believe it. The proprietor sprang out of the door and grabbed Meyer by the sleeve. "Come in here, fella, and check out this parrot . . . "

Meyer stood in front of an African Grey that cocked his little head and said: "Vus? Kenst reddin Yiddish?"

Meyer turned excitedly to the store owner. "He speaks Yiddish?"

"Vuh den? Chinese maybe?"

In a matter of moments, Meyer had placed five hundred dollars down on the counter and carried the parrot in his cage away with him. All night he talked with the parrot in Yiddish. He told the parrot about his father's adventures coming to America. About how beautiful his mother was when she was a young bride. About his family. About his years of working in the garment center. About Florida. The parrot listened and commented. They shared some walnuts. The parrot told him of living in the pet store, how he hated the weekends. They both went to sleep.

Next morning, Meyer began to put on his tfillin all the while, saying his prayers. The parrot demanded to know what he was doing and when Meyer explained, the parrot wanted some too. Meyer went out and hand-made a miniature set of tfillin for the parrot. The parrot wanted to learn to daven, and learned every prayer. He wanted to learn to read Hebrew so Meyer spent weeks and months, sitting and teaching the parrot, teaching him Torah. In time, Meyer came to love and count on the parrot as a friend and a Jew. He had been saved.

One morning, on Rosh Hashanah, Meyer rose and got dressed and was about to leave when the parrot demanded to go with him. Meyer explained that Shul was not a place for a bird but the parrot made a terrific argument and was carried to Shul on Meyer's shoulder. Needless to say, they made quite a spectacle, and Meyer was questioned by everyone, including the Rabbi and Cantor. They refused to allow a bird into the building on the High Holy Days but Meyer convinced them to let him in this one time, swearing that parrot could daven. Wagers were made with Meyer. Thousands of dollars were bet (even odds) that the parrot could NOT daven, 'could not speak Yiddish or Hebrew, etc.

All eyes were on the African Grey during services. The parrot perched on Meyer's shoulder as one prayer and song passed—Meyer heard not a peep from the bird. He began to become annoyed, slapping at his shoulder and mumbling under his breath, "Daven!"

Nothing.

"Daven . . . parrot, you can daven, so daven . . . come on, everybody's looking at you!" Nothing.

After Rosh Hashanah services were concluded, Meyer found that he owed his Shul buddies and the Rabbi over four thousand dollars. He marched home, upset as hell, saying nothing. Finally several blocks from the Temple the bird began to sing an old Yiddish song and was happy as a lark. Meyer stopped and looked at him.

"You miserable bird, you cost me over four thousand dollars. Why? After I made your tfillin and taught you the morning prayers, and taught you to read Hebrew and the Torah. And after you begged me to bring you to Shul on Rosh Hashanah, why? Why did you do this to me?"

"Don't be a schmuck," the parrot replied. "Think of the odds on Yom Kippur!"

A Texan bought a round of drinks for all in the bar and said that his wife had just produced "a typical Texas baby" weighing twenty pounds.

Wow! . . . and congratulations from all around . . ., Two weeks later he returned to the same bar. The bartender recognized him and asked, "Aren't you the father of the typical Texas baby that weighted twenty pounds at birth? How much does he weigh now?"

"The proud father answered, "10 pounds."

The bartender said, "Why . . . what happened? He did weigh TWENTY pounds!"

The proud Texas father pulled a slow hard drink on a Lone Star long neck beer, wiped his lips on his shirtsleeve, leaned into the bartender and proudly said, "Just had him circumsized!"

Ten top reasons how you know if you are a Jewish redneck

1) You think a hora is a high priced call girl

2) You light your shabbos candles from your cigarette

3) Your belt buckle is bigger than your yarmulke

4) Instead of a noisemaker, you've fired a shotgun at the sound of haman's name

5) You have a gun rack in your sukkah

6) You think "KKK" is a symbol for really Kosher.

7) You think marrying your first cousin is required according to Jewish law.

8) You don't ride on shabbat because your car is up on blocks.

9) When someone shouts l'chaim your respond l'howdy

10) You are saving a bottle of Mogen David wine for some special occasion

After months of negotiation with the authorities, a Talmudist from Odessa was granted permission to visit Moscow. He boarded the train and found an empty seat. At the next stop a young man got on and sat next to him. The scholar looked at the young man and thought: This fellow doesn't look like a peasant, and if he isn't a peasant he probably comes from this district.

If he comes form this district, then he must be Jewish because this is, after all, a Jewish district. On the other hand, if he is a Jew, where could he be going? I'm the only Jew in our district who has permission to travel to Moscow.

Ahh, but just outside Moscow there is a little village called Samvet, and Jews don't need special permission to go there. But why would he be going to Samvet? He's probably going to visit one of the Jewish families there, but how many Jewish families are there in Samvet? Only two—the Bernsteins and the Steinbergs.

The Bernsteins are a terrible family, and a nice-looking fellow like him must be visiting the Steinbergs. But why is he going? The Steinbergs have only daughters, so maybe he's their son-in-law. But if he is, then which daughter did he marry? They say that Sarah married a nice lawyer from Budapest, and Esther married a businessman from Zhitomir, so it must be Sarah's husband.

Which means that his name is Alexander Cohen, if I'm not mistaken.

But if he comes from Budapest, with all the anti-Semitism they have there, he must have changed his name. What's the Hungarian equivalent of Cohen? Kovacs! But if they allowed him to change his name, he must have some special status. What could it be? A doctorate from the University.

At this point the scholar turns to the young man and says, "How do you do, Dr. Kovacs?"

"Very well, thank you, sir," answered the startled passenger. "But how is it that you know my name?"

"Oh," replied the Talmudist, "it was obvious."

At the emergency meeting of the UN regarding another conflict in the Middle East, the floor has been given to the Israeli Consul. The Israeli Consul began, "Ladies and gentlemen before I commence with my speech, I wanted to relay an old story to all of you. When Moses was leading the Jews out of Egypt he had to go through deserts, and prairies, and even more deserts, the people became thirsty and needed water.

"So Moses struck the side of a mountain with his cane and at that time a pond appeared with crystal clean, cool water. And the people rejoiced and drank to their hearts' content. Moses wished to cleanse his whole body, so he went over to the other side of the pond, took all of his clothes off and dove into the cool waters of the pond. Only when Moses came out of the water he discovered that all his clothes have been stolen. And I have reasons to believe that the Palestinians stole his clothes."

Yassir Arafat, hearing this accusation, jumps out of his seat and screams, "This is a travesty. It is widely known that there were no Palestinians there at the time!!!"

"And with that in mind", said the Israeli Consul, "let me begin my speech . . ."

A young woman brings home her fiancé to meet her parents. After dinner, her mother tells her father to find out about the young man.

The father invites the fiancé to his study for a drink. "So what are your plans?" the father asks the young man.

"I am a Torah scholar." he replies.

"A Torah scholar. Hmmm," the father says. "admirable, but what will you do to provide a nice house for my daughter to live in, as she's accustomed to?"

"I will study," the young man replies, "and God will provide for us."

"And how will you buy her a beautiful engagement ring, such as she deserves?" aks the father.

"I will concentrate on my studies," the young man replies, "God will provide for us,"

"And children?" asks the father. "How will you support children?"

"Don't worry, sir, God will provide," replies the fiancé. The conversation proceeds like this, and each time the father questions him the young idealist insists that God will provide.

Later, the mother asks, "How did it go, Honey?"

The father answers, "He has no job and no plans, but the good news is he thinks I'm God."

Once upon a time a powerful Emperor of the Rising Sun advertised for a new Chief Samurai. After a year, only three applied for the job: a Japanese, a Chinese and a Jewish samurai.

"Demonstrate your skills!", commands the Emperor. The Japanese samurai steps forward, opens a tiny box releasing one fly, draws his samurai sword and Swoosh!, the fly falls to the floor neatly divided in two pieces!

"Wow! what a feat! O.K., #2, show me what you can do." The Chinese samurai smiles confidently, steps forward, opens a tiny box releasing one fly, draws his samurai sword and Swoosh! Swoosh!, the fly falls to the floor neatly divided into 4 pieces!

"Man! That's skill! How are you going to top that, #3?" The Jewish samurai thinks, "well, if it worked for them, it oughtta work for me," he steps forward, opens a tiny box releasing one fly, draws his samurai sword and Swoooooosh!, flourishes his sword so mightily that a gust of wind blows through the room. But the fly is still buzzing around!

In disappointment, the Emperor says, "What kind of skill is that? The fly isn't even dead."

"Dead, schemed," replies the Jewish samurai. "Dead is easy. I circumcised him!"

Hirako and his friend Izumata are at the baths in Tokyo and are making small talk.

Hirako then says to Izumata; "Izumata-san. I regret to inform you that your wife is dishonoring your bed with a man of the Hebrew persuasion."

Izumata thanks his friend for the information and goes home to confront his wife.

"I know you are dishonoring our bed with a man of the Hebrew persuasion. How could you do this?"

The wife protests her innocence: "That is absolutely not true, Izumata-san. I deny it completely. Who has been telling you such mishigoss?"

Isaac and Sarah got married and left on their honeymoon.

When they got back, Sarah immediately telephoned her mother Leah. "Well," said Leah, "how was the honeymoon, darling?"

"Oh mom," Sarah replied, "the honeymoon was fantastic. It was so romantic!"

Then Sarah started to cry. "Oh Mom, as soon as we got back, Isaac started using terrible language. He said things I'd never hoped to hear, all those 4-letter words. Please Mom, get into your car now and come and take me home."

"Calm down, darling," said Leah, "tell your mother what could be that awful.

"Don't be shy, tell me what 4-letter words Isaac used."

"Cook, wash and dust"

The first Jewish President of the U.S. calls his mother in Brooklyn, N.Y. and invites her to come down for Thanksgiving. She says "I'd like to, but it's so much trouble. I mean, I have to get a cab to the airport, and I hate waiting on Ocean Pkway." He replies, "Mom! I'm the President! You won't need a cab. I'll send a limousine for you". His mother replies, "I know, but then I'll have to get my ticket at the airport, and try to get a seat on the plane and I hate to sit in the middle . . . it's just too much trouble." He replies, "Mom! I'm the President of the United States! I'll send AIR FORCE ONE for you, it's my private jet!" To which she replies, "Oh well but when we land, I'll have to carry my luggage through the airport and try to get a cab . . . it's really too much trouble for someone my age". He replies, "Mom! I'm the President! I'll send a helicopter for you! You won't have to lift a finger, the Secret Service will handle everything." She answers "That's nice. . but you know I'll still need a hotel room and the rooms are so expensive and I really don't care for hotels that much". Exasperated, the answers, "Mom! I'm the President! You'll stay in the White House in the Lincoln Bedroom". She responds, "Well . . . all right. I guess I'll come". The next day she is on the phone with her friend, Esther: "Hello, Sylvia . . . so what's new?" Sylvia; "I'm visiting my son for Thanksgiving" Esther: "That's wonderful. Which son?" Sylvia: You know my son, Marvin, the doctor?" Esther: "Yes" Sylvia: "It's his brother."

A priest, a Pentecostal preacher and a Rabbi all served as Chaplains to the students of the University of Montana at Missoula. They would get together two or three times a week For coffee and to talk shop.

One day, someone made the comment that preaching to people Isn't really all that hard. A real challenge would be to preach to a bear. One thing led to another and they decided to do an experiment. They would all go out into the woods, find a bear, preach to it, and attempt to convert it.

Seven days later, they're all together to discuss the experience. Father Flannery, who has his arm in a sling, is on crutches, and has various bandages, goes first. "Well," He says, "I went into the woods to find me a bear. And when I found him began to read to him from the Catechism. Well, that bear wanted nothing to do with me and began to slap me around. So I quickly grabbed my holy water, sprinkled him and, Holy Mary Mother of God, he became as gentle a lamb. The bishop is coming out next week to give him first communion and confirmation."

Reverend Billy Bob spoke next. He was in a wheelchair, with an arm and both legs in casts, and an IV drip. In his best fire and brimstone oratory he claimed, "Well, brothers, you know that we don't sprinkle! I went out and I found me a bear. And then I began to read to my bear from God's HOLY WORD! But that bear wanted nothing to do with me. So I took hold of him and we began to wrestle. We wrestled down one hill, up another and down another until we came to a creek. So I quickly dunked him and baptized his soul. And just Like you said, he became as gentle as a lamb. We spent the rest of the day praising Jesus."

They both looked down at the rabbi, who was lying in a hospital bed. He was in a body cast and traction with IVs and monitors running in and out of him. He was in bad shape.

The rabbi looks up and says, "Looking back on it, circumcision may not have been the best way to start."

THINGS YOU DON'T LEARN IN HEBREW SCHOOL

1. The High Holidays have absolutely nothing to do with marijuana.

2. Where there's smoke, there may be salmon.

3. No meal is complete without leftovers.

4. According to Jewish dietary law, pork and shellfish may be eaten only in Chinese restaurants.

5. A shmata is a dress that your husband's ex is wearing.

6. You need ten men for a minyan, but only four, in polyester pants and white shoes, for pinochle

7. One mitzvah can change the world; two will just make you tired.

8. After the destruction of the Second Temple, God created Neiman-Marcus.

9. Anything worth saying is worth repeating a thousand times.

10. Never take a front row seat at a Bris.

11. Next year in Jerusalem. The year after that, how about a nice cruise?

12. Never leave a restaurant empty-handed.

13. Spring ahead, Fall back, Winter in Boca.

14. WASP's leave and never say good bye; Jews say good bye and never leave.

15. Always whisper the names of diseases.

16. If it tastes good, it's probably not kosher.

17. The important Jewish holidays are the ones on which alternate side of the street parking is suspended.

18. Without Jewish mothers, who would need therapy?

19. If you have to ask the price, you can't afford it. But, if you can afford it, make sure to tell everybody what you paid.

20. Laugh now, but one day you'll be driving a Lexus and eating dinner at 4:00 PM in Florida.

SIGNS ON SYNAGOGUE BULLETIN BOARDS:

1. Under same management for over 5765 years.
2. Don't give up. Moses was once a basket case.
3. What part of "Thou shalt not" don't you understand?
4. Shul committees should be made up of three members, two of whom should be absent at every meeting.
5. Sign over the urinal in a bathroom at Hebrew University: "The future of the Jewish people is in your hands."
6. Any time a person goes into a delicatessen and orders a pastrami on white bread, somewhere a Jew dies.
7. It was mealtime during a flight on El Al. "Would you like dinner?," the flight attendant asked Moshe, seated in front. "What are my choices?," Moshe asked. "Yes or no" she replied.
8. An elderly Jewish man is knocked down by a car and is brought to the local hospital. A pretty nurse tucks him into bed and says, "Mr. Schwartz, are you comfortable?" Schwartz replies, "I make a nice living . . ."
9. A rabbi was opening his mail one morning. Taking a single sheet of paper from an envelope he found written on it only one word: "Shmuck." At the next Friday night service, the Rabbi announced, "I have known many people who have written letters and forgot to sign their names, but his week I received a letter from someone who signed his name. . . . . and forgot to write a letter."

CHURCH BULLETIN BLOOPERS: ENTERTAINING MESSAGES FOR THE CONGREGATION.

The Scouts are saving aluminum cans, bottles and other items to be recycled. Proceeds will be used to cripple children.

The Outreach Committee has enlisted 25 visitors to make calls on people who are not afflicted with any church.

Evening Message—6 PM the pastor would appreciate if the ladies of the congregation would lend him their electric girdles for the pancake breakfast next Sunday morning.

The audience is asked to remain seated until the end of the recession.

Low Self Esteem Group will meet Thursday at 7 PM. Please use the back door.

Ushers will eat latecomers.

The third verses of Blessed Assurance will be sung without musical accomplishment.

For those of you who have children and don't know it, we have a nursery downstairs.

The Rev. Merriwether spoke briefly, much to the delight of the congregation.

The pastor will preach his farewell message, after which the choir will sing "Break Forth Into Joy."

A songfest was hell at the Methodist Church Wednesday.

Next Sunday Mrs. Vinson will be the soloist for the morning service. The pastor will then speak on "It's a Terrible Experience."

Due to the Rector's illness. Wednesday's healing service will be discontinued until further notice.

Stewardship Offertory: "Jesus Paid It All."

The music for today's service was all composed by George Friedrich Handel in celebration of the 300th anniversary of his birth.

Remember in prayer the many who are sick of our church and community.

The eighth graders will be presenting Shakespeare's Hamlet in the church basement Friday at 7 PM. The congregation is invited to attend this tragedy.

The concert held in Fellowship Hall was a great success. Special thanks are due to the minister's daughter, who labored the whole evening at the piano, which as usual fell upon her.

Twenty-two members were present at the church meeting held

at the home of Mrs. Marsha Crutchfield last evening. Mrs. Crutchfield and Mrs. Rankin sang a duet, The Lord Knows Why.

Don't let worry kill you. Let the church help.

Thursday night potluck supper. Prayer and medication to follow.

The rosebud on the altar this morning is to announce the birth of David Alan Belzer, the sin of Rev. and Mrs. Julius Belzer.

This afternoon there will be a meeting in the south and north ends of the church. Children will be baptized at both ends.

Tuesday there will be an ice cream social at 4 PM. All ladies giving milk, please come early.

Wednesday the Ladies Liturgy Society will meet. Mrs. Jones will sing "Put Me In My Little Bed" accompanied by the pastor.

Thursday at 5 PM there will be a meeting of the Little Mothers Club. All wishing to become Little Mothers, please see the minister in his private study.

This being Easter Sunday, we will ask Mrs. Lewis to come forward and lay an egg on the altar.

The service will close with "Little Drops of Water." One of the ladies will start (quietly) and the rest of the congregation will join in.

Next Sunday, a special collection will be taken to defray the cost of the new carpet. All those wishing to do something on the new carpet will come forward and get a piece of paper.

The ladies of the church have cast off clothing of every kind and they may be seen in the church basement Friday.

The bean supper will be held on Tuesday evening in the church basement. Music will follow.

At the early evening service tonight, the sermon topic will be "What is Hell?" Come early and listen to our choir practice.

Weight Watchers will meet at 7 PM at the Presbyterian Church. Pleas use large double door at the side entrance.

8 new choir robes are needed, due to the addition of several new members and to the deterioration to some older ones.

Mrs. Johnson will be entering the hospital this week for testes.

The Senior Choir invites any member of the congregation who enjoys sinning to join the choir.

Please join us as we show our support for Amy and Alan who are preparing for the girth of their first child.

The Lutheran Men's group will meet at 6 PM. Steak, mashed

potatoes, green beans, bread and dessert will be served for a nominal feel.

The Associate Minister unveiled the church's new tithing slogan last Sunday: "I Upped My Pledge—Up Yours!

JEWISH JEOPARDY: (We give the answer, you add the question. . . .)

A: Midrash
Q: What is a Middle East skin disease?

A: The Gaza Strip
Q: What is an Egyptian Belly Dance?

A: A classroom, a Passover ceremony, and a latke
Q: What is a cheder, a seder, and a tater?

A: Sofer
Q: On what do Jews recline on Passover?

A: Babylon
Q: What does the rabbi do during some sermons?

A: Kishka, sukkah, and circumcision
Q: What are a gut, a hut, and a cut?
And speaking of circumcisions:
An enterprising Rabbi is offering circumcisions via the Internet. . . . . The service is to be called "E-MOHEL

OY WHO WANTS TO BE A JEWISH MILLIONAIRE?

$100
Which of these names is least likely to be found at temple?
A. Cohen
B. Rosenberg
C. Schwartz
D. Christensen

$200
The term "Bloomies" refers to
A. Underpants

B. A wonderful store
C. Flowers
D. The British

$300
The person your therapist is most likely to hear about is
A. Your boss
B. Your roommate
C. Your mother
D. Your dog

$400
How many Jewish mothers does it take to screw in a lightbulb?
A. One
B. Four
C. Three
D. None, I'll just sit here in the dark.

$500
The most disturbing thing about the TV show "Friends" is
A. Monica needs a meal
B. Rachel needs a haircut
C. Joey needs a brain
D. Ross and Monica are siblings, but Monica is so obviously gentile and Ross is so obviously Jewish.

$1,000
You should call your mother
A. Every single day
B. Weekly
C. Monthly
D. Annually

$2,000
Your son will least likely be
A. A doctor
B. A lawyer
C. A fireman
D. A rabbi

$4,000
Houserobe is to Slippers as Little Black Dress is to
A. Heels

B. Sandals
C. Sneakers
D. A Nice Pair of Prada Slides

$8,000
Murphy Brown's producer was
A. Miles Silverberg
B. Simon Goldenstein
C. Brian Rosengold
D. David Bergsteiner

$16,000
Which of the following comedians is not Jewish but could be?
A. Jon Stewart
B. Billy Crystal
C. Robin Williams
B. Ben Stiller

$32,000
Fill in the blank: During the summer, I go ______ the shore.
A. Up
B. To
C. See
D. Down

$50,000
What popular game is played by many Jewish college students?
A. Chutzpah and Ladders
B. Pin the Tallis on the Rabbi
C. Go Gefilte Fish
D. Jewish Geography

$100,000
Which of the following is not a traditional bagel variety?
A. Poppy
B. Sesame
C. Onion
D. Asiago Cheese

$250,000
Which food is least likely to appear in a Jewish Deli?
A. A Knish
B. Matzoh Ball Soup

C. Corned Beef on Rye
D. Beef Wellington

$500,000

When preparing a meal for a family of five, the actual number of people you should prepare food for is:

A. 5
B. 6
C. 8
D. The population of Long Island.

$1,000,000

What celebrity told Oprah her favorite present was a mezuzah she got from her grandmother?

A. Sally Field
B. Gwyneth Paltrow
C. Cameron Diaz
D. Angelina Jolie

ARE THESE YOUR FINAL ANSWERS? CHECK THEM AGAINST THE ANSWER KEY BELOW.

$100 = D
$200 = B
$300 = C
$400 = D
$500 = E
$1,000 = A
$2,000 = C
$4,000 = D
$8,000 = A
$16,000 = C
$32,000 = D
$50,000 = D
$100,000 = D
$250,000 = D
$500,000 = D
$1,000,000 = B

An Arab had spent many days in the desert without finding a source of water. It got so bad that his camel died of thirst. He crawled through the sands, certain that he was breathing his last breath, when suddenly, he saw a shiny object sticking out of the sand several yards ahead of him.

He crawled to the object, pulled it out of the sand, and discovered that he had a Manischewitz wine bottle.

It appeared that there may be a drop or two left in the bottle, so he unscrewed the top, and out popped a genie. But this was no ordinary genie. This genie appeared to be a Chasidic Rabbi, complete with black alpaca coat, black hat, side curls, and tzitzies . . .

"Vell kid," said the genie, "you know how it voiks. You got three vishes."

"I'm not going to trust you," says the Arab. "I'm not going to trust a Jewish genie!"

"Vott'ya you got to lose? Looks to me—you're a gonner anyvay!"

The Arab thought about this for a minute, and decided that the genie was right. "Okay, I wish I were in a lush oasis, with plentiful food and drink."

POOF.

The Arab found himself in the most beautiful oasis he had ever seen and he was surrounded with jugs of wine and platters of delicacies.

"Okee-dokee kiddo, vat's your second vish?"

"My second wish is that I were rich beyond my wildest dreams."

POOF.

The Arab found himself surrounded by treasure chests filled with rare old coins and precious gems.

"Okay kid, you got just vone more vish. Better you should make it a good vone!"

After thinking for a few minutes, the Arab says, "I wish that no matter where I go, beautiful women will always need and want me!"

POOF.

He was turned into a tampon.

The Moral of the Story:

If you're an Arab doing business with a Jewish genie, there's going to be a string attached!

An Irish daughter had not been home for over 5 years. Upon her return, her father cussed her.

"Where have you been all this time? Why did ye not write to us, not even a line? Why didn't ye call? Can ye not understand what ye put yer old mother through?"

The girl, crying, replied, "Sniff, sniff . . . Dad . . . I became a prostitute . . ."

"Ye what!!? Out of here, ye shameless harlot! Sinner! You're a disgrace to this Catholic family."

"OK, Dad—as ye wish. I just came back to give mum this luxurious fur coat, title deed to a ten bedroom mansion plus a $5 million savings certificate. For me little brother, this gold Rolex. And for ye Daddy, the sparkling new Mercedes limited edition convertible that's parked outside plus a membership to the country club . . . (takes a breath) . . . and an invitation for ye all to spend New Year's Eve on board my new yacht in the Riviera and . . .

"Now what was it ye said ye had become?" says Dad.

Girl, crying again, "Sniff, sniff . . . a prostitute Daddy! Sniff, sniff."

"Oh! Be Jesus! Ye scared me half to death, girl! I thought ye said a Protestant. Come here and give yer old Dad a hug.

At the end of the tax year, the Tax Office sent an inspector to audit the books of a synagogue.

While he was checking the books he turned to the Rabbi and said: "I notice you buy a lot of candles, what do you do with the candle drippings?"

"Good question," retorted the Rabbi. "We save them up and send them back to the candle makers, and every now and then they send us a free box of candles."

"Oh," replied the auditor, somewhat disappointed that his unusual question had a practical answer.

But on he went, in his obnoxious way, "What about all these biscuit purchases? What do you do with the crumbs?"

"Ah, yes," replied the Rabbi, realizing that the inspector was trying to trap him with an unanswerable question. "We collect them and send them back to the manufacturers, and every now and then they send a free box of biscuits."

"I see!" replied the auditor, thinking hard about how he could fluster the know-it-all Rabbi. "Well, Rabbi", he went on, "what do you do with all the leftover foreskins from the circumcisions you perform?"

"Here, too, we do not waste", answered the Rabbi. "What we do is save up all the foreskins and send them to the Tax Office, and about once a year they send a complete dick like you."

Jesus was wandering around Jerusalem when He decided that He really needed a new robe.

After looking around for a while, He saw a sign for Finkelstein, the Tailor. So He went in and made the necessary arrangements to have Finkelstein prepare a new robe for Him. A few days later, when the robe was finished, Jesus tried it on and it was a perfect fit!

He asked how much He owed. Finkelstein brushed him off: "No, no, no, for the Son of God? There's no charge! However, may I ask for a small favor? Whenever you give a sermon, perhaps you could just mention that your nice new robe was made by Finkelstein, the tailor?"

Jesus readily agreed and as promised, extolled the virtues of his Finkelstein robe whenever He spoke to the masses.

A few months later, while Jesus was again walking through Jerusalem, He happened to walk past Finkelstein's shop and noted a huge line of people waiting for Finkelstein's robes.

He pushed his way through the crowd to speak to him and as soon as Finkelstein spotted him he said: "Jesus, Jesus, look what you've done for my business! Would you consider a partnership?"

"Certainly," replied Jesus. "Jesus and Finkelstein it is."

"Oh, no, no," said Finkelstein. "Finkelstein and Jesus. After all, I am the craftsman." The two of them debated this for some time."

Their discussion was long and spirited, but ultimately fruitful, and they finally came up with a mutually acceptable compromise. A few days later, the new sign went up over Finkelstein's shop: LORD & TAILOR.

A Jewish father was troubled by the way his son turned out, and went to see his Rabbi about it. "I brought him up in the faith, gave him a very expensive bar mitzvah, cost me a fortune to educate him. Then he tells me last week he has decided to be a Christian! Rabbi, where did I go wrong?"

"Funny you should come to me," said the Rabbi. "Like you I, too, brought my boy up in the faith, put him through University, cost me a fortune, then one day he, too, tells me he has decided to become a Christian."

"What did you do?" asked the father.

"I turned to God for the answer," replied the Rabbi.

"And what did he say?" pressed the father.

"God said, 'Funny you should come to me . . .'"

GOLF JOKES

Bill was having a really bad day on the golf course. Right around the 14th hole, it seems he had missed one putt too many. He let loose with a fairly impressive string of profanities, grabbed his putter, and stormed off toward the lake by the 15th tree.

"Uh-oh," said his caddie to one of his playing partners, "There goes that club."

"You think so?" said his partner. "I've got five bucks says he misses the water!"

A pastor, a doctor and an engineer were waiting one morning for a particularly slow group of golfers.

Engineer: What's with these guys? We must have been waiting for 15 minutes!

Doctor: I don't know, but I've never seen such ineptitude!

Pastor: Hey, here comes the ranger. Let's have a word with him. [dramatic pause] Hi George. Say, what's with that group ahead of us? They're rather slow, aren't they?

George: Oh, yes, that's a group of blind fire fighters. They lost their sight saving our clubhouse from a fire last year, so we always let them play for free anytime.

The group was silent for a moment.

Pastor: That's so sad. I think I will say a special prayer for them tonight.

Doctor: Good idea. And I'm going to contact my ophthalmologist buddy and see if there's anything he can do for them.

Engineer: Why can't these guys play at night?

A golfer, playing a round by himself, is about to tee off, and a greasy little salesman runs up to him, and yells, "Wait! Before you tee off, I have something really amazing to show you!"

The golfer, annoyed, says, "What is it?"

"It's a special golf ball," says the salesman. "You can never lose it!"

"Whattaya mean," scoffs the golfer, "you can never lose it? What if you hit it into the water?"

"No problem," says the salesman. "It floats, and it detects where the shore is, and spins towards it."

"Well, what if you hit it into the woods?"

"Easy," says the salesman. "It emits a beeping sound, and you can find it with your eyes closed."

"Okay," says the golfer, impressed. " But what if your round goes late and it gets dark?"

"No problem, sir, this golf ball glows in the dark! I'm telling you, you can never lose this golf ball!"

The golfer buys it at once. "Just one question," he says to the salesman. "Where did you get it?"

"I found it."

A gushy reporter told Jack Nicklaus, "You are spectacular, your name is synonymous with the game of golf. You really know your way around the course. What's your secret?"

Nicklaus replied, "The holes are numbered"

A young man and a priest are playing together.

At a short par-3 the priest asks, "What are you going to use on this hole my son?"

The young man says, "An 8-iron, father. How about you?"

The priest says, "I'm going to hit a soft seven and pray."

The young man hits his 8-iron and puts the ball on the green.

The priest tops his 7-iron and dribbles the ball out a few yards.

The young man says, "I don't know about you father, but in my church when we pray, we keep our head down."

An American went to Scotland and played golf with a newly acquainted Scottish golfer.

After a bad tee shot, he played a "Mulligan" which was an extremely good one.

He then asked the Scot, "What do you call a Mulligan in Scotland?"

"We call it hitting 3."

Police are called to an apartment and find a woman holding a bloody 5-iron standing over a lifeless man.

The detective asks: "Ma'am, is that your husband?"

"Yes," says the woman.

"Did you hit him with that golf club?"

"Yes, yes, I did." The woman begins to sob, drops the club, and puts her hands on her face.

"How many times did you hit him?"

"I don't know, five, six, maybe seven times. . . . just put me down for a five."

A golfer set up his ball on the first tee, took a mighty swing and hit his ball into a clump of trees.

He found his ball and saw an opening between two trees he thought he could hit through.

Taking out his 3-wood, he took another mighty swing; the ball hit a tree, bounced back, hit him in the forehead and killed him.

As he approached the gates of Heaven, St. Peter saw him coming and asked, "Are you a good golfer?"

He replied, "Got here in two, didn't I?"

The bride came down the aisle and when she reached the altar, the groom was standing there with his golf bag and clubs at his side.

She said: "What are your golf clubs doing here?"

He looked her right in the eye and said, "This isn't going to take all day, is it?"

An octogenarian who was an avid golfer moved to a new town and joined the local Country Club. He went to the Club for the first time to play, but was told that there wasn't anybody he could play with because they were already out on the course. He repeated several times that he really wanted to play today. Finally, the assistant Pro said he would play with him and asked him how many strokes he wanted for a bet. The 80-year-old said, "I really don't need any strokes as I have been playing quite well. The only real problem I have, is getting out of sand traps." And he did play well. Coming to the par four 18th, they were all even. The Pro had a nice drive and was able to get on the green and two-putt for a par. The old man had a nice drive, but his approach shot landed in a sand trap next to the green. Playing from the bunker he hit a high ball, which landed on the green and rolled into the cup. Birdie, match and all the money! The Pro walked over to the sand trap where his opponent was still standing. He said: "nice shot, but I thought you said you have a problem getting out of sand traps?" Replied the octogenarian, "I do, would you please give me a hand."

A woman goes to the local newspaper office to see that the obituary for her recently deceased husband is published. The obit editor informs her that there is a charge of 50 cents per word. She pauses, reflects, and then she says, well then, let it read "Fred Brown died." Amused at the woman's thrift, the editor tells her that there is a seven-word minimum for all obituaries. She thinks it over and in a few seconds says, "In that case, let it read, "Fred Brown died: golf clubs for sale."

A 75-year-old woman went to the doctor for a check up. The doctor told her she needed more cardiovascular activity and recommended that she engage in sexual activity three times a week. A bit embarrassed, she said to the doctor, "Please tell my husband." The doctor went out into the waiting room and told the husband that his wife needed sex three times a week. The 78-year-old husband replied, "Which days?" The doctor answered, "Monday, Tuesday, and Friday would be ideal." The husband said, "I can bring her on Mondays, but on Tuesdays and Fridays I golf, so she'll have to take the bus."

Don't buy a putter until you've had a chance to throw it.

Never try to keep more than 300 separate thoughts in your mind during your swing.

When your shot has to carry over a water hazard, you can either hit one more club or two more balls.

If you're afraid a full shot might reach the green while the foursome ahead of you is still putting out, you have two options: you can immediately shank a lay-up or you can wait until the green is clear and top a ball halfway there.

The less skilled the player, the more likely he is to share his ideas about the golf swing.

No matter how bad you are playing, it is always possible to play worse.

The inevitable result of any golf lesson is the instant elimination of the one critical unconscious motion that allowed you to compensate for all of your many other errors.

If it ain't broke, try changing your grip.

Golfers who claim they don't cheat also lie.

Everyone replaces his divot after a perfect approach shot.

A golf match is a test of your skill against your opponents luck.

It is surprisingly easy to hole a fifty foot putt . . . for an 8.

Counting on your opponent to inform you when he breaks a rule is like expecting him to make fun of his own haircut.

Nonchalant putts count the same as chalant putts.

It's not a gimme if you're still away.

The shortest distance between any two points on a golf course is a straight line that passes directly through the center of a very large tree.

There are two kinds of bounces; unfair bounces and bounces just the way you meant to play it.

You can hit a two acre fairway 10% of the time and a two-inch branch 90% of the time.

If you really want to get better at golf, go back and take it up at a much earlier age.

The game of golf is 90% mental and 10% mental.

Since bad shots come in groups of three, a fourth bad shot is actually the beginning of the next group of three.

When you look up, causing an awful shot, you will always look down again at exactly the moment when you ought to start watching the ball if you ever want to see it again.

Every time a golfer makes a birdie, he must subsequently make two triple bogeys to restore the fundamental equilibrium of the universe.

If you want to hit a 7 iron as far as Tiger Woods does, simply try to layup just short of a water hazard.

To calculate the speed of a players downswing, multiply the speed of his backswing by his handicap; i.e., backswing 20 mph, handicap 15, downswing = 600 mph.

There are two things you can learn by stopping your backswing at the top and checking the position of your hands: how many hands you have, and which one is wearing the glove.

Hazards attract, fairways repel.

You can put a draw on the ball, you can put a fade on the ball, but no golfer can put a straight on the ball.

A ball you can see in the rough from 50 yards away is not yours. If there is a ball in the fringe and a ball in the bunker, your ball is in the bunker. If both balls are in the bunker, yours is in the footprint.

A blonde is standing by the first tee waiting for her golf lesson from the resident professional. A foursome is in process of teeing off. The first golfer addresses the ball and swings, hitting it 230 yards straight down the middle of the fairway.

"That was a good shot," said the blonde.

"Not bad considering my impediment," said the golfer.

"What do you mean?" said the blonde.

"I have a glass eye," said the golfer.

"I don't believe you, show me," said the blonde.

He popped his eye out and showed her.

The next golfer addresses the ball and swings, hitting it 240 yards, straight down the middle of the fairway.

"That was a good shot," said the blonde.

"Not bad considering my impediment," said the golfer.

"What's wrong with you?" said the blonde.

"I have a prosthetic arm," said the golfer.

"I don't believe you, show me," said the blonde, so he screwed his arm off and showed her.

The next golfer addresses the ball and swings, hitting it 250 yards straight down the middle of the fairway. "That was a good shot," said the blonde.

"Not bad considering my impediment," said the golfer.

"What's wrong with you?" said the blonde.

"I have a prosthetic leg," said the golfer.

"I don't believe you, show me" said the blonde, so he screwed his leg off and showed her.

The fourth golfer addresses the ball and swings, hitting it 280 yards straight down the middle of the fairway.

"That was a wonderful shot," said the blonde.

"Not bad considering my impediment," said the golfer.

"What's wrong with you?" said the blonde.

"I have an artificial heart," said the golfer.

"I don't believe you, show me" said the blonde.

"I can't show you out here in the open," said the golfer. "Come around here behind the Pro-Shop." As they had not returned within five minutes, his golfing mates decided to go and see what was holding them up.

As they turned the corner behind the Pro-Shop, sure enough, there he was, screwing his heart out.

At a golf course, four men approached the sixteenth tee. The straight fairway ran along a road and bike path fenced off on the left.

The first golfer teed off and hooked the ball in that direction. But the ball went over the fence and bounced off the bike path onto the road, where it hit the tire of a moving bus and was knocked back on to the fairway.

As they all stood in silent amazement, one man finally asked him, "How on earth did you do that?"

He shrugged his shoulders and said, "You have to know the bus schedule."

The duffer muffed his tee shot into the woods, then hit into a few trees, then proceeded to hit across the fairway into some other woods. Finally, after banging away several more times, he proceeded to hit into a sand trap.

All the while, he'd noticed that the club professional had been watching.

"What club should I use now?" he asked the pro.

"I don't know," the pro replied.

"What game are you playing?"

A lady golfer who visits a driving range to tone up before a game, is about to tee off, when she notices the man next to her. "Pardon me, sir." she said. "You are aiming in the wrong direction—back towards the golf shop."

"Oy!—tanks for dat. Vitout you, I vouldn't know. I'm blindt." He then turns around and starts hitting out into the range. After a few minutes, he asks the lady how he is doing.

"Not bad," she answers. "Most of your shots are straight and fairly long. Only a few of them are slicing."

"Tanks, again, Missus," he replies. "Vitout you telling, I vouldn't know dese tings." A few shots later, he enquires again. "Do you mind I should ask a poisonal qvestion?"

"Not at all," she replies.

"I don't do vell vit the ladies. Am I ugly or vat?"

"You're quite presentable," she replies. "I don't think that should be a problem."

Smiling now, he exults, "Vat a relief. I vas always afraid to ask. Again, I got to tank you."

He was about to hit another ball when the lady interrupts him. "Do you mind if I give you a bit of advice?" she asks.

"Vit gladness. All de help you got I vill take," he answers.

"Lose the Jewish accent," she replies. "You're Chinese."

My life has not been quite the same
Since I chose to play this game.
It rules my mind for hours on end
A fortune it has made me spend

It has made me curse and cry.
I hate myself and want to die.
It promises a thing called "par"
If I can hit it straight and hit it far,

To master such a tiny ball
Should not be very hard at all.
But my desires the ball refuses
And does exactly as it chooses.

It hooks and slices, dribbles, or dies
Or disappears before my very eyes.
Often it will have a whim
To hit a tree or take a swim.

With miles of grass on which to land
It finds a tiny patch of sand,
Then has me offering up my soul
If it will just drop in the hole.

It's made me whimper like a pup,
And swear that I will give it up.
And take to drink to ease my sorrow.
But "The Ball" knows . . .

I'll be back . . . tomorrow.

LAWYER JOKES

In a trial, a Southern small-town prosecuting attorney called his first witness, a grandmotherly, elderly woman to the stand. He approached her and asked, “Mrs. Jones, do you know me?” She responded, ‘Why, yes, I do know you, Mr. Williams. I’ve known you since you were a boy, and frankly, you’ve been a big disappointment to me. You lie, you cheat on your wife, and you manipulate people and talk about them behind their backs. You think you’re a big shot when you haven’t the brains to realize you’ll never amount to anything more than a two-bit paper pusher. Yes, I know you.’

The lawyer was stunned. Not knowing what else to do, he pointed across the room and asked, “Mrs. Jones, do you know the defense attorney?”

She again replied, “Why yes, I do. I’ve known Mr. Bradley since he was a youngster, too. He’s lazy, bigoted, and he has a drinking problem. He can’t build a normal relationship with anyone, and his law practice is one of the worst in the entire state. Not to mention he cheated on his wife with three different women. One of them was your wife. Yes, I know him.”

The defense attorney nearly died.

The judge asked both counselors to approach the bench and, in a very quiet voice, said, ‘If either of you idiots asks her if she knows me, I’ll send you both to the electric chair.’

A dying man gathered his Lawyer, Doctor and Clergyman at his bed side and handed each of them an envelope containing $25,000 in cash. He made them each promise that after his death and during his repose, they would place the three envelopes in his coffin. He told them that he wanted to have enough money to enjoy the next life.

A week later the man died. At the Wake, the Lawyer and Doctor and Clergyman, each concealed an envelope in the coffin and bid their old client and friend farewell. By chance, these three met several months later. Soon the Clergyman, feeling guilty, blurted out a confession saying that there was only $10,000 in the envelope he placed in the coffin. He felt, rather than waste all the money, he would send it to a Mission in South America. He asked for their forgiveness.

The Doctor, moved by the gentle Clergyman's sincerity, confessed that he too had kept some of the money for a worthy medical charity. The envelope, he admitted, had only $8,000 in it. he said he too could not bring himself to waste the money so frivolously when it could be used to benefit others.

By this time the Lawyer was seething with self-righteous outrage. He expressed his deep disappointment in the felonious behavior of two of his oldest and most trusted friends. "I am the only one who kept his promise to our dying friend. I want you both to know that the envelope I placed in the coffin contained the full amount. Indeed, my envelope contained my personal check for the entire $25,000."

There was a job opening in the country's most prestigious law firm and it finally comes down to Bill and John. Both graduated magna cum laude from law school. Both came from good families. Both are equally attractive and well spoken. It's up to the senior partner to choose one, so he takes each aside and asks, "Why did you become a lawyer?"

In seconds, he chooses Bill.

Baffled, John takes Bill aside.

"I don't understand why I was rejected. When Mr. Jones asked me why I became a lawyer, I said that I had the greatest respect for the law, that I'd lay down my life for the Constitution and that all I wanted was to do right by my clients. What in the world did you tell him?"

"I said I became a lawyer because of my hands," Bill replies.

"Your hands? What do you mean?"

"Well, I took a look one day and there wasn't any money in either of them!"

A tourist wanders into a back alley shop in San Francisco's Chinatown. He discovers a detailed, life-sized bronze rat. The sculpture is so interesting and unique that he asks the shop owner what it costs.

"Twelve dollars for the rat," says the shop owner, "and a thousand dollars for the story behind it." "You can keep the story, old man," he replies, "but I'll take the rat."

The transaction complete, the tourist leaves the store with the bronze rat under his arm.

As he crosses the street in front of the store, two live rats emerge from a sewer drain and fall in step behind him.

Nervously looking over his shoulder, he begins to walk faster, but every time he passes another sewer drain, more rats come out and follow him.

By the time he's walked two blocks, at least a hundred rats are at his heels, and people begin to point and shout. Multitudes of rats swarm from sewers, basements, vacant lots, and abandoned cars. Rats by the thousands are at his heels, and as he sees the waterfront at the bottom of the hill, he panics and starts to run full tilt.

No matter how fast he runs, the rats keep up, squealing hideously, now not just thousands but millions, so that by the time he comes rushing up to the water's edge a trail of rats twelve city blocks long is behind him.

He jumps onto a light post, grasping it with one arm while he hurls the bronze rat into San Francisco Bay with the other, as far as he can heave it.

He watches as the seething tide of rats surges over the breakwater, following one another like a huge wave into the sea, where they all drown.

Shaken, he makes his way back to the antique shop. "Ah, so you have come back for the rest of the story," says the owner. "Actually," says the tourist, "I was wondering if you have a bronze lawyer."

On their way to get married, a young Catholic couple are involved in a fatal car accident. The couple find themselves sitting outside the Pearly Gates waiting for St. Peter to process them into Heaven.

While waiting, they begin to wonder: Could they possibly get married in Heaven?

When St. Peter shows up, they ask him. St. Peter says, "I don't know. This is the first time anyone has asked. Let me go find out," and he leaves.

The couple sit and wait, and wait. Two months pass and the couple is still waiting. As they wait, they discuss that IF they were allowed to get married in Heaven, what was the eternal aspect of it all.

"What if it doesn't work?" they wonder, "Are we stuck together FOREVER?"

After yet another month, St. Peter finally returns, looking somewhat bedraggled. "Yes," he informs the couple, "you CAN get married in Heaven."

"Great!" say the couple. "But we were just wondering, what if things don't work out? Could we also get a divorce in Heaven?"

St. Peter, red-faced with anger, slams his clipboard onto the ground.

"What's wrong?" asked the frightened couple.

"OH, COME ON!" St. Peter shouts, "It took me three months to find a priest up here! Do you have ANY idea how long it'll take me to find a lawyer?"

The Judge admonished the witness, "Do you understand that you have sworn to tell the truth?"

"I do."

"Do you understand what will happen if you are not truthful?"

"Sure," said the witness. "My side will win."

One afternoon, a wealthy lawyer was riding in the back of his limousine when he saw two men eating grass by the road side. He ordered his driver to stop and he got out to investigate. Why are you eating grass? He asked one man.

We don't have any money for food, the poor man replied.

Oh, well, you can come with me to my house, instructed the lawyer.

But, sir, I have a wife and two children with me!

Bring them along! replied the lawyer. He turned to the other man and said, You come with us, too.

But, sir, I have a wife and six children! the second man answered.

Bring them as well! answered the lawyer as he headed for his limo.

They all climbed into the car, which was no easy task, even for a car as large as the limousine. Once underway, one of the poor fellows says, Sir, you are too kind. Thank you for taking all of us with you.

The lawyer replied, Glad to do it. You'll love my place, the grass is almost a foot tall . . .

A lawyer's wife dies. At the cemetery, people are appalled to see that the tombstone reads, "Here lies Phyliis, wife of Murray, L.L.D., Wills, Divorce, Malpractice." Suddenly, Murray bursts into tears. His brother says, "You should cry, pulling a stunt like this!" Through his tears, Murray croaks, "You don't understand! They left out my office phone number!"

The devil visited a lawyer's office and made him an offer. "I can arrange some things for you," the devil said. "I'll increase your income five-fold. Your partners will love you; your clients will respect you; you'll have four months of vacation each year and live to be a hundred. All I require is that your wife's soul, your children's souls, and their children's souls rot in hell for eternity."

The lawyer thought for a moment. "What's the catch?" he asked.

A man goes to a brain store to get some brain to complete a study. He sees a sign remarking on the quality of professional brain offered at this particular brain store. He begins to question the butcher about the cost of these brains.

"How much does it cost for engineer brain?"

"Three dollars an ounce."

"How much does it cost for programmer brain?"

"Four dollars an ounce."

"How much for lawyer brain?"

"$1,000 an ounce."

"Why is lawyer brain so much more?"

"Do you know how many lawyers we had to kill to get one ounce of brain?"

A lawyer phoned the governor's mansion shortly after midnight. "I need to talk to the governor, it's an emergency!" exclaimed the lawyer. After some cajoling, the governor's aide eventually agreed to wake him up. "So, what is it that's so important that it can't wait until morning?" grumbled the governor. "Judge Brown just died, and I want to take his place," pleaded the attorney. "Well, it's OK with me if its OK with the mortuary," came the reply.

A law firm receptionist answered the phone the morning after the firm's senior partner had passed away unexpectedly. "Is Mr. Smith there?", asked the client on the phone. "I'm very sorry," the receptionist answered, "but Mr. Smith passed away last night." "Is Mr. Smith there?", repeated the client. The receptionist was perplexed. "Perhaps you didn't understand me, I'm afraid Mr. Smith passed away last night." "Is Mr. Smith there?", the client again asked. "Ma'am, do you understand what I'm saying?" said the exasperated receptionist, "Mr. Smith is DEAD!" "Oh I understand you perfectly," said the client, "I just can't hear it often enough."

A defendant was asked if he wanted a bench trial or a jury trial. "Jury trial," the defendant replied. "Do you understand the difference?" asked the judge. "Sure," replied the defendant, "That's where twelve ignorant people decide my fate instead of one."

At the United Way in a fairly small town a volunteer worker noticed that the most successful lawyer in the whole town hadn't made a contribution. This guy was making about $600,000 a year so the volunteer thought, "Why not call him up?"

He calls up the lawyer.

"Sir, according to our research you haven't made a contribution to the United Way, would you like to do so?"

The lawyer responds, "A contribution? Does your research show that I have an invalid mother who requires expensive surgery once a year just to stay alive?"

The worker is feeling a bit embarrassed and says, "Well, no sir, I'm . . ."

"Does your research show that my sister's husband was killed in a car accident? She has three kids and no means of support!"

The worker is feeling quite embarrassed at this point. "I'm terribly sorry . . ."

"Does your research show that my brother broke his neck on the job and now requires a full time nurse to have any kind of normal life?"

The worker is completely humiliated at this point. "I am sorry sir, please forgive me . . ."

"The gall of you people! I don't give them anything, so why should I give it to you!"

A lawyer was driving his big BMW down the highway, singing to himself, "I love my BMW, I love my BMW." Focusing on his car, not his driving, he smashed into a tree. He miraculously survived, but his car was totaled. "My BMW! My BMW!" he sobbed.

A good Samaritan drove by and cried out, "Sir, sir, you're bleeding! And my god, your left arm is gone!"

The lawyer, horrified, screamed, "My Rolex! My Rolex!"

A group of dinner guests were blaming all of America's troubles on lawyers when a woman said, "They aren't all so bad. Why, last year a lawyer gave me $1,000."

"I don't believe it," the host responded.

"It's true, I swear it," said the woman. "I had a complicated personal injury case and what with the lawyer's fee, the cost of expert witnesses, the expense of the appeal and so on, my bill was $41,000. When the judgment only amounted to $40,000, my lawyer simply forgave the difference."

A judge was riding horses one day with a young lawyer friend. They came upon an open stretch of country and noticed a hangman's noose hanging from a tree, solemnly waving in the wind. The judge turned to his riding companion and jokingly said, "Jacob, if that gallows had its due, where do you suppose you would be?" "Riding alone," quickly came the reply.

An Amish man named Samuel was injured when he and his horse were struck by a car at an intersection. Samuel sued the driver of the car. In court, he was cross-examined by the driver's lawyer:

Lawyer: Samuel, you've told us all about your injuries. However, according to the accident report, you told the investigating officer at the scene that you weren't injured at all, isn't that true?"

Samuel: Well . . . let me explain.

Lawyer: Go right ahead (thinking he now had the plaintiff on the ropes). Please tell the jury.

Samuel: When the officer arrived at the scene, he first looked upon my fallen horse. Finding him injured, the officer said to me, "Looks like he has a broken leg," and then he took out his weapon and shot my horse dead. The officer next looked upon me and asked how I was doing. Suffering from the same injury as my horse, I of course immediately replied, "I'm OK!"

After an electrician finished repairing some faulty wiring in an attorney's home he handed him the bill. "Five hundred dollars! For an hour's work?" cried the attorney, "That's ridiculous! Why I'm an attorney and I don't make that much." "Funny," replied the electrician, "when I was an attorney, I didn't either!"

A farmer walks into a lawyer's office wanting to file for divorce. The attorney asks, "May I help you?" The farmer said, "Yeah, I want to get one of them thar divorces." The attorney said, "Well do you have any grounds?" The farmer said, "Yeah, I got me about 140 acres." The attorney says, "No, you don't understand. Do you have a case?" The farmer says, "No, I don't have a Case, I have a John Deere." The attorney says, "No, you don't understand. I mean do you have a grudge?" The farmer says, "Yeah, I got me a grudge, that's where I parks me John Deere." The attorney says, "No sir, I mean do you have a suit?" The farmer says, "Yes sir, I got me a suit. I wear it to church on Sundays." The exasperated attorney says, "Well sir, does your wife beat you up or anything?" The farmer says, "Oh no sir. We both get up about the same time, around 4:30." Finally, the attorney says, "Okay, let me put it to you this way. "Why do you want a divorce from your wife?" To which the farmer replies, "Well," says the farmer, "I can never have me a meaningful conversation with her."

A lawyer and an engineer were fishing in the Caribbean. The lawyer, wanting to start a conversation with the gentleman next to him said, "I'm here because my house burned down and everything I owned was destroyed by the fire. The insurance company paid for everything." "That's quite a coincidence," said the engineer, "I'm here because my house and all my belongings were destroyed by a flood, and my insurance company also paid for everything." The lawyer pondered the engineer's plight for a moment and, looking somewhat confused, asked, "How do you start a flood?"

Your attorney and your mother-in-law are trapped in a burning building. You only have time to save one of them. Do you: (1) have lunch?, or (2) go to a movie?

George and Harry set out in a trans-Atlantic hot air balloon race. After 37 hours in the air and appearing lost, George offers, "We had better lose some altitude Harry so we can see exactly where we are." Hesitantly, Harry lets some hot air out of the balloon, and it begins to slowly descend below the cloud cover. Still confused as to their exact location George again offers, "I still can't tell where we are Harry, let's ask that gentleman down there on the ground." Harry yells down to the stranger, "Hey, Mister can you tell us where we are?" "You're in a balloon about 100 feet up in the air," came the reply. "That man must be a lawyer," George quipped. "How can you tell?" said Harry. "Because the advice he just gave us is 100 percent accurate and totally useless!"

A Mexican bandit made a specialty of crossing the Rio Grande from time to time, robbing banks in Texas. Finally, a reward was offered for his capture, DEAD or ALIVE! A trigger happy, young, enterprising Texas Ranger decided to track down the bandit on his own and collect the reward. After a lengthy search, the Ranger tracked the bandit to his favorite cantina and snuck up behind him. At the sound of the Ranger's guns cocking and preparing to fire, the surprised bandit sped around only to see both of the Ranger's six-shooters aimed at him. The Ranger announced, "You're under arrest! Tell me where you hid the loot or I'll drop you where you stand," his finger becoming itchy on the trigger. However, the bandit didn't speak English and the Ranger didn't speak Spanish. Fortunately for the Ranger, a bilingual lawyer was present in the cantina and translated the Ranger's demand to the bandit. The terrified bandit blurted out, in Spanish, that the loot was buried next to an old oak tree behind the cantina. "What did he say, what did he say?", the Ranger hurriedly asked. To which the lawyer replied, "Well, the best I can make out he said . . . you don't have the nerve to shoot me."

A man walked into a lawyer's office and inquired about the lawyer's rates. "$50.00 for three questions," replied the lawyer. "Isn't that kinda steep?", asked the man while doling out the $50.00. "Yes," answered the lawyer, "what's your third question?"

An attorney ran over to the office of his client. "I can't believe it!" said the angered attorney. "You sent a case of Dom Perignon to the judge in our case? That judge is as straight as an arrow. Now we're certain to lose this case!" "Relax," said the client, "I sent it in the prosecutor's name."

While summing up the State's case against the alleged despicable conduct of the defendant, the Prosecutor addressed the jury, "Ladies and gentlemen—all I can say is that if Moses had known the defendant, there would have been two or three more Commandments."

A recent admittee to the bar accepted a job at a prestigious law firm in Los Angeles. Many law firms competed for the new attorney because of his top class ranking and because of his well known wit and intellect as shown while he was editor of his school's law review.

The new attorney packed his bags and boarded a flight to Los Angeles. As the attorney is stowing his carry on luggage in the overhead compartment, he notices a very attractive woman coming down the aisle towards him. The attorney takes his seat just as the woman stops, checks her seat assignment and sits down right next to him. The attorney is on cloud nine. Three hours sitting next to a goddess. It was sheer heaven the attorney thought to himself.

Eager to strike up a conversation with the woman, he asks, "Business or vacation?" With a warm smile the woman turns towards him and says, "Business. I'm going to the annual Nymphomaniac Convention in L.A." The young attorney can't believe his luck. Here is the most gorgeous woman he has ever seen, sitting right next to him and heading to a convention for nymphomaniacs! Woooohooooo!!

Pondering for a moment about what this beautiful woman might be doing at the convention his curiosity gets the best of him. Retaining his court like composure, the attorney asks, “What’s your role at the convention if I may be so bold to ask?” A coy question fit for the supreme court he thought. “Lecturer,” she replied. “I use my experience to debunk some of the most popular myths about sexuality.” “Really,” he says, “what myths are those?” “Well,” she explains, “one popular myth is that African American men are the most endowed when, in fact, it’s Native American Indian men who are most likely to possess that trait. Another popular myth is that French men are the best lovers in the world, when in actuality, it’s men of Jewish descent that . . .” Suddenly, the woman stops in mid-sentence and becomes embarrassed about her rambling and begins to blush. “I’m sorry,” she says, “I shouldn’t even be discussing this with you. You’re a total stranger. I don’t even know your name.” Smiling, the bright attorney offers his hand for an introductory handshake and says, “Oh, by all means, allow me to introduce myself. My name is Geronimo—Geronimo Goldstein!!”

After her conviction of murder in the second degree, the District Attorney, during her sentencing hearing said, “Mrs. Smith—after you put the arsenic in the stew and served it to your husband, didn’t you feel even a little remorse for what you were doing?” “I did,” she said calmly. “And when was that?” quipped the D.A. “When he asked for seconds!” came the reply.

After his motion to surpress evidence was denied by the court the angered attorney spoke up, “Your Honor,” he said, “what would you do if I called you a stupid, degenerate, old fool.” The Judge, now also angered, answered, “I would hold you in contempt of court and seek to have you suspended from practicing before this court again!” “What if I only thought it?” asked the attorney. “In that case, there is nothing I could do, you have the right to think whatever you want." "Oh, I see. If it pleases the court, let the record reflect, that I 'think' you're a stupid, degenerate, old fool."

A certain lawyer was quite wealthy and had a summer house in the country where he retreated for several weeks every year. Each summer, the lawyer would invite a different friend of his to spend a week or two at this home, which happened to be in the backwoods. On one particular occasion, he invited a Czechoslovakian friend to stay with him. The friend, eager to get a freebee off of the lawyer, agreed. They had a splendid time in the country—rising early and living in the great outdoors. Early one morning, the lawyer and his Czechoslovakian companion went out to pick berries for their morning breakfast. As they went around the berry patch, gathering blueberries and raspberries in tremendous quantities, along came two huge Bears—a large male and a smaller female. The lawyer, seeing the two bears and sensing danger, immediately dashed for cover. His friend, however, being ignorant of nature, was not so lucky. The male bear charged the paralyzed Czechoslovakian, then swallowed him whole. The lawyer, stiff with fright, rushed back to his car and sped into town to get the local sheriff. The sheriff, upon hearing the lawyer's story, grabbed his rifle and dashed back to the berry patch with the lawyer following closely behind. Sure enough, the two bears were still there. "He's in THAT one!", cried the lawyer, pointing to the large male bear, all the while visions of lawsuits from his friend's family lagged in the back of his mind. He just had to save his friend. The sheriff looked at the two bears, and without batting an eye, leveled his rifle, took careful aim, and SHOT THE FEMALE. "What did you do that for!," exclaimed the lawyer, "I said he was in the other one!" "Exactly, replied the sheriff, "Would YOU believe a lawyer who told you the Czech was in the male?"

What do you call a smiling, sober, courteous person at a bar association convention?

The caterer.

Why are lawyers like nuclear weapons?

1. If one side has one, the other side has to get one;
2. Once launched, they can't be recalled; and
3. When they land, they screw everything up for the next 20 years.

Why does the Bar prohibit lawyers from having sex with their clients?

To prevent clients from being billed twice for the same service.

A man walking along the beach one day finds a bottle. He rubs it and, sure enough, out popped a genie. "I will grant you three wishes," said the genie. "But there is a catch." "What catch?" the man asked. The genie replied, "Every time you make a wish, every lawyer in the world will receive double the wish you were granted." "Well, I can live with that! No problem!" replied the elated man. "What is your first wish?" asked the genie. "Well, I've always wanted a Ferrari!" POOF! A Ferrari appeared in front of the man. "Now every lawyer in the world has TWO Ferraris," said the genie. "Next wish?" "I'd love a million dollars," replied the man. POOF! One million dollars appeared at his feet. "Now every lawyer in the world has TWO million dollars," said the genie. "Well, that's okay, as long as I've got my million," replied the man. "What is your third and final wish?" The man though long and hard, and finally said, "Well, you know, I've always wanted to donate a kidney!"

A bored truck driver had a nasty habit of swerving to hit attorneys he found walking along side of the highway. One day as he was driving along he came across a Nun who appeared to be having car trouble. Pulling over to offer the Nun a ride to the nearest service station, the Nun graciously thanked the driver for stopping and accepted his offer. After driving a few miles the truck driver saw an attorney walking along the highway. As was his custom, the truck driver swerved to hit the attorney but, at the last moment, remembered he had the Nun as a passenger and abruptly swerved away to avoid hitting the attorney. Surprised upon hearing a loud 'thump' as he passed the attorney, the truck driver peered in his rear view only to see the attorney lying injured along side of the road. "I'm so sorry Sister, I thought I missed hitting that attorney!" the truck driver pleaded. "You did my son, but I got him with the door!" said the Nun.

A man walks into a bar with an alligator. "Do you serve lawyers in here?", the man inquires. "Sure do!", replied the bartender. "Great!," said the man. "I'll have a Coors Light, and how 'bout a lawyer for my 'gator."

The lawyer's son wanted to follow in his father's footsteps, so he went to law school. He graduated with honors, and then went home to join his father's firm. At the end of his first day at work he rushed into his father's office, "Father, father, in one day I broke that accident case that you've been working on for the past four years!" "You did what!" his father exclaimed. "You idiot, what do you think put you through law school!"

A man was sent to Hell for his sins. As he was being taken to his place of eternal torment, he passed a room where a lawyer was having an intimate encounter with a beautiful young woman. "What a ripoff," the man muttered. "I have to roast for all eternity, and that lawyer gets to spend it with a beautiful woman." Jabbing the man with his pitchfork, the escorting demon snarled, "Who are you to question that woman's punishment?"

A lawyer named "Strange" was shopping for a tombstone. After he had made his selection, the stonecutter asked him what inscription he would like on it. "Here lies an honest man and a lawyer," responded the lawyer. "Sorry, but I can't do that," replied the stonecutter giving the lawyer a little elbow nudge, "In this state, it's against the law to bury two people in the same grave. The stonecutter then suggested, I could put 'Here lies an honest lawyer'." "But that won't let people know who it is," protested the lawyer. "It most certainly will," retorted the stonecutter. "People will read it and exclaim, "That's Strange!"

An attorney passed on and found himself in Heaven. Not at all happy with his accommodations, he complained to St. Peter, who told him that his only recourse was to appeal his assignment. The attorney immediately advised St. Peter that he intended to appeal. The attorney was informed that it would be at least three years before his appeal could be heard. The attorney protested that a three-year wait was unconscionable. However, his words fell on deaf ears. The lawyer was then approached by Satan, who told him that he would be able to arrange his appeal to be heard in just a few days, but only if the attorney stipulated to change the venue to Hell. When the attorney inquired as to why appeals could be heard so much faster in Hell, Satan gleefully exclaimed, "Who do you think has all of the judges!"

Two divorce lawyers were having drinks in a lounge after a grueling day in the courts. In walks the most stunning woman either of the lawyers had seen in a long time. One of the lawyers says, "Boy! I sure would like to screw her!" To which the other replies, "Out of what?"

A judge of some thirty years passed away unexpectedly. Upon his passing he is greeted by an angel who explained he was there to guide the judge to heaven. The angel introduced himself and added, "and I must say it is truly an honor to meet you." As they slowly headed closer to the pearly gates the judge suddenly stopped dead in his tracks and in no uncertain terms said, "Listen, I don't care how rare it is for someone of my stature to make it up here, but if there are any attorneys in there, I'm not going in. I'm tired of them all. I'd rather suffer an eternity in hell than argue another minute with an attorney."

Arriving at the pearly gates, and with much eyebrow raising by the heavenly host, the judge was determined to be worthy to enter heaven. "One moment, St. Peter," said the judge as the gates to heaven swung open for him, "just one thing, I'm tired of being around attorneys. I've been around them all of my life. Are there any inside? Because if there are, the deal's off and you can just send me to hell right now!" "Certainly not!" cried St. Peter, "You're quite safe. There are no attorneys in here." Feeling reassured, the judge pressed on and through the pearly gates into heaven. The judge found heaven very enjoyable until one day when all of a sudden a very elderly gentleman with a long white beard, wearing a suit and carrying a briefcase in one hand and a handful of papers in the other pushed past him mumbling something about being late for court. Enraged, the judge stormed back to St. Peter. "Hey! St. Peter!" cried the judge, "You said there were no attorneys here." "There aren't," stammered St. Peter. "I beg to differ," the angered judge promptly retorted, then pointing to the elderly man, "What does that elderly guy over there look like to you?" demanded the judge. "Oh my," St. Peter said laughingly, "That's not an attorney!—That's God. He just thinks he's an attorney!"

"To me, a lawyer is basically the person that knows the rules of the country. We're all throwing dice, playing the game, moving our pieces around the board, but if there is a problem, the lawyer is the only person who has read the inside top of the box."

What's the difference between a lawyer and a trampoline?
You take off your shoes before you jump on a trampoline.

A lawyer is standing at the gates to Heaven and St. Peter is listing his sins:

1. Defending a large corporation in a pollution suit where he knew they were guilty;

2. Defending an obviously guilty murderer because the fee was high;

3. Overcharging fees to many clients;

4. Prosecuting an innocent woman because a scapegoat was needed in a controversial case;

And the list goes on for quite awhile. The lawyer objects and begins to argue his case. He admits to all of these things, but argues, "Wait, I've done some charity stuff in my life also." St. Peter looks in his book and says, "Oh yes, I see. Once you gave a dime to a panhandler and once you gave an extra nickel to the shoeshine boy, correct?" The lawyer gets a smug look on his face and replies, "Yes, yes!" St. Peter turns to the angel next to him and whispers, "Give this guy 15 cents and tell him to go to hell!"

"You seem to have more than the average share of intelligence for a man of your background," sneered the lawyer at a witness on the stand. "If I wasn't under oath, I'd return the compliment," replied the witness.

What's the difference between a lawyer and a catfish?

One is a slimy, bottom dwelling, scum sucker. The other is a fish.

A plaintiff lawyer had a jury trial in a very difficult business case. The client who had attended the trial was out of town when the jury came back with its decision. Verdict for Plaintiff! The lawyer immediately sent a telegram to his client, reading "Justice has triumphed!" The client immediately wired back, "Appeal at once!"

Humpty Dumpty, the tooth fairy, an old drunk and an honest attorney are all walking down the street together. Simultaneously, they each spot a one-hundred dollar bill lying on the sidewalk. Who gets the money?

The old drunk, of course. The other three individuals only exist in fairy tales.

A Russian, a Cuban, an American and a Lawyer are seated in the same compartment on a train. The Russian takes a bottle of vodka out of his luggage, pours some into a glass, drinks it, and firmly stated, "In Russia, we have best vodka in the world, nowhere in the world you can find vodka as good as one we make in mother Russia. And, we have much of it, so much we can just throw it away like water . . ." That said, the Russian opens the train's window and hurls the vodka out of the train. The others in the compartment are quite impressed. Just then the Cuban removes a box of Havana cigars from his luggage, removes one, lights it and begins to smoke. "In Cuba, we have the best cigars in the world 'Havanas', nowhere in the world are there such good cigars, and we have much of them also, so many that we can just throw them away . . ." Making that bold statement, the Cuban sends the box of Havanas the way of the vodka. Once again, the compartment's occupants are quite impressed. At that moment, not to be out done, the American abruptly stands up, opens the window, and throws the lawyer out!

A lawyer died and arrived at the pearly gates. To his dismay, there were thousands of people ahead of him in line to see St. Peter. To his surprise, St. Peter left his desk at the gate and came down the long line to where the lawyer was standing, and greeted him warmly. Then St. Peter and one of his assistants took the lawyer by the hand and guided him up to the front of the line, and into a comfortable chair by his desk. The lawyer said, "I don't mind all this attention, but what makes me so special?" St. Peter replied, "Well, I've added up all the hours that you billed your clients, and by my calculation you must be about 180 years old!"

A housewife, an accountant and a lawyer were asked "How much is 2 plus 2?" The housewife replies: "Four!" The accountant says: "I think it's either 3 or 4. Let me run those figures through my spreadsheet one more time." The lawyer pulls the drapes, dims the lights and asks in a hushed voice, "How much do you want it to be?"

A lawyer's dog, running about unleashed, beelines for the local butcher shop and steals a roast off the counter. The butcher goes to the lawyer's office and asks, "If a dog, running unleashed, steals a piece of meat from my store, do I have a right to demand payment for the meat from the dog's owner?" "Absolutely," the lawyer responded. The butcher immediately shot back, "Good! You owe me $7.99 for the roast your dog stole from me this morning." The lawyer, without a word, writes the butcher a check for $7.99. A few days later, the butcher, browsing through his mail, finds an envelope from the lawyer. The contents read "Consultation: $100.00."

A Dublin lawyer died in poverty and many barristers of the city subscribed to a fund for his funeral. The Lord Chief Justice was asked to donate a shilling. "Only a shilling to bury an attorney?" said the Justice, "Here's a guinea, go and bury 20 of them."

A man walked into the local Chamber of Commerce of a small town, obviously desperate. Seeing a man at the counter, the stranger asks, "Is there a criminal attorney in town?" To which the man behind the counter immediately quipped, "Yeah, but we can't prove it yet!"

A lawyer charged a client $500.00 for legal services. The client paid him with crisp new $100.00 bills. After the client left, the lawyer discovered that two of the bills had stuck together—he'd been overpaid by $100.00. The ethical dilemma for the lawyer: Should he tell his partner?

Kids Will Be Kids. On a business trip in Philadelphia, a gentleman took one afternoon off to see the Liberty Bell and other historic sites. He soon found himself in line with two young families waiting to see the sites as he overheard this conversation between their two small boys, not yet old enough to be in school:

Child 1: My name is Billy. What's yours?
Child 2: Tommy.
Child 1: My Daddy's an accountant. What does your Daddy do?
Child 2: My Daddy's a lawyer.
Child 1: Honest?
Child 2: No—just the regular kind.

Having been propositioned by a well endowed and pretty prostitute one evening, a successful single gentleman agreed to have consensual sex with the young lady for the sum of $500.00. After the evening ended the gentleman handed the young lady $250.00. The prostitute immediately demanded the balance and threatened to sue if she didn't get it. "That's a laugh!" the man stated, "I'd like to see you try." A few days later the man was surprised to receive a summons ordering him to appear in court as a defendant in a lawsuit. The man hurried to his lawyer's office and explained the details of the case. His lawyer said, "She can't possibly get a judgment against you on such grounds, but it will be interesting to see how she presents her case." After the usual preliminaries, the parties appeared in court ready for trial.

The prostitute's lawyer addressed the court first, "Your Honor, my client, this lady here, is the owner of a piece of property, a garden spot surrounded by a profuse growth of shrubbery, which property she agreed to rent to the defendant for a specific length of time for the sum of $500.00. The defendant obtained exclusive possession of the property, using it extensively for the purpose for which it was rented. However, upon evacuating the premises, he paid only one-half of the amount agreed upon. The rent was not excessive since it is restricted and exclusive property and we ask that judgment be granted for plaintiff and against defendant in the amount of $250.00.

The defendant's lawyer, thrown back by what he had just heard, pondered the opening remarks for a moment and stood to present his off-the-cuff version of the case, "Your Honor, my client agrees that the young lady has a fine piece of property, and that he rented such property for a period of time, and that he even derived a degree of pleasure from the transaction. However, my client found a well on the property upon which he placed his own stones, sunk a shaft, and erected a pump. All equipment belonging to my client and all labor being performed by him. We allege that these improvements to the property were sufficient to effect an offset of the unpaid portion of rent and further allege that the plaintiff was adequately compensated for the fair market rental value of such property. We, therefore, ask that judgment not be granted for plaintiff and that the defendant be awarded his attorney's fees and costs incurred in the defense of this frivolous action."

The prostitute's lawyer replied, "If it pleases the court your Honor, my client agrees that the defendant did find a well on the property, and that he made the improvements to the property as alleged. However, had the defendant not known the well existed, he would have never rented the property. Furthermore, upon evacuating the premises, the defendant removed the stones, pulled out the shaft, and took the pump with him. In doing so, he not only dragged his equipment through the well-manicured shrubbery, but left the well with a hole much larger than it was prior to his occupancy, making it easily accessible to small children, thereby creating a possible danger to the health and general welfare of the public. We, therefore, ask that judgment be granted as requested in the complaint.

Judgment for the plaintiff in the amount of $250.00!

A millionaire informs his attorney, "I want a stipulation in my Will that my wife is to inherit everything, but only if she remarries within six months of my death." "Why such an odd stipulation?" asked the attorney. "Because I want someone to be sorry I died!" came the reply.

In questioning potential jurors for an upcoming trial the Judge inquired, "Is there any reason why any of you cannot see this trial through to its conclusion?" A lone juror spoke up, "I can't!" stated the woman, "Why, just looking at the woman I'm convinced she's guilty!" "Madam," said the Judge, "that's the prosecutor."

These are things people actually said in court, word for word, taken down and now published by court reporters who had the torment of staying calm while these exchanges were actually taking place.

ATTORNEY: Are you sexually active?
WITNESS: No, I just lie there.

ATTORNEY: What gear were you in at the moment of the impact?
WITNESS: Gucci sweats and Reeboks.

ATTORNEY: This myasthenia gravis, does it affect your memory at all?
WITNESS: Yes.
ATTORNEY: And in what ways does it affect your memory?
WITNESS: I forget.
ATTORNEY: You forget? Can you give us an example of something you forgot?
WITNESS: I forgot what I didn't remember.

ATTORNEY: What was the first thing your husband said to you that morning?
WITNESS: He said, "Where am I, Cathy?"
ATTORNEY: And why did that upset you?
WITNESS: My name is Susan!

ATTORNEY: Now doctor, isn't it true that when a person dies in his sleep, he doesn't know about it until the next morning?
WITNESS: Are you kidding?

ATTORNEY: The youngest son, the twenty-year-old, how old is he?
WITNESS: How old is the twenty-year-old?
ATTORNEY: Yes.
WITNESS: Is this a trick question?

ATTORNEY: Were you present when your picture was taken?
WITNESS: Man . . . you have got to be shittin' me!

ATTORNEY: So the date of conception (of the baby) was August 8th?
WITNESS: Yes.
ATTORNEY: And what were you doing at that time?
WITNESS: DUH . . . I was gettin' laid!

ATTORNEY: She had three children, right?
WITNESS: Yes.
ATTORNEY: How many were boys?
WITNESS: None.
ATTORNEY: Were there any girls?
WITNESS: Oh God. Your Honor, can I get a new attorney?

ATTORNEY: How was your first marriage terminated?
WITNESS: By death.
ATTORNEY: And by whose death was it terminated?
WITNESS: Well it sure as hell wasn't mine!

ATTORNEY: Can you describe the individual?
WITNESS: He was about medium height and had a real full thick beard.
ATTORNEY: Was this a male or a female?
WITNESS: Guess.

ATTORNEY: Is your appearance here this morning pursuant to a deposition notice which I sent to your attorney?

WITNESS: No, this is how I dress when I go to work.

ATTORNEY: Doctor, how many of your autopsies have you performed on dead people?
WITNESS: All my autopsies are performed on dead people. Are you crazy?

ATTORNEY: ALL your responses MUST be oral, OK? What school did you go to?
WITNESS: Oral.

ATTORNEY: Do you recall the time that you examined the body?
WITNESS: The autopsy started around 8:30 p.m.
ATTORNEY: And Mr. Denton was dead at the time?
WITNESS: No, he was sitting on the table wondering why I was doing an autopsy on him!

ATTORNEY: Are you qualified to give a urine sample?
WITNESS: Huh . . . are you qualified to ask that question?

A doctor and a lawyer were attending a cocktail party when the doctor was approached by a man who asked advice on how to handle his ulcer.

The doctor mumbled some medical advice, then turned to the lawyer and asked, "How do you handle the situation when you are asked for advice during a social function?"

"Just send a bill for such advice," replied the lawyer.

On the next morning the doctor arrived at his surgery and issued the ulcer-stricken man a $50 bill. That afternoon he received a $100 bill from the lawyer.

A gang of robbers broke into a lawyer's club by mistake. The old legal lions gave them a fight for their life and their money. The gang was very happy to escape.

"It ain't so bad," one crook noted. "We got $25 between us."

The boss screamed: "I warned you to stay clear of lawyers—we had $100 when we broke in!"

A golfer hooked his tee shot over a hill and onto the next fairway. Walking toward his ball, he saw a man lying on the ground, groaning with pain.

"I'm an attorney," the wincing man said, "and this is going to cost you $5,000."

"I'm sorry, I'm really sorry," the concerned golfer replied. "But I did yell 'fore'."

"I'll take it," the attorney said.

The day after a verdict had been entered against his client, the lawyer rushed to the judge's chambers, demanding that the case be reopened, saying: "I have new evidence that makes a huge difference in my client's defense."

The judge asked, "What new evidence could you have?"

The lawyer replied, "My client has an extra $10,000, and I just found out about it!"

OLD AGE JOKES

Just when you have lost faith in human kindness, someone who teaches at an Elementary School forwarded the following letter.

The letter was sent to the principal's office after the school had sponsored a luncheon for the elderly. An old lady received a new radio at the lunch as a door prize and was writing to say thank you. This story is a credit to all humankind.

Dear Principal:

God bless you for the beautiful radio I won at your recent senior citizens luncheon. I am 84 years old and live a the Johnson Home for the Aged. All of my family has passed away. I am all alone now and it's nice to know that someone is thinking of me. God bless you for your kindness to an old forgotten lady.

My roommate is 95 and has always had her own radio, but before I received one, she would never let me listen to hers, even when she was napping. The other day her radio fell off the nightstand and broke into a lot of pieces. It was awful and she was in tears. She asked if she could listen to mine, and I told her to kiss my butt.

Thank you for that opportunity.

Sincerely, Mary Jones

THIS IS THE WORST VIRUS

Even the most advanced programs from Norton or McAfee cannot take care of this one. It appears to affect those who were born prior to 1960.

Symptoms:

1. Causes you to send the same e-mail twice.
2. Causes you to send a blank e-mail.
3. Causes you to send an e-mail to the wrong person.
4. Causes you to send it back to the person who sent it to you.
5. Causes you to forget to attach the attachment.

6. Causes you to hit “send” before you’ve finished.
7. Causes you to hit “delete” instead of “send”.
8. Causes you to hit “send” when you should “delete”.

It is called “The C-NILE virus”!!!

After retiring, I went to the Social Security office to apply for Social Security. The woman behind the counter asked me for my driver’s license to verify my age. I looked in my pockets and realized I had left my wallet at home.

I told the woman that I was very sorry, but I would have to go home and come back later.

The woman said, ‘Unbutton your shirt’.

So I opened my shirt revealing my curly silver hair.

She said, ‘That silver hair on your chest is proof enough for me’ and she processed my Social Security application.

When I got home, I excitedly told my wife about my experience at the Social Security office.

She said, ‘You should have dropped your pants. You might have gotten disability, too’

Some of the artists of the 60’s are revising their hits with new lyrics to accommodate aging Baby Boomers.

They Include:

Herman’s Hermits—Mrs. Brown, You’ve Got a Lovely Walker.
Ringo Starr—I Get By With a Little Help From Depends.
The Bee Gees—How Can You Mend a Broken Hip.
Bobby Darin—Splish, Splash, I Was Havin’ a Flash.
Roberta Flack—The First Time Ever I Forgot Your Face.
Johnny Nash—I Can’t See Clearly Now.
Paul Simon—Fifty Way to Lose Your Liver.
The Commodores—Once, Twice, Three Times to the Bathroom.
Procol Harem—A Whiter Shade of Hair.
Leo Sayer—You Make Me Feel Like Napping.
The Temptations—Papa’s Got a Kidney Stone.
Abba—Denture Queen.

Tony Orlando—Knock 3 Times On The Ceiling If You Hear Me Fall.

Helen Reddy—I Am Woman, Hear Me Snore.

Leslie Gore—It's My Procedure, and I'll Cry If I Want To.

Willie Nelson—On the Commode Again.

Mrs. Goldberg and Mrs. Murphy were friends for many years. After both their husbands died they each moved into a different retirement home. Sometime later they met and chatted to get caught up on their current situation. Mrs. Goldberg said that her residence was OK, but she now had a boyfriend. After lunch, they would go to her room, and "He would touch me up here, then he would touch me down here, and then we would sing Jewish songs."

Mrs Murphy responded that her home was also OK, and that she also had a boyfriend. After lunch, they would go to HER room, and "He would touch me up here, then he would touch me down there, They didn't know any Jewish songs, so they just screwed."

Miss Beatrice, the church organist, was in her eighties and had never been married.

She was admired for her sweetness and kindness to all.

One afternoon the pastor came to call on her and she showed him into her quaint sitting room.

She invited him to have a seat while she prepared tea.

As he sat facing her old Hammond organ, the young minister noticed a cut-glass bowl sitting on top of it.

The bowl was filled with water, and in the water floated, of all things, a condom!

When she returned with tea and scones, they began to chat.

The pastor tried to stifle his curiosity about the bowl of water and its strange floater, but soon it got the better of him and he could no longer resist.

'Miss Beatrice', he said, 'I wonder if you would tell me about this?' pointing to the bowl.

'Oh, yes,' she replied, 'Isn't it wonderful? I was walking through the Park a few months ago and I found this little package on the ground.

The directions said to place it on the organ, keep it wet and that it would prevent the spread of disease.

Do you know I haven't had the flu all winter.'

A teenage granddaughter comes downstairs for her date with this see-through blouse on and no bra.

Her grandmother just pitched a fit, telling her not to dare go out like that!

The teenager tells her "Loosen up Grams. These are modern times. You gotta let your rose buds show!

And out she goes.

The next day the teenager comes down stairs, and the grandmother is sitting there with no top on.

The teenager wants to die. She explains to her grandmother that she has friends coming over and that it is just not appropriate.

The grandmother says, "Loosen up, Sweetie. If you can show off your rose buds, then I can display my hanging baskets.

An older couple were lying in bed one night. The husband was falling asleep but the wife was in a romantic mood and wanted to talk. She said: "You used to hold my hand when we were courting." Wearily he reached across, held her hand for a second and tried to get back to sleep. A few moments later she said: "Then you used to kiss me. "Mildly irritated, he reached across, gave her a peck on the cheek and settled down to sleep. Thirty seconds later she said: Then you used to bite my neck." Angrily, he threw back the bed clothes and got out of bed. "Where are you going?" she asked. "To get my teeth!"

80-year old Bessie bursts into the rec room at the retirement home. She holds her clenched fish in the air and announces,

"Anyone who can guess what's in my hand can have sex with me tonight!!" An elderly gentleman in the rear shouts out, "An elephant?" Bessie thinks a minute and says, "Close enough."

Two elderly ladies had been friends for many decades. Over the years, they had shared all kinds of activities and adventures. Lately, their activities had been limited to meeting a few times a week to play cards. One day, they were playing cards when one looked at the other and said, "Now don't get mad at me . . . I know we've been friends for a long time . . . but I just can't think of your name! I've thought and thought, but I can't remember it. Please tell me what your name is." Her friend glared at her. For at least three minutes she just stared and glared at her. Finally she said, "How soon do you need to know?"

As a senior citizen was driving down the freeway, his car phone rang. Answering, he heard his wife's voice urgently warning him, "Herman, I just heard on the news that there's a car going the wrong way on Interstate 77. Please be careful!" "Hell," said Herman, "It's not just one car, there are hundreds of them!"

I've often been asked, 'What do you old folks do now that you're retired?'

Well . . . I'm fortunate to have a few friends who have chemical engineering backgrounds, and one of the things we enjoy most is turning beer, wine, bourbon, and martinis into urine.

And, we're pretty darn good at it too!!'

Six retired Floridians were playing poker in the condo clubhouse when Meyerwitz loses $500 on a single hand, clutches his chest and drops dead at the table. Showing respect for their fallen comrade, the other five continued playing standing up.

Finkelstein looks around and asks, “So, who is going to tell his wife?”

They draw straws. Goldberg picks the short one.

They tell him to use good judgment, be discreet and be gentle. Don’t make a bad situation any worse.

“Discreet?” he asked. “I’ll be the most discreet person you will ever meet. Discretion is my middle name. Just leave it to me.”

So, Goldberg goes over to the Meyerwitz apartment and knocks on the door.

The wife answers and asks what he wants. Goldberg declares, “Your husband just lost $500 and is afraid to come home.”

“Tell him to drop dead!” she yells.

“I’ll go tell him,” says Goldberg.

The other day I went downtown to run a few errands. I went into the local coffee shop for a snack. I was only there for about 5 minutes. When I came out, there was this cop writing out a parking ticket. I said to him, ‘Come on, man, how about giving a retired person a break?’ He ignored me and continued writing the ticket. His insensitivity annoyed me, so I called him a ‘Nazi.’ He glared at me and then wrote out another ticket for having worn tires. So I proceeded to call him ‘doughnut eating Gestapo.’ He finished the second ticket and put it on the windshield with the first. Then he wrote a third ticket when I called him a *moron in blue.* This went on for about 15 minutes. The more I talked back to him the more tickets he wrote.

Personally, I didn’t really care. I came downtown on the bus. I try to have a little fun each day now that I’m retired. The doctor tells me that it’s important to my health.

Seems an elderly gentleman had serious hearing problems for a number of years.

He went to the doctor and the doctor was able to have him fitted for a set of hearing aids that allowed the gentleman to hear 100%.

The elderly gentleman went back in a month to the doctor and the doctor said, "Your hearing is perfect. Your family must be really pleased that you can hear again."

To which the gentleman said, "Oh, I haven't told my family yet. I just sit around and listen to the conversations. I've changed my will three times!"

I have feared for some time my wife wasn't hearing as well as she used to, and I thought she might need a hearing aid. Not quite sure how to approach her, I called our family doctor to discuss the problem.

He told me there was is a simple informal test I could perform to give him a better idea about my wife's hearing loss.

"Here's what you do," said the doctor; "Stand about 40 feet away from her, and talk in a normal conversational speaking tone see if she hears you. if not, go to 30 feet, then 20 feet, and so on until you get a response."

That evening, my wife was in the kitchen cooking dinner, and I was in the family room, about 40 feet away.

In a normal tone I asked, "What's for dinner?'

No response.

So I moved closer to the kitchen, about 30 feet away. I asked, "Honey, what's for dinner?"

Still no response.

Next I moved into the breakfast area where I was about 20 feet from her. I asked, "So—what's for dinner?"

Again, I got no response.

So, I walked right into the kitchen, no more than about 5 feet away. "Hey!" I said. "I wanna know—what's for dinner?" Again there was no response.

Determined, I walked right up behind her. "For the last time—what's for dinner?"

"For the FIFTH time: CHICKEN!"

While on a road trip, an elderly couple stopped at a roadside restaurant for lunch. After finishing their meal, they left the restaurant and resumed their trip.

When leaving, the elderly woman unknowingly left her glasses on the table and she didn't miss them until they had been driving about twenty minutes.

By then, to add to the aggravation, they had to travel quite a distance before they could find a place to turn around—in order to return to the restaurant to retrieve her glasses.

All the way back, the husband became the classic grouchy old man. He fussed and complained and scolded his wife relentlessly during the entire return drive. The more he chided her—the more agitated he became. He just wouldn't let up.

To her relief, they finally arrived at the restaurant. As the woman got out of the car and hurried inside to retrieve her glasses, the old geezer yelled to her. . "While you're in there, you might as well get my hat and the credit card!!"

An elderly man goes into a brothel and tells the madam he would like a young girl for the night. Surprised, she looks at the ancient man and asks how old he is.

"I'm 90 years old," he says.

"90!" replies the woman. "Don't you realize you've had it?"

"Oh, sorry," says the old man. "How much do I owe you?"

Because they had no reservations at a busy restaurant, my elderly neighbor and his wife were told there would be a 45 minute wait for a table. "Young man, we're both 90 years old," the husband said.

"We may not have 45 minutes."

They were seated immediately.

Mildred was a 93 year old woman who was particularly despondent over the recent death of her husband. She decided that she would just kill herself and join him in death. Thinking that it would be best to get it over with quickly, she took out his old Army pistol and made the decision to shoot herself in the heart since it was so badly broken in the first place. Not wanting to miss the vital organ and became a vegetable and a burden to someone, she called her doctor's office to inquire as to just exactly where the heart would be. "On a woman", the doctor said, "your heart would be just below your left breast."

Later that night, Mildred was admitted to the hospital with a gunshot wound to her knee.

An elderly gentleman went to the local drug store and asked the pharmacist for Viagra. The pharmacist said "That's no problem. How many do you want?"

The man answered, "Just a few, maybe four, but cut each one in four pieces."

The pharmacist said, "That won't do you any good."

The elderly gentleman said, "That's alright. I don't need them for sex anymore. I am over 80 years old. I just want it to stick out far enough so I don't piss on my shoes."

I was sitting in the waiting room for my first appointment with a new dentist when I noticed his DDS diploma, which bore his full name.

Suddenly, I remembered a tall, handsome, dark-haired boy with the same name had been in my high school class some 40-odd years ago. Could he be the same guy that I had a secret crush on, way back then?

Upon seeing him, however, I quickly discarded any such thought. This balding, gray-haired man with the deeply lined face was way too old to have been my classmate! After he examined my teeth, I asked him if he had attended Morgan Park High School.

"Yes. Yes, I did. I'm a mustang," he gleamed with pride.

"When did you graduate?" I asked.

He answered, "In 1959. Why do you ask?"

I exclaimed, "You were in my class!".

He looked at me closely. Then . . . that ugly, old, wrinkled, fat, bald, gray, decrepit son-of-a-bitch asked, ... "What did you teach?

An 80 year old Italian man goes to the doctor for a check-up. The doctor is amazed at what good shape the guy is in and asks, "How do you stay in such great physical condition?"

I'm Italian and I'm a golfer," says the old guy, "and that's why I'm in such good shape. I'm up well before daylight and out golfing up and down the fairways. Have a glass of vino, and all is well."

"Well," says the doctor, "I'm sure that helps, but there's got to be more to it. How old was your Dad when he died?"

"Who said my Dad's dead?" The doctor is amazed. "You mean you're 80 years old and your Dad's still alive. How old is he?"

"He's 100 years old" says the old Italian golfer. "In fact he golfed with me this morning and then we went to the topless beach for a walk, that's why he's still alive . . . he's Italian and a golfer too."

"Well." The doctor says, "that's great, but I'm sure there's more to it than that. How about your Dad's Dad? How old was he when he died?"

'Who said my grandpa's dead? He's still kicking. ." Stunned, the doctor asks, "You mean your grandfather's still living! Incredible, how old is he?"

"He's 118 years old," says the old Italian golfer. The doctor is getting frustrated at this point. "So I guess he went golfing with you this morning too?"

"No, Grandpa couldn't go this morning because he's getting married today."

At this point, the doctor is close to losing it. "Getting married! Why would a 118 year old guy want to get married?"

"Who said he wanted to?"

HOW TO KNOW WHEN YOU'RE GROWING OLD

Everything hurts, and what doesn't hurt, doesn't work.

The gleam in your eyes is from the sun hitting your bifocals.

You feel like the morning after, and you haven't been anywhere the night before.

Your little black book contains only names ending in M.D.

You get winded playing chess.

Your children begin to look middle-aged.

You finally reach the top of the ladder and find it leaning against the wrong wall.

You join a health club and don't go.

You begin to outlive enthusiasm.

You decide to procrastinate but then never get around to it.

You're still chasing women, but can't remember why.

Your mind makes contracts that your body can't meet.

A dripping faucet causes an uncontrollable bladder urge.

You know all the answers, but nobody asks you the questions.

You look forward to a dull evening.

You walk with your head held high trying to get used to your bifocals.

Your favorite part of the newspaper is "25 years ago today."

You turn out the light for economic rather than romantic reasons.

You have too much room in the house and not enough in the medicine cabinet.

When I went to lunch today, I noticed an old lady sitting on a park bench sobbing her eyes out. I stopped and asked her what was wrong. She said, "I have a 22 year old husband at home. He makes love to me every morning and then gets up and makes me pancakes, sausage, fresh fruit and freshly ground coffee."

I said, "Well, then why are you crying?" She said, "He makes me homemade soup for lunch and my favorite brownies and then makes love to me for half the afternoon.

I said, "Well, why are you crying?" She said, "For dinner he makes me a gourmet meal with wine and my favorite dessert and then makes love to me until 2:00 a.m." I said, "Well, why in the world would you be crying?" She said, "I can't remember where I live!"

Grant me the senility to forget the people I never liked anyway, the good fortune to run into the ones I do, and the eyesight to tell the difference.

I, being of sound mind and body, do not wish to be kept alive indefinitely by artificial means. Under no circumstances should my fate be put in the hands of pinhead politicians who couldn't pass ninth-grade biology if their lives depended on it, or lawyers or doctors interested in simply running up the bills. If a reasonable amount of time passes and I fail to ask for at least one of the following:

Glass of wine
chocolate
Margarita
chocolate
Martini
Cold Beer
chocolate
Chicken fried steak
cream gravy
chocolate
Mexican food
chocolate
French fries
chocolate
Pizza
chocolate
ice cream
cup of tea
chocolate
Sex
chocolate

It should be presumed that I won't ever get better.

When such a determination is reached, I hereby instruct my appointed person and attending physician to pull the plug, reel in the tubes, and call it a day.

Just came across this exercise suggested for seniors, to build muscle strength in the arms and shoulders. It seems so easy, so I thought I'd pass it on to some of my friends and family. The article suggests to do it three days a week.

Begin by standing on a comfortable surface, where you have

plenty of room at each side. With a 5-lb potato sack in each hand, extend your arms straight out from your sides and hold them there as long as you can.

Try to reach a full minute, then relax. Each day, you'll find that you can hold this position for just a bit longer.

After a couple of weeks, move up to 10-lb potato sacks. Then 50-lb potato sacks.

Eventually try to get to where you can lift a 100-lb potato sack in each hand and hold your arms straight for more than a full minute.

(I'm at this level)

After you feel confident at that level, put a potato in each of the sacks.

No nursing home for me.

I am checking into the Holiday Inn!

With the average cost for a nursing home per day reaching $188.00, there is a better way when we get old & feeble.

I have already checked on reservations at the Holiday Inn. For a combined long term stay discount and senior discount, it's $49.23 per night. That leaves $138.77 a day for: Breakfast, lunch and dinner in any restaurant I want, or room service. Laundry, gratuities and special TV movies.

Plus, they provide a swimming pool, a workout room, a lounge, washer, dryer, etc.

Most have free toothpaste and razors, and all have free shampoo and soap.

They treat you like a customer, not a patient. $5 worth of tips a day will have the entire staff scrambling to help you. There is a city bus stop out front, and seniors ride free. To meet other nice people, call a church bus on Sundays. For a change of scenery, take the airport shuttle bus and eat at one of the nice restaurants there. While you're at the airport, fly somewhere. Otherwise, the cash keeps building up.

It takes months to get into decent nursing homes. Holiday Inn will take your reservation today. And you are not stuck in one place forever, you can move from Inn to Inn, or even from city to city. Hawaii? They have a Holiday Inn there too.

T.V. broken? Light bulbs need changing?

Need a mattress replaced? No problem. They fix everything, and apologize for the inconvenience.

The Inn has a night security person and daily room service.

The maid checks to see if you are ok. If not, they will call the undertaker or an ambulance. If you fall and break a hip, Medicare will pay for the hip, and Holiday Inn will upgrade you to a suite for the rest of your life.

And no worries about visits from family. They will always be glad to find you, and probably check in for a few days mini-vacation. The grandkids can use the pool. What more can you ask for?

So, when I reach the golden age I'll face it with a grin. Just forward all my email to: me @ Holiday.Inn

A father, son and twenty-one year old grandson went out to the country club for their weekly round of golf. Just as they were about to tee-off, a beautiful, blonde young woman, carrying her clubs, ran up and said, "Hi, guys! Listen, the member who brought me here for a round of golf was called away for an emergency, so I'm left high and dry. Would you let me join you?"

All three men immediately agreed, and the smiling blonde thanked them. Then she added, "Look, guys, I work in a topless bar as a dancer, so nothing shocks me. If any of you wants to smoke cigars, have a beer, bet, swear or tell off-color stories, just go ahead. All I ask for you is please don't try to coach me on how to play my shots. I like to make my own plays."

The guys readily agreed and invited her to drive first. Three pairs of eyes were fastened on her shapely behind as she leaned over to place her ball on the tee. She then drove the ball 270 yards down the middle of the fairway, right in front of the green. The father's mouth dropped in awe as he gasped, "That was beautiful!"

The blonde put her driver away and muttered, "I really didn't get into it, and I should have faded it a little."

The three guys then made their drives and their second shots. Being closest to the pin, the blonde took out a nine iron and lofted the ball within five feet of the hole. The son muttered, "Damn, lady, you played that perfectly!"

The blonde frowned and commented, "Well, it was a little weak, and I've left myself a tricky putt.!

The son then buried a long putt for a par, dad two putted for a bogey, and grand dad overran the green with his pitching wedge. He then chipped back and putted twice for a double bogey. The blonde tapped in the five-footer for a birdie, and the guys all congratulated her.

As she slipped her putter back into the bag, she said, "Well, thanks, but I really haven't played much lately, and I'm a little rusty. Maybe I'll get into this next drive." Having the honor on the second hole, she whacked the ball 300 yards, smack down the middle of the fairway.

For the rest of the round, the statuesque blonde continued to amaze the guys, shooting for par or less on every hole. When they got to the 18th green, the blonde was three under par, but was faced with a nasty, twelve-foot shot on an undulating green for a par. She turned to the three guys and said, "I really wanna thank you all for not acting like a bunch of chauvinists and telling me what club to use or how to play a shot. However, I need this putt for a sixty-nine, and I'd REALLY like to break seventy on this course. If any one of you can tell me how to make par on this hole, I'll take him back to my apartment, pour some twenty-five year old Jameson's in him, fix him dinner and then show him a good time the rest of the night."

The yuppie grandson jumped at the offer. He strolled across the green and carefully eyed the line of the putt. Finally, he said, "Honey, aim about six inches to the right of the hole and hit it firmly. It'll get over that little hump and break right into the cup!"

The father kneeled down and checked the putt, using his putter as a plumb. "Don't listen to the kid, darlin'. You want to hit it softly about ten inches to the right, and run it down that little hogback, so it falls right into the cup!"

The gray haired grandfather walked over to the blonde's ball on the green and picked it up and handed it to her. He grinned as he confided, "That's a 'gimme', sweetheart! Your car or mine?"

I passed by the nursing home & there were six old ladies lying naked in the front yard in the grass. I thought this was a little peculiar, but continued on my way because it's a long walk and I wanted to get it over with before it got truly hot again today.

On my way back, the ladies were still lying in the yard and to quench my curiosity, I went inside and asked to speak to the director of the facility.

When I asked him if he knew there were six naked old ladies lying on his front lawn, he replied, "Yes, I know. They're retired prostitutes and they're having a yard sale!"

Three sisters, ages 92, 94 and 96, live in a house together. One night the 96-year-old draws a bath. She puts her foot in and pauses. She yells to the other sisters, "Was I getting in or out of the bath?"

The 94-year-old yells back, "I don't know. I'll come up and see." She starts up the stairs and pauses "Was I going up the stairs or down?"

The 92-year-old is sitting at the kitchen table having tea listening to her sisters. She shakes her head and says, "I sure hope I never get that forgetful, knock on wood." She then yells, "I'll come up and help both of you as soon as I see who's at the door."

Three retirees, each with a hearing loss, were playing golf on fine March day. One remarked to the other, "Windy, isn't it?"

"No," the second man replied, "It's Thursday."

And the third man chimed in, "So am I. Let's have a beer."

A little old lady was running up and down the halls in a nursing home. As she walked, she would flip up the hem of her nightgown and say "Supersex." She walked up to an elderly man in a wheelchair. Flipping her gown at him, she said, "Supersex."

He sat silently for a moment or two and finally answered, "I'll take the soup."

Two elderly women were out driving in a large car—both could barely see over the dashboard. As they were cruising along, they came to an intersection. The stoplight was red, but they just went on through. The woman in the passenger seat thought to herself "I must be losing it. I could have sworn we just went through a red light." After a few more minutes, they came to another intersection and the light was red again. Again, they went right through. The woman in the passenger seat was almost sure that the light had been red but was really concerned that she was losing it. She was getting nervous. At the next intersection, sure enough, the light was red and they went on through. So, she turned to the other woman and said, "Mildred, did you know that we just ran through three red lights in a row? You could have killed us both!"

Mildred turned to her and said, "Oh, crap, am I driving?"

Old people have problems that you haven't even considered yet! An 85-year-old man was requested by his doctor for a sperm count as part of his physical exam. The doctor gave the man a jar and said, "Take this jar home and bring back a semen sample tomorrow."

The next day the 85-year-old man reappeared at the doctor's office and gave him the jar, which was as clean and empty as on the previous day. The doctor asked what happened and the man explained, "Well, doc, it's like this—first I tried with my right hand, but nothing. Then tried with my left hand, but still nothing. Then I asked my wife for help. She tried with her right hand, then with her left, still nothing. She tried with her mouth, first with the teeth in, then with her teeth out, still nothing.

We even called up the lady next door and she tried too, first with both hands, then an armpit, and she even tried squeezin' it between her knees, but still nothing.

The doctor was shocked! "You asked your neighbor?"

The old man replied, "Yep, none of us could get the jar open."

LOVEMAKING TIPS FOR SENIORS

1. Put on your glasses. Double check that your partner is actually in bed with you.

2. Set timer for 3 minutes, in case you doze off in the middle.
3. Set the mood with lighting. Turn them ALL OFF!
4. Make sure you put 911 on your speed dial before you begin.
5. Write partner's name on your hand in case you can't remember it.
6. Keep extra poly-grip close by so your teeth don't end up under the bed or between the thighs.
7. Have Tylenol ready in case you actually complete the act.
8. Make all the noise you want. The neighbors are deaf too.
9. If it works, call everyone you know with the good news.
10. Don't even think about trying it twice.

We went to breakfast at a restaurant where the "seniors' special" was two eggs, bacon, hash browns and toast for $1.99. "Sounds good," my wife said. "But I don't want the eggs."

"Then I'll have to charge you two dollars and forty-nine cents because you're ordering a la carte," the waitress warned her.

"You mean I'd have to pay for not taking the eggs?" My wife asked incredulously. "I'll take the special."

"How do you want your eggs?"

"Raw and in the shell," my wife replied.

She took the two eggs home.

A college student challenged a senior citizen, saying it was impossible for their generation to understand his. "You grew up in a different world," the student said. "Today we have television, jet planes, space travel, nuclear energy, computers . . ."

Taking advantage of a pause in the student's litany, the geezer said, "You're right. We didn't have those things when we were young; so we invented them! What are you doing for the next generation??"

A very elderly gentleman, very well dressed, hair well groomed, great looking suit, flower in his lapel smelling slightly of a good after shave, presenting a well looked after image, walks into an upscale cocktail lounge. Seated at the bar is an elderly lady, The gentleman walks over, sits along side of her, orders a drink, takes a sip, turns to her and says, "So tell me, do I come here often?"

Two elderly gentlemen from a retirement center were sitting on a bench under a tree when one turns to the other and says . . .

"Slim, I'm 83 years old now and I'm just full of aches and pains. I know you're about my age. How do you feel?"

Slim says, "I feel just like a new-born baby."

"Really!? Like a new-born baby!?"

"Yep. No hair, no teeth, and I think I just wet my pants.

An elderly couple had dinner at another couple's house, and after eating, the wives left the table and went into the kitchen. The two gentlemen were talking, and one said, "Last night we went out to a new restaurant and it was really great. I would recommend it very highly."

The other man said, "What is the name of the restaurant?"

The first man thought and thought and finally said, "What is the name of that flower you give to someone you love? You know . . . the one that's red and has thorns."

"Do you mean a rose?"

"Yes, that's the one," replied the man. He then turned towards the kitchen and yelled, "Rose, what's the name of that restaurant we went to last night?

Two old men were sitting on a park bench outside the local town hall where a flower show was in progress.

One leaned over to the other and said, "Cripes! life is boring, we never have any fun these days. For two bucks, I'd take my clothes off and streak through the flower show!"

"You're on!" said the other old fellow, holding up two dollars.

As fast as he could, the first old man fumbled his way out of his clothes and completely naked, streaked through the front door of the town hall.

Waiting outside, his friend heard a huge commotion inside the hall, followed by loud applause. The naked old man burst out through the door surrounded by a cheering crowd.

"How did it go?" asked his friend.

"Great!" he said,

"I WON FIRST PRIZE AS A DRIED ARRANGEMENT!!!"

A senior citizen goes in for his yearly physical with his wife tagging along.

When the doctor enters the examination room he says, "I will need a urine sample, a stool sample, and a sperm sample."

The man, being hard of hearing, turns to his wife and asks, "What did he say?"

The wife yells back to him, "GIVE HIM YOUR UNDERWEAR!

An eighty year old woman goes to the Doctor for a check up. She was required to bring with her all types of medicine she had at home. As the Doctor was looking through these he came across Birth Control pills. "Mrs. Smith do you realize that these are Birth Control pills"? he said. "Yes, they help me sleep at night." "But Mrs. Smith there is nothing in them that would help you to sleep!" "I know that, but when I grind one up each morning and put it in the glass of orange juice that my 17 year old Granddaughter drinks, believe me, it helps me sleep at night"!

THE PERKS OF BEING 60 & OVER AND OTHER WORDS OF WISDOM

1. Kidnappers are not very interested in you.
2. In a hostage situation you are likely to be released first.
3. No one expects you to run into a burning building
4. People call at 9 PM and ask, "Did I wake you?"

5. People no longer view you as a hypochondriac.
6. There is nothing left to learn the hard way.
7. Things you buy now won't wear out.
8. You can eat dinner at 4 PM.
9. You can live without sex but not without glasses.
10. You enjoy hearing arguments about pension plans.
11. You have a party and the neighbors don't even realize it.
12. You no longer think of speed limits as a challenge.
13. You quit trying to hold your stomach in, no matter who walks into the room.
14. You sing along with elevator music.
15. Your eyes won't get much worse.
16. Your investment in health insurance is finally beginning to pay off.
17. Your joints are a more accurate meteorologist than the national weather service.
18. Your secrets are safe with your friends because they can't remember them either.
19. Your supply of brain cells is finally down to manageable size.

I feel like my body has gotten totally out of shape, so I got my doctor's permission to join a fitness club and start exercising . . . I decided to take an aerobics class for seniors. I bent, twisted, gyrated, jumped up and down, and perspired for an hour. But, by the time I got my leotards on, the class was over.

Reporters interviewing a 104 year-old woman: "And what do you think is the best thing about being 104?" the reporter asked. She simply replied, "No peer pressure."

Just before the funeral services, the undertaker came up to the very elderly widow and asked, "How old was your husband?

"98," she replied. "Two years older than me."

"So you're 96," the undertaker commented.
She responded, "Hardly worth going home is it?"

A 97 year old man goes into his doctor's office and says, "Doc, I want my sex drive lowered."

"Sir", replied the doctor, "You're 97. Don't you think your sex drive is all in your head?"

"You're darned right it is!" replied the old man. "That's why I want it lowered!"

An elderly woman from Brooklyn decided to prepare her will and make her final requests. She told her rabbi she had two final requests. First, she wanted to be cremated, and second, she wanted her ashes scattered over Bloomingdales.

"Bloomingdales?" the rabbi exclaimed. "Why Bloomingdales?"

"Then I'll be sure my daughters visit me twice a week."

A man was telling his neighbor, "I just bought a new hearing aid. It cost me four thousand dollars, but its state of the art. It's perfect."

"Really," answered the neighbor. "What kind is it?"

"Twelve thirty."

Morris, an 82 year-old man, went to the doctor to get a physical. A few days later the doctor saw Morris walking down the street with a gorgeous young woman on his arm.

A couple of days later the doctor spoke to Morris and said, "You're really doing great, aren't you?"

Morris replied, "Just doing what you said, Doc: 'Get a hot mamma and be cheerful.' "

The doctor said, "I didn't say that. I said, 'You've got a heart murmur. Be careful' "

If my body were a car, this is the time I would be thinking about trading it in for a newer model.

I've got bumps and dents and scratches in my finish and my paint job is getting a little dull, but that's not the worst of it.

My headlights are out of focus and it's especially hard to see things up close.

My traction is not as graceful as it once was.

I slip and slide and skid and bump into things even in the best of weather.

My whitewalls are stained with varicose veins.

It takes me hours to reach my maximum speed.

My fuel rate burns inefficiently.

But here's the worst of it—

Almost every time I sneeze, cough or sputter. . . . . either my radiator leaks or my exhaust backfires!

Jacob, age 92 and Rebecca, age 89, are all excited about their decision to get married. They go for a stroll to discuss the wedding, and on the way they pass a drugstore. Jacob suggest they go in.

Jacob addresses the man behind the counter:

"Are you the owner?"

The pharmacist answers "Yes."

Jacob: "We're about to get married.; Do you sell heart medication?"

Pharmacist: "Of course we do".

Jacob: "How about medicine for circulation?"

Pharmacist: "All kinds."

Jacob "Medicine for rheumatism, scoliosis?"

Pharmacist: "Definitely".

Jacob: "How about Viagra?"

Pharmacist "Of course."

Jacob: "Medicine for memory problems, arthritis, jaundice?"

Pharmacist: "Yes a large variety. The works."

Jacob: "What about vitamins, sleeping pills, Geritol, antidotes for Parkinson's disease?"

Pharmacist: "Absolutely".

Jacob: You sell wheelchairs and walkers?"

Pharmacist: "All speeds and sizes."

Jacob says to the pharmacist: "We'd like to register here for our wedding gifts, please."

A little old couple walked slowly into McDonalds one cold winter evening. They looked out of place amid the young families and young couples eating there that night. Some of the customers looked admiringly at them.

You could tell what the admirers were thinking. "Look, there is a couple who has been through a lot together, probably for 60 years or more!"

The little old man walked right up to the cash register, placed his order with no hesitation and then paid for their meal.

The couple took a table near the back wall and started taking food off of the tray. There was one hamburger, one order of French fries and one drink. The little old man unwrapped the plain hamburger and carefully cut it in half. He placed one half in front of his wife. Then he carefully counted out the French fries, divided them in two piles and neatly placed one pile in front of his wife. He took a sip of the drink, his wife took a sip and then set the cup down between them. As the man began to eat his few bites of hamburger the crowd began to get restless. Again you could tell what they were thinking. "That poor old couple. All they can afford is one meal for the two of them."

As the man began to eat his French fries one young man stood and came over to the old couples' table. He politely offered to buy another meal for the couple to eat.

The old man replied that they were just fine. They were used to sharing everything. Then the crowd noticed that the little old lady hadn't eaten a bite. She just sat there watching her husband eat and occasionally taking turns sipping the drink. Again the young man came over and begged them to let him buy them something to eat.

This time the lady explained that no, they were used to sharing everything together. As the little old man finished eating and was wiping his face neatly with a napkin the young man could stand it no longer.

Again he came over to their table and offered to buy some food. After being politely refused again he finally asked a question of the little old lady. "Ma'am, why aren't you eating? You said that you share everything. What is it that you are waiting for?" She answered . . .

'THE TEETH'

A group of Florida senior citizens were sitting around talking about their ailments.

"My arms are so weak I can hardly hold this cup of coffee," said one.

"Yes, I know. My cataracts are so bad, I can't even see my coffee," replied another.

"I can't turn my head because of the arthritis in my neck," said a third, to which several nodded weakly in agreement.

"My blood pressure pills make me dizzy," claimed another.

"I guess that's the price we pay for getting old," winced an old man as he shook his head.

Then there was a short moment of silence . . .

"Well, it's not that bad," said one woman cheerfully. "Thank God we can all still drive."

What happens when we get old!

1. You and your teeth don't sleep together.

2. Your try to straighten out the wrinkles in your socks and discover you aren't wearing any.

3. At the breakfast table you hear snap, crackle, pop and you're not eating cereal.

4. Your back goes out but you stay home.

5. You wake up looking like your driver's license picture.

6. It takes two tries to get up from the couch.

7. Your idea of a night out is sitting on the patio.

8. Happy hour is a nap.

9. When you're on vacation your energy runs out before your money does.

10. When all you want for your birthday is to not be reminded of your age.

11. When you step off a curb and look down one more time to make sure the street is still there.

12. Your idea of weight lifting is standing up.
13. It takes longer to rest than it did to get tired.
14. Your memory is shorter and your complaining lasts longer.
15. Your address book has mostly names that start with Dr.
16. You sit in a rocking chair and can't get it going.
17. The pharmacist has become your new best friend.
18. Getting "lucky" means you found your car in the parking lot.
19. The twinkle in your eye is merely a reflection from the sun on your bifocals.
20. It takes twice as long—to look half as good.
21. Everything hurts, and what doesn't hurt—doesn't work.
22. You look for your glasses for half an hour and they were on your head the whole time.
23. You sink your teeth into a steak—and they stay there.
24. You give up all your bad habits and still don't feel good.
25. You have more patience, but it is actually that you just don't care anymore.
26. You finally get your head together and your body starts falling apart.
27. You wonder how you could be over the hill when you don't even remember being on top of it.

Two elderly people lived in a Florida mobile home park. He was a widower and she a widow. They had known one another for a number of years. Now, one evening there was a community supper in the big activity center. These two were at the same table, across form one another. As the meal went on, he made a few admiring glances at her and finally gathered up his courage to ask her, "Will you marry me?"

After about six seconds of 'careful consideration,' she answered. "Yes. Yes, I will."

The meal ended and with a few more pleasant exchanges, they went to their respective places.

Next morning, he was troubled. "Did she say 'yes' or did she say 'no'?" He couldn't remember. Try as he would, he just could not recall, not even a faint memory. With trepidation, he went to the telephone and called her. First, he explained to her that he didn't remember as well as he used to. Then he reviewed the lovely evening past. As he gained a little more courage, he then inquired of her, "When I asked if you would marry me, did you say 'Yes' or did you say 'No'?" He was delighted to hear her say, "Why, I said, 'Yes, yes I will' and I meant it with all my heart." Then she continued, "And I am so glad that you called, because I couldn't remember who had asked me."

An elderly couple decide to celebrate their fiftieth anniversary by reliving their honeymoon. They get a reservation for the honeymoon suite in the same hotel at the same resort. After waking the next morning to a room service breakfast they begin eating in the nude.

The wife says "Oh Harold! This is just like fifty years ago! My breasts feel all warm and tingly!" To which he replies "Well, they ought to, Gladys . . . One is a hanging in your oatmeal, and the other is in your coffee!"

I took my dad to the mall the other day to buy some new shoes. We decided to grab a bite at the food court. I noticed he was watching a teenager sitting next to him. The teenager had spiked hair in all different colors: green, red, orange, and blue. My dad kept staring at him.

The teenager would look and find him staring every time.

When the teenager had enough, he sarcastically asked, "What's the matter old man, never done anything wild in your life?"

Knowing my Dad, I quickly swallowed my food so that I would not choke on his response; knowing he would have a good one. And in classic style he did not bat an eye in his response, "Got drunk once and had sex with a peacock. I was just wondering if you were my son."

Hospital regulations require a wheel chair for patients being discharged. However, while working as a student aide, I found one elderly gentleman already dressed and sitting on the bed with a suitcase at his feet, who insisted he didn't need my help to leave the hospital. After a chat about rules being rules, he reluctantly let me wheel him to the elevator.

On the way down I asked him if his wife was meeting him.

I don't know," he said "She's still upstairs in the bathroom changing out of her hospital gown"

Couple in their nineties are both having problems remembering things. During a checkup, the doctor tells them that they're physically okay, but they might want to start writing things down to help them remember.

Later that night, while watching TV, the old man gets up from his chair. "Want anything while I'm in the kitchen?" he asks.

"Will you get me a bowl of ice cream?"

"Sure."

"Don't you think you should write it down so you can remember it?" she asks.

"No, I can remember it."

"Well, I'd like some strawberries on top, too. Maybe you should write it down, so's not to forget it?"

He says, "I can remember that. You want a bowl of ice cream with strawberries."

"I'd also like whipped cream. I'm certain you'll forget that, write it down?" she asks.

Irritated, he says, "I don't need to write it down, I can remember it! Ice cream with strawberries and whipped cream—I got it, for goodness sake!"

Then he toddles into the kitchen. After about 20 minutes, the old man returns from the kitchen and hands his wife a plate of bacon and eggs. She stares at the plate for a moment.

"Where's my toast?"

A senior citizen said to his eighty-year old buddy:

"So I hear you're getting married?"

"Yep!"

"Do I know her?"
"Nope!"
"This woman, is she good looking?"
"Not really."
"Is she a good cook?"
"Naw, she can't cook too well."
"Does she have lots of money?"
"Nope! Poor as a church mouse."
"Well, then, is she good in bed?"
"I don't know."
"Why in the world do you want to marry her then?"
"Because she can still drive!"

A little old man shuffled slowly into an ice cream parlor and pulled himself slowly, painfully, up onto a stool. . After catching his breath, he ordered a banana split.

The waitress asked kindly, "Crushed nuts?"

"No," he replied, "Arthritis."

Q: Where can women over the age of 60 find young, sexy men, who are interested in them?

A: Try a bookstore under fiction.

Q: What can a man do while his wife is going through menopause?

A: Keep busy. If you're handy with tools, you can finish the basement. When you are done you will have a place to live.

Q: How can you increase the heart rate of your 60+ year old husband?

A: Tell him you're pregnant.

Q: How can you avoid spotting a wrinkle every time you walk by a mirror?

A: The next time you're in front of a mirror, take off your glasses.

Q: Why should 60+ year old people use valet parking?

A: Valets don't forget where they park your car.

Q: Is it common for 60+ year olds to have problems with short term memory storage?

A: Storing memory is not a problem, retrieving it is a problem.

Q: As people age, do they sleep more soundly?

A: Yes, but usually in the afternoon.

Q: Where do 60+ year olds look for fashionable glasses?

A: Their foreheads.

Q: What is the most common remark made by 60+ year olds when they enter antique stores?

A: "I remember these!

At 85 years of age, Roger married Jenny, a lovely 25 year old.

Since her new husband is so old, Jenny decided that after their wedding she and Roger should have separate bedrooms, because she is concerned that her new but aged husband may overexert himself if they spend the entire night together.

After the wedding festivities Jenny prepares herself for bed and the expected knock" on the door. Sure enough the knock comes, the door open and there is Roger, her 85 year old groom, ready for action. They unite as one.

All goes well, Roger takes leave of his bride, and she prepares to go to sleep. After a few minutes, Jenny hears another knock on her bedroom door, and it's Roger. Again he is ready for more "action".

Somewhat surprised, Jenny consents to more coupling. When the newlyweds are done, Roger kisses his bride, bids her a fond good night and leaves.

She is set to go to sleep again, but, aha you guessed it—Roger is back again, rapping on the door, and is as fresh as a 25-year-old, ready for more "action".

And, once more they enjoy each other. But as Roger gets set to leave again, his young bride says to him, "I am thoroughly impressed that at your age you can perform so well and so often. I have been with guys less than a third of your age who were only good once. You are truly a great lover, Roger."

Roger, somewhat embarrassed, turns to Jenny and says: "You mean I was here already?"

The couple were 85 years old, and had been married for sixty years.

Though they were far from rich, they managed to get by because they watched their pennies.

Though not young, they were both in very good health, largely due to the wife's insistence on healthy foods and exercise for the last decade. One day, their good health didn't help when they went on a rare vacation and their plane crashed, sending them off to Heaven.

They reached the pearly gates, and St. Peter escorted them inside.

He took them to a beautiful mansion, furnished in gold and fine silks, with a fully stocked kitchen and a waterfall in the master bath. A maid could be seen hanging their favorite clothes in the closet.

They gasped in astonishment when he said, "Welcome to Heaven. This will be your home now."

The old man asked St. Peter how much all this was going to cost. "Why, nothing," St. Peter replied, "remember, this is your reward in Heaven."

The old man looked out the window and right there he saw a championship golf course, finer and more beautiful than any ever built on Earth.

"What are the green fees?", grumbled the old man.

"This is heaven," St. Peter replied. "You can play for free, every day."

Next they went to the clubhouse and saw the lavish buffet lunch, with every imaginable cuisine laid out before them, from seafood to steaks to exotic deserts, free flowing beverages.

"Don't even ask," said St. Peter to the man. "This is Heaven, it is all free for you to enjoy."

The old man looked around and glanced nervously at his wife.

"Well, where are the low fat and low cholesterol foods, and the decaffeinated tea?" he asked.

"That's the best part," St. Peter replied. "You can eat and drink as much as you like whatever you like, and you will never get fat or sick. This is Heaven!"

The old man pushed, "No gym to work out at?"

"Not unless you want to," was the answer.

"No testing my sugar or blood pressure or . . ."

"Never again. All you do here is enjoy yourself."

The old man glared at his wife and said, "You and your bran muffins.

We could have been here ten years ago!

Chapter 1: GAMES FOR WHEN WE ARE OLDER

1. Sag, you're it.
2. Pin the toupee on the bald guy.
3. 20 questions shouted into your good ear.
4. Kick the bucket.
5. Red Rover, Red Rover, the nurse says Bend Over.
6. Doc Goose.
7. Simon says something incoherent.
8. Hide and Go Pee.
9. Spin the Bottle of Mylanta.
10. Musical Recliners.

Chapter 2: SIGNS OF MENOPAUSE

1. You sell your home heating system at a yard sale.
2. Your husband jokes that instead of buying a wood stove, he is using you to heat the family room this winter. Rather than just saying you are not amused, you shoot him.
3. You have to write post-it notes with your kids' names on them.
4. The Phenobarbital dose that wiped out the Heaven's Gate Cult gave you four hours of decent rest.
5. You change your underwear after every sneeze.
6. You're on so much estrogen that you take your Brownie troop on a field trip to Chippendale's.

Chapter 3: SIGNS OF WEAR

OLD" IS WHEN. . Your sweetie says, "Let's go upstairs and make love," and you answer, "pick one, I can't do both!"

"OLD" IS WHEN. . Your friends compliment you on your new alligator shoes but you're barefoot.

"OLD" IS WHEN. . A sexy babe catches your fancy and your pacemaker opens the garage door.

"OLD" IS WHEN. . Going braless pulls all the wrinkles out of your face.

"OLD" IS WHEN. . You don't care where your spouse goes, just as long as you don't have to go along.

"OLD" IS WHEN. . You are cautioned to slow down by the doctor instead of by the police.

"OLD" IS WHEN. . "Getting a little action" means I don't need to take any fiber today.

"OLD" IS WHEN. . "Getting lucky" means you find your car in the parking lot.

"OLD" IS WHEN. . An "all-nighter" means not getting up to pee.

Two elderly ladies are sitting on the front porch, doing nothing.

One lady turns and asks, "Do you still get horny?" The other replies, "Oh sure I do." The first old lady asks, "What do you do about it?" The second old lady replies, "I suck a lifesaver."

After a few moments, the first old lady asks, "Who drives you to the beach?"

An old lady was standing at the railing of the cruise ship holding her hat on tightly so that it would not blow off in the wind. A gentleman approached her and said: "Pardon me, madam. I do not intend to be forward, but did you know that your dress is blowing up in this high wind?"

"Yes, I know," said the lady, "I need both hands to hold onto this hat." "But, madam, you must know that your privates are exposed!" said the gentleman in earnest.

The woman looked down, then back up at the man and replied, "Sir, anything you see down there is 85 years old. I just bought this hat yesterday!"

Ethel and Mabel, two elderly widows, were watching the folks go by from their park bench. Ethel said, “You know, Mabel, I’ve been reading this ‘Sex and Marriage’ book and all they talk about is ‘mutual orgasm’. ‘Mutual orgasm’ here and ‘mutual orgasm’ there—that’s all they talk about.

Tell me, Mabel, when your husband was alive, did you two ever have mutual orgasms?”. Mabel thought for a long while. Finally, she shook her head and said,

“No, I think we had State Farm.

Three old ladies were sitting side by side in their retirement home reminiscing. The first lady recalled shopping at the green grocers and demonstrated with her hands, the length and thickness of a cucumber she could buy for a penny. The second old lady nodded, adding that onions used to be much bigger and cheaper also, and demonstrated the size of two big onions she could buy for a penny a piece. The third old lady remarked, “I can’t hear a word you’re saying, but I remember the guy you’re talking about.”

Two elderly women were eating at a restaurant one morning. Ethel noticed something funny about Mabel’s ear and she said, “Mabel, did you know you’ve got a suppository in your left ear?”

Mabel answered, “I have? A suppository?” She pulled it out & stared at it. Then she said,

“Ethel, I’m glad you saw this thing. Now I think I know where my hearing aid is.”

When the husband finally died his wife put the usual death notice in the paper, but added that he died of gonorrhea. No sooner were the papers delivered when a good friend of the family phoned and complained bitterly, “You know very well that he died of diarrhea, not gonorrhea.” Replied the widow, “I nursed him night and day so of course I know he died of diarrhea, but I thought it would be better for posterity to remember him as a great lover rather than the big shit he always was."

An elderly couple was on a cruise and it was really stormy. They were standing on the stern of the boat watching the moon, when a wave came up and washed the old woman overboard. They searched for days and couldn't find her, so the captain sent the old man back to shore with the promise that he would notify him as soon as they found something.

Three weeks went by and finally the old man got a fax from the boat. It read: "Sir, sorry to inform you, we found your wife dead at the bottom of the ocean. We hauled her up to the deck and attached to her butt was an oyster and in it was a pearl worth $50,000 . . . please advise"

The old man faxed back: "Send me the pearl and re-bait the trap"

Upon hearing that her elderly grandfather had just passed away, Katie went straight to her grandparent's house to visit her 95 year old grandmother and comfort her.

When she asked how her grandfather had died, her grandmother replied, "He had a heart attack while we were making love on Sunday morning."

Horrified, Katie told her grandmother that 2 people nearly 100 years old having sex would surely be asking for trouble.

"Oh no, my dear," replied granny. Many years ago, realizing our advanced age, we figured out the best time to do it was when the church bells would start to ring. It was just the right rhythm. Nice and slow and even. Nothing too strenuous, simply in on the Ding and out on the Dong. She paused, wiped away a tear, and continued, and if that damned ice cream truck hadn't come along, he'd still be alive today. . . . ."

There is more money being spent on breast implants and Viagra today than on Alzheimer's research. This means that by 2040, there should be a large elderly population with perky boobs and huge erections and absolutely no recollection of what to do with them.

A Florida couple, both well into their 80's, goes to a sex therapist's office.

The doctor says, "What can I do for you?"

The man says, "Will you watch us have sexual intercourse?"

The doctor raises both eyebrows, but he is so amazed that such an elderly couple is asking for sexual advice that he agrees.

When the couple finishes, the doctor says, "There's absolutely nothing wrong with the way you have intercourse."

He thanks them for coming, he wishes them good luck, he charges them $50 and he says good-bye. The next week, the couple returns and asks the sex therapist to watch again.

The sex therapist is a bit puzzled, but agrees.

This happens several weeks in a row.

The couple makes an appointment, has intercourse with no problems, pays the doctor, then leaves.

Finally, after 3 months of this routine, the doctor says, "I'm sorry, but I have to ask. Just what are you trying to find out?"

The man says, "We're not trying to find out anything.

She's married and we can't go to her house. I'm married and we can't go to my house.

The Holiday Inn charges $98.

The Hilton charges $139.

We do it here for $50, and I get $43 back from Medicare."

MILITARY JOKES

Letter from a Farm Kid (Now at San Diego Marine Corps Recruit Training)

Dear Ma and Pa,

I am well. Hope you are. Tell Brother Walt and Brother Elmer the Marine Corps beats working for old man Minch by a mile. Tell them to join up quick before all of the places are filled.

I was restless at first because you got to stay in bed till nearly 6 a.m. but I am getting so I like to sleep late. Tell Walt and Elmer all you do before breakfast is smooth your cot, and shine some things. No hogs to slop, feed to pitch, mash to mix, wood to split, fire to lay. Practically nothing.

Men got to shave but it is not so bad, there's warm water. Breakfast is strong on trimmings like fruit juice, cereal, eggs, bacon, etc., but kind of weak on chops, potatoes, ham, steak, pie and other regular food, but tell Walt and Elmer you can always sit by the two city boys that live on coffee. Their food plus yours holds you until noon when you get fed again. It's no wonder these city boys can't walk much.

We go on "route marches," which the platoon sergeant says are long walks to harden us. If he thinks so, it's not my place to tell him different. A "route march" is about as far as to our mailbox at home. Then the city guys get sore feet and we all ride back in trucks. The country is nice but awful flat.

The sergeant is like a school teacher. He nags a lot. The Captain is like the school board. Majors and colonels just ride around and frown. They don't bother you none.

This next will kill Walt and Elmer with laughing. I keep getting medals for shooting. I don't know why. The bulls-eye is near as big as a chipmunk head and don't move, and it ain't shooting back at you like the Higgett boys at home. All you got to do is lie there all comfortable and hit it. You don't even load your own cartridges. They come in boxes.

Then we have what they call hand-to-hand combat training. You get to wrestle with them city boys. I have to be real careful though, they break real easy. It ain't like fighting with that ole bull at home. I'm about the best they got in this except for that Tug Jordan from over in Silver Lake. I only beat him once. He joined up the same time as me, but I'm only 5'6" and 130 pounds and he's 6'8" and near 300 pounds dry.

Be sure to tell Walt and Elmer to hurry and join before other fellers get onto this setup and come stampeding in.

Your loving daughter,

The Captain called the Sergeant in. "Sarge, I just got a telegram that Private Jones' mother died yesterday. Better go tell him and send him in to see me."

So the Sergeant calls for his morning formation and lines up all the troops. "Listen up, men," says the Sergeant. "Johnson, report to the mess hall for KP. Smith, report to Personnel to sign some papers. The rest of you men report to the Motor Pool for maintenance. Oh by the way, Jones, your mother died, report to the commander."

Later that day the Captain called the Sergeant into his office. "Hey, Sarge, that was a pretty cold way to inform Jones his mother died. Couldn't you be a bit more tactful, next time?"

"Yes, sir," answered the Sarge.

A few months later, the Captain called the Sergeant in again with, "Sarge, I just got a telegram that Private McGrath's mother died. You'd better go tell him and send him in to see me. This time be more tactful."

So the Sergeant calls for his morning formation. "Ok, men, fall in and listen up." "Everybody with a mother, take two steps forward." "Not so fast, McGrath!"

Admiral McKenzie was in charge of the Navy, and he was visiting his colleague General Marshall, who was in charge of the Army. McKenzie arrives at the military camp and is greeted by Marshall. They both walk around the place, and McKenzie asks: "So how are your men?"

"Very well trained, Admiral McKenzie."

"I hope so. You see, my men over at the Navy are so well trained, you could see they're the bravest men all over the country."
"Well, my men are very brave, too."

"I'd like to see that."

So Marshall calls Private Cooper and says: "Private Cooper! I want you to stop that tank coming here with your body!"

"Are you crazy? It'd kill me, you idiot! I'm out of here!" As Private Cooper ran away, Marshall turned to a bewildered McKenzie and said: "You see? You have to be pretty brave to talk like that to a general."

It was a dark, stormy, night. The Marine was on his first assignment, and it was guard duty.

A General was taking his dog for a walk. The nervous young Private snapped to attention, made a perfect salute, and snapped out, "Sir, Good Evening, Sir!"

The General, out for some relaxation, returned the salute and said "Good evening marine, nice night, isn't it?"

Well it wasn't a nice night, but the Private wasn't going to disagree with the General, so he saluted again and replied "Sir, Yes Sir!".

The General continued, "You know there's something about a stormy night that I find soothing, it's really relaxing. Don't you agree?"

The Private didn't agree, but them the private was just a private, and responded "Sir, Yes Sir!"

The General, pointing at the dog, "This is a Golden Retriever, the best type of dog to train."

The Private glanced at the dog, saluted yet again and said "Sir, Yes Sir!"

The General continued "I got this dog for my wife."

The Private simply said "Good trade Sir!"

You've all heard of the Air Force's ultra-high-security, super-secret base in Nevada, known simply as "Area 51?"

Well, late one afternoon, the Air Force folks out at Area 51 were very surprised to see a Cessna landing at their "secret" base. They immediately impounded the aircraft and hauled the pilot into an interrogation room.

The pilot's story was that he took off from Vegas, got lost, and spotted the Base just as he was about to run out of fuel. The Air Force started a full FBI background check on the pilot and held him overnight during the investigation.

By the next day, they were finally convinced that the pilot really was lost and wasn't a spy. They gassed up his airplane, gave him a terrifying "you-did-not-see-a-base" briefing, complete with threats of spending the rest of his life in prison, told him Vegas was that-a-way on such-and-such a heading, and sent him on his way.

The day after that though, to the total disbelief of the Air Force, the same Cessna showed up again. Once again, the MP's surrounded the plane . . . only this time there were two people in the plane.

The same pilot jumped out and said, "Do anything you want to me, but my wife is in the plane and you have to tell her where I was last night!"

One reason the Services have trouble operating jointly is that they don't speak the same language.

For example, if you told Navy personnel to "secure a building," they would turn off the lights and lock the doors.

Army personnel would occupy the building so no one could enter.

Marines would assault the building, capture it, and defend it with suppressive fire and close combat.

The Air Force, on the other hand, would take out a three-year lease with an option to buy.

The 1982 Israeli invasion of Lebanon resulted in many dogfights between Syrian and Israeli jet fighters.

In the end, the Syrians lost over 80 planes and had a number of SAM batteries knocked out, while the Israelis lost no planes.

Sometime later, the Syrian Defense Minister was shopping for weapons in Moscow.

His host, the Soviet Defense Minister, was embarrassed about the scorecard from Lebanon.

He told his Syrian guest, "Take anything you want—our best tanks, rifles, or surface-to-air missiles."

"No, no—you don't understand!" the Syrian replied. "Last time you gave us surface-to-air missiles. This time we need surface-to-*jet* missiles!"

The new Ensign was assigned to subs, where he'd dreamed of working since a young boy. He was trying to impress the Master Chief with his expertise learned in Sub School.

The Master Chief cut him off quickly and said, "Listen, 'sir', it's real simple. Add the number of times we dive to the number of times we surface. Divide that number by two. If the result doesn't come out even, don't open the hatch."

On some air bases the Air Force is on one side of the field and civilian aircraft use the other side of the field, with the control tower in the middle. One day the tower received a call from an aircraft asking, "What time is it?"

The tower responded, "Who is calling?"

The aircraft replied, "What difference does it make?"

The tower replied, "It makes a lot of difference. If it is an American Airlines flight, it is 3 o'clock. If it is an Air Force plane, it is 1500 hours. If it is a Navy aircraft, it is 6 bells. If it is an Army aircraft, the big hand is on the 12 and the little hand is on the 3. If it is a Marine Corps aircraft, it's Thursday afternoon and 120 minutes to "Happy Hour."

During training exercises, the lieutenant who was driving down a muddy back road encountered another car stuck in the mud with a red-faced colonel at the wheel. "Your jeep stuck, sir?" asked the lieutenant as he pulled alongside. "Nope," replied the colonel, coming over and handing him the keys, "Yours is."

Having just moved into his new office, a pompous, new colonel was sitting at his desk when an airman knocked on the door. Conscious of his new position, the colonel quickly picked up the phone, told the airman to enter, then said into the phone, “Yes, General, I'll be seeing him this afternoon and I'll pass along your message. In the meantime, thank you for your good wishes, sir.” Feeling as though he had sufficiently impressed the young enlisted man, he asked, “What do you want?” “Nothing important, sir,” the airman replied, “I'm just here to hook up your telephone.”

An Israeli soldier who just enlisted asked the Commanding Officer for a 3-day pass.

The CO says, “Are you crazy? You just join the Israeli army, and you already want a 3-day pass? You must do something spectacular for that recognition!”

So the soldier comes back a day later in an Arab tank!

The CO was so impressed, he asked, “How did you do it?”

“Well, I jumped in a tank, and went toward the border with the Arabs. I approached the border, and saw an Arab tank. I put my white flag up, the Arab tank put his white flag up. I said to the Arab soldier, “Do you want to get a three-day pass? So we exchanged tanks!”

The drill sergeant making his morning announcements to a group of newcomers in a training camp, stated: “Today, gentlemen, I have some good news and some bad news. First, the good. Private Peters will be setting the pace on our morning run.”

With this the platoon was overjoyed, as Private Peters was overweight and terribly slow. But then the drill sergeant finished his statement:” Now for the bad news. Private Peters will be driving a truck.”

STUPID JOKES

Did you hear about the guy from Alabama who passed away and left his entire estate to his beloved widow? But she can't touch it 'til she's 14.

-How do you know when you're staying in a Kentucky hotel? When you call the front desk and say, "I gotta leak in my sink" and the front desk replies, "Go ahead".

-How can you tell if a Tennessee redneck is married? There is dried tobacco juice on BOTH sides of his pickup truck.

-What do they call reruns of "Hee Haw" in Alabama? Documentaries.

-Where was the toothbrush invented?
Mississippi. If it was invented anywhere else, it would have been called a teethbrush.

-A Georgia State trooper pulls over a pickup on I-75 and says to the driver, "Got any I.D.?" and the driver replies, "Bout wut?".

-Did you hear about the $3 million Arkansas State Lottery?
The winner gets $3 a year for a million years.

-A new law recently passed in West Virginia:
When a couple gets divorced, they're STILL brother and sister.

The sheriff in a small town walks out in the street and sees a blonde cowboy coming down the walk with nothing on but his cowboy hat, gun and his boots.

So the sheriff arrests him for indecent exposure. As he is locking him up he asks "Why in the world are you dressed like this?"

Cowboy says "Well it's like this Sheriff . . . I was in the bar down the road and this pretty little redhead asks me to go out to her motor home with her. . . . and I did.

We go inside and she pulls off her top and asks me to pull off my shirt. . . . . So I did. . . .

Then she pulls off her skirt and asks me to pull off my pants. . . . . So I did . . .

Then she pulls off her panties and asks me to pull off my shorts. . . . . So I did . . .

Then she gets on the bed and looks at me kind of funny and says, Now go to town cowboy. . . . So here I am.

Bubba's sister is pregnant and is in a bad car accident, which caused her to fall into a deep coma. After nearly six months, she awakens and sees that she is no longer pregnant.

Frantically, she asks the doctor about her baby.

The doctor replies, "Ma'am, you had twins—a boy and a girl. The babies are fine. Your brother came in and named them."

The woman thinks to herself. "Oh, no! Not Bubba; he's an idiot!"

Expecting the worst, she asks the doctor, "Well, what's the girl's name?"

"Denise," the doctor answers.

The new mother thinks, "Wow! That's a beautiful name! I guess I was wrong about my brother. I really like the name Denise." Then she asks the doctor, "What's the boy's name?"

The doctor replies, "Denephew."

Two blondes are walking down the street. One notices a compact on the sidewalk & leans down to pick it up. She opens it, looks in the mirror & says, "Hmm, this person looks familiar." She hands it to the 2nd blonde, who looks in the mirror & says, "You dummy, it's me!"

A blonde suspects her boyfriend of cheating on her, so she goes out & buys a gun. She goes unexpected to his apartment & when she opens the door, finds him in the arms of a redhead. Well, the blonde is really angry. She opens her purse, takes out the gun, & is overcome with grief. She puts the gun to her head. The boyfriend yells, "No, honey, don't do it." The blonde replies, "Shut up, you're next!"

A blonde brags about her knowledge of state capitals & proudly says, "Go ahead, ask me; I know them all." A friend says, "OK, what's the capital of Wisconsin?" The blonde replies, "Oh that's easy: W."

Returning home from work, a blonde was astonished to see that she'd been robbed. She telephoned the police at once & reported the crime. The police dispatcher broadcast the call, & a K-9 unit patrolling nearby was 1st to respond. As the officer approached the house with his dog on a leash, the blonde ran out on the porch, shuddered at the sight of the cop & his dog, then sat down on the steps. With her face in her hands, she moaned, "I come home, find all my possessions stolen, call the police for help, & what do they do? Send me a BLIND policeman!"

A State Trooper pulls a car over on a lonely back road and approaches the blonde lady driver. "Ma'am, is there a reason that you're weaving all over the road"? The woman replied, "Oh officer, thank goodness you're here!! I almost had an accident! I looked up and there was a tree right in front of me. I swerved to the left and there was another tree in front of me. I swerved to the right and there was another tree in front of me!"

Reaching through the side window to the rear view mirror, the officer replied, "Ma'am . . . that's your air freshener."

She was Sooooooo Blonde . . .
She thought a quarterback was a refund.
She thought General Motors was in the army.

She thought Meow Mix was a CD for cats.

At the bottom of an application where it says "Sign here:" she wrote "Sagittarius."

She Was Sooooooooooooo Blonde . . .

She took the ruler to bed to see how long she slept.

She sent a fax with a stamp on it.

Under "education" on her job application, she put "Hooked On Phonics."

She was Soooooooooooooooo Blonde . . .

She tripped over a cordless phone.

She spent 20 minutes looking at the orange juice can because it said "Concentrate."

She told me to meet her at the corner of "WALK" and "DON'T WALK."

She tried to put M&M's in alphabetical order.

She was Soooooooooooooooooo Blonde . . .

She studied for a blood test.

She sold the car for gas money.

When she missed bus #44 she took bus #22 twice instead.

When she went to the airport and saw a sign that said, "Airport Left," she turned around and went home.

She Was Sooooooooooooooooooo Blonde . . .

When she heard that 90% of all crimes occur around the home, she moved.

She thought if she spoke her mind, she'd be speechless.

She thought that she could not use her AM radio in the evening.

She had a shirt that said "TGIF," which she thought stood for "This Goes In Front."

She is sooooooooooooooooooooooooo Blonde . . .

She thinks Taco Bell is the Mexican phone company.

A blonde goes on "Who wants to be a Millionaire."

Regis: "Barbara, you've done very well so far—$500,000 and one lifeline left—phone a friend.

The next question will give you the top prize of One Million dollars if you get it right . . . but if you get it wrong you will drop back to $32,000—are you ready?"

Barbara: "Sure, I'll have a go!"

Regis: "Which of the following birds does not build it's own nest?

Is it. . . . .

A-Robin

B-Sparrow

C-Cuckoo

D-Thrush

Remember Barbara its worth 1 Million dollars."

"I think I know who it. . but I'm not 100% . . .

I'd like to phone a friend Regis, just to be sure.

Regis: "Yes, who, Barbara, do you want to phone?

Barbara: "I'll phone my friend Maggie back home in Brooklyn." (ringing)

Maggie (also a blonde): "Hello . . ."

Regis: "Hello Maggie, its Regis here from Who Wants to be a Millionaire-I have Barbara here and she is doing really well on $500,000, but needs your help to get a Million.

The next voice you hear will be Barbara's and she'll read you the question.

There are 4 possible answers and 1 correct answer and you have 30 seconds to answer—fire away Barbara."

Barbara: "Maggie, which of the following birds does not build it's own nest? Is it:

A-Robin

B-Sparrow

C-Cuckoo

D-Thrush"

Maggie: "Oh Gees, Barbara that's simple. . . . . It's a Cuckoo."

Barbara: "You think?"

'Maggie: "I'm sure."

Barbara: "Thanks Maggie." (hangs up)

Regis: "Well, do you want to stick on $500,000 or play on for the Million, Barbara?"

Barbara: "I want to play, I'll go with C-Cuckoo"

Regis: "Is that your final answer?"

Barbara: "It is."

Regis: “Are you confident?”

Barbara: “Yes fairly, Maggie’s a sound bet.”

Regis: “Barbara. . . . . you had $500,000 and you said C-Cuckoo . . . you’re right!—You have just won ONE MILLION DOLLARS.

Here is your check. You have been a great contestant and a real gambler. Audience please put your hands together for Barbara.”

That night Barbara calls Maggie and brings her down to a local bar for a celebration drink and, as they are sipping their Champagne, Barbara turns to Maggie and asks “Tell me Maggie, How in God’s name did you know that it was the Cuckoo that does not build its own nest?

Maggie: “Listen Barbara, everybody knows that a Cuckoo lives in a clock.”

After their 11th child, an Alabama couple decided that was enough as they could not afford a larger bed. So the husband went to his veterinarian and told him that he and his cousin didn’t want to have any more children.

The doctor told him that there was a procedure called a vasectomy that could fix the problem but that it was expensive.

‘A less costly alternative,’ said the doctor, ‘is to go home, get a cherry bomb, (fireworks are legal in Alabama) light it, put it in a beer can, then hold the can up to your ear and count to 10.’

The Alabamian said to the doctor, ‘I may not be the sharpest tool in the shed, but I don’t see how putting a cherry bomb in a beer can next to my ear is going to help me.’

Trust me,’ said the doctor.

So the man went home, lit a cherry bomb and put it in a beer can.

He held the can up to his ear and began to count on one hand ‘1’, 2, 3, 4, 5 . . .

At which point he paused, placed the beer can between his legs and resumed counting on his other hand.

This procedure also works in Tennessee, Kentucky, Texas, Oklahoma, Mississippi, Georgia, South Carolina, and parts of Arkansas and Louisiana . . .

Two redneck farmers, Jim and Bob, are sitting at their favorite bar, drinking beer.

Jim turns to Bob and says, "You know, I'm tired of going through life without an education. Tomorrow, I think I'll go to the community college and sign up for some classes." Bob thinks it's a good idea and the two leave.

The next day, Jim goes down to the college and meets the Dean of Admissions who signs him up for the four basic classes: Math, English, History, and Logic.

"Logic?" Jim says, "What's that?"

The Dean says, "I'll give you an example. Do you own a weed eater?"

"Yeah."

"Then logically speaking, because you own a weed eater, I think that you would have a yard."

"That's true, I do have a yard."

"I'm not done," the dean says. "Because you have a yard, I think logically that you would have a house."

"Yes, I do have a house."

"And because you have a house, I think that you might logically have a family."

"Yes, I have a family."

"I'm not done yet. Because you have a family, then logically you must have a wife. And because you have a wife, then logic tells me you must be a heterosexual."

"I am a heterosexual. That's amazing; you were able to find out all of that because I have a weed eater."

Excited to take the class now, Jim shakes the Dean's hand and leaves to go meet Bob at the bar. He tells Bob about his classes, how he is signed up for Math, English, History, and Logic.

"Logic?" Bob says, "What's that?"

Jim says, "I'll give you an example. Do you have a weed eater?"

"No."

"Then you're gay."

Three blondes were all applying for the last available position on the Texas Highway Patrol.

The detective conducting the interview looked at the three of them and said, 'So y'all want to be cops, huh?'

The blondes all nodded.

The detective got up, opened a file drawer and pulled out a folder. Sitting back down, he opened it and pulled out a picture, and said,

'To be a detective, you have to be able to detect. You must be able to notice things such as distinguishing features and oddities, such as scars and so forth.'

So saying, he stuck the photo in the face of the first blonde and withdrew it after about two seconds. 'Now,' he said, 'did you notice any distinguishing features about this man?'

The blonde immediately said, 'Yes, I did. He has only one eye!'

The detective shook his head and said, 'Of course he has only one eye in this picture! It's a profile of his face! You're dismissed!'

The first blonde hung her head and walked out of the office.

The detective then turned to the second blonde, stuck the photo in her face for two seconds, pulled it back and said, 'What about you? Notice anything unusual or outstanding about this man?'

'Yes! He only has one ear!'

The detective put his head in his hands and exclaimed, 'Didn't you hear what I just told the other lady? This is a profile of the man's face! Of course you can only see one ear!! You're excused too!'

The second blonde sheepishly walked out of the office.

The detective turned his attention to the third and last blonde and said, 'This is probably a waste of time, but . . .' He flashed the photo in her face for a couple of seconds and withdrew it, saying, 'All right, did you notice anything distinguishing or unusual about this man?'

The blonde said, 'I sure did. This man wears contact lenses.'

The detective frowned, took another look at the picture and began looking at some of the papers in the folder.

He looked up at the blonde with a puzzled expression and said, 'You're absolutely right! His bio says he wears contacts! How in the world could you tell that by looking at his picture?'

The blonde rolled her eyes and said, 'Well, Helloooo! With only one eye and one ear, he certainly can't wear glasses.'

Two blondes living in Oklahoma were sitting on a bench talking. . . . . . . and one blonde says to the other, "Which do you think is farther away . . . Florida or the moon?"

The other blonde turns and says "Hellooooooooo, can you see Florida . . . ?"

A blonde pushes her BMW into a gas station. She tells the mechanic it died. After he works on it for a few minutes, it is idling smoothly.

She says, "What's the story?"

He replies, "Just crap in the carburetor"

She asks, "How often do I have to do that?"

A police officer stops a blonde for speeding and asks her very nicely if he could see her license.

She replied in a huff, "I wish you guys would get your act together. Just yesterday you take away my license and then today you expect me to show it to you!"

There's this blonde out for a walk. She comes to a river and sees another blonde on the opposite bank. "Yoo-hoo!" she shouts, "How can I get to the other side?"

The second blonde looks up the river then down the river and shouts back, "You ARE on the other side."

A gorgeous young redhead goes into the doctor's office and said that her body hurt wherever she touched it.

"Impossible!" says the doctor. "Show me."

The redhead took her finger, pushed on her left breast and screamed, then she pushed her elbow and screamed even more. She pushed her knee and screamed; likewise she pushed her ankle and screamed. Everywhere she touched made her scream.

The doctor said, “You’re not really a redhead, are you?
“Well, no” she said, “I’m actually a blonde.”
“I thought so,” the doctor said. “Your finger is broken.”

A highway patrolman pulled alongside a speeding car on the freeway. Glancing at the car, he was astounded to see that the blonde behind the wheel was knitting! Realizing that she was oblivious to his flashing lights and siren, the trooper cranked down his window, turned on his bullhorn and yelled, “PULL OVER!”
“NO!” the blonde yelled back, “IT’S A SCARF!”

A Russian, an American, and a Blonde were talking one day. The Russian said, “We were the first in space!”
The American said, “We were the first on the moon!”
The Blonde said, “So what? We’re going to be the first on the sun!”
The Russian and the American looked at each other and shook their heads. “You can’t land on the sun, you idiot! You’ll burn up!” said the Russian.
To which the Blonde replied, “We’re not stupid, you know. We’re going at night!”

A blonde was playing Trivial Pursuit one night.
It was her turn. She rolled the dice and she landed on Science & Nature. Her question was, “If you are in a vacuum and someone calls your name, can you hear it?”
She thought for a time and then asked, “Is it on or off?”

A girl was visiting her blonde friend, who had acquired two new dogs, and asked her what their names were. The blonde responded by saying that one was named Rolex and one was named Timex.

Her friend said, "Whoever heard of someone naming dogs like that?"

"HELLLOOOOOOO . . . . . . ," answered the blond.

"They're watch dogs!"

Norman and his blonde wife live in Calgary. One winter morning while listening to the radio, they hear the announcer say, "We are going to have 8 to 10 centimeters of snow today. You must park your car on the even numbered side of the street, so the snowplow can get through." Norman's wife goes out and moves her car.

A week later while they are eating breakfast, the radio announcer says, "We are expecting 10 to 12 centimeters of snow today. You must park your car on the odd numbered side of the street, so the snowplow can get through." Norman's wife goes out and moves her car again.

The next week they are having breakfast again, when the radio announcer says "We are expecting 12 to 14 centimeters of snow today. You must park. . . . . "then the electric power goes out. Norman's wife is very upset, and with a worried look on her face she says, "Honey, I don't know what to do. Which side of the street do I need to park on so the snowplow can get through?"

With the love and understanding in his voice like all men who are married to Blondes exhibit, Norman says, "Why don't you just leave it in the garage this time?"

A week after their marriage, the redneck newlyweds, Bubba and Betty Lou, paid a visit to their doctor.

"You ain't gonna believe this, Doc," said the husband. "My thingy's turnin' blue."

"That's pretty unusual," said the doctor. "Let me examine you."

The doctor takes a look. Sure enough, the redneck's "thingy" really was blue.

The doctor turns to the wife, "Are you using the diaphragm that I prescribed for you?"

"Yep, shore am," she replied brightly.

"And what kind of jelly are you using with it?"
"Grape."

A couple of redneck hunters are out in the woods when one of them falls to the ground.

He doesn't seem to be breathing and his eyes are rolled back in his head.

The other redneck starts to panic, then whips out his cell phone and calls 911.

He frantically blurts out to the operator, "O my gawd! Help! My friend just died.

He's Dead! What can I do?"

The operator, trying to calm him says, "Take it easy. I can help.

Just listen to me and follow my instructions.

First, lets make sure he's dead."

There's a short pause, and then the operator hears a loud gun shot!!!

The redneck comes back on the line and says, "OK, now what?"

A small zoo in Arkansas obtained a very rare species of gorilla. Within a few weeks the gorilla, a beautiful female, became very difficult to handle. Upon examination the zoo veterinarian determined the problem. The gorilla was in heat. To make matters worse, there was no male gorilla available.

Thinking about their problem, the zoo keeper thought of Bobby Lee Jones a redneck part-time worker responsible for cleaning the animal cages. Bobby Lee, like most rednecks, had little sense but possessed ample ability to satisfy a female of any species.

The zoo keeper thought they might have a solution. Bobby Lee was approached with a proposition. Would he be willing to mate with the gorilla for $500.00? Bobby Lee showed some interest but said he would have to think the matter over carefully. The following day he announced that he would accept their offer but only under four conditions.

"First", Bobby Lee said, "I ain't gonna kiss her on the lips." The Keeper quickly agreed to this condition.

"Second", he said, "You can't never tell no one about this." The keeper again readily agreed to this condition.

"Third", Bobby Lee said, "I want all the children raised Southern Baptist." Once again, it was agreed.

"And lastly", Bobby Lee said, "I'll need another week to come up with the $500.00."

Billy Bob and Luther were talking one afternoon when Billy Bob tells Luther, "Ya know, I reckon I'm 'bout ready for a vacation.

Only this year I'm gonna do it a little different. The last few years, I took your advice about where to go.

Three years ago you said to go to Hawaii. I went to Hawaii and Earlene got pregnant.

Then two years ago, you told me to go to the Bahamas, and Earlene got pregnant again.

Last year you suggested Tahiti and darned if Earlene didn't get pregnant again."

Luther asks Billy Bob, "So, what you gonna do this year that's different?"

Billy Bob says, "This year I'm taking Earlene with me."

A Norwegian took a trip to Fargo, North Dakota.

While in a bar, an Indian on the next stool spoke to the Norwegian in a friendly manner.

"Look," he said, "let's have a little game. I'll ask you a riddle. If you can answer it, I'll buy YOU a drink. If you can't then you buy ME one. OK?"

"Ja, dat sounds purty good," said the Norwegian.

The Indian said, "My father and mother had one child.

It wasn't my brother. It wasn't my sister. Who was it?"

The Norwegian scratched his head and finally said, "I give up. Who vas it?"

"It was ME," chortled the Indian.

So the Norwegian paid for the drinks.

Back in Sioux Falls the Norwegian went into the bar and spotted one of his cronies. “Sven,” he said, “I got a game. If you can answer a question, I’ll buy you a drink. If you can’t, YOU have to buy ME vun. Fair enough?” “Fair enough,” said Sven.

“OK . . . my fadder and mudder had vun child. It vasn’t my brudder. It vasn’t my sister. Who vas it?”

“Search me,” said Sven. “I give up, who vas it?”

“It vas some Indian up in Fargo, North Dakota.

Ole and Lena got married. On their honeymoon trip they were nearing Minneapolis when Ole put his hand on Lena’s knee.

Giggling, Lena said, “Ole, you can go farther dan dat if you vant to.” So Ole drove to Duluth.

When the Norwegian accidentally lost 50 cents in the outhouse, he immediately threw in his watch and billfold and went into the house to tell his wife.

“Vy did you do dat?” she asked.

He explained, “By yimminyy, I’m not going down dere yust for 50 cents.”

A Norwegian appeared with five other men in a police line-up. All were suspects in a rape case.

As the victim entered the room, the Norwegian blurted, “Yep dat’s her!”

A Norwegian woman competed with a French woman and an English woman in the Breast Stroke division of an English Channel swim competition. The French woman came in first, the English woman second.

Finally the Norwegian woman reached shore completely

exhausted. After being revived with blankets and coffee, she remarked, "I don't vant to complain, but I tink those other two girls used dere arms."

Two Norwegians from Minnesota went fishing in Canada and returned with only one fish.

"The way I figger it, dat fish cost us $400" said the first Norwegian.

"Vell," said the other one, "At dat price it's a good ting we didn't catch any more."

Year after year Bubba's wife pleaded with him to take her fishing but he kept telling her she would not enjoy it. She, finally, wore him down, he consented, and early one morning they took off to the lake.

They had not been there very long when the fish began biting. Almost as fast as they cast, a fish would bite, and they reeled it in. After catching their limit, Bubba said, "Martha, sweet thang, I'm sorry. You've been good luck and I'm gonna bring you with me the next time. If you'll mark the spot where we caught all these fish, we'll go home."

On the way home, Bubba turned to Martha and said, "Sweet thang, how did you mark the spot were all the fish are so next time I'll know?"

"Bubba, darlin', I put a big 'X' on the side of the boat right down closest to the water."

"Sweet thang, that's about the dumbest thing I ever seed you do. Don't you know that won't work? We may not get the same boat the next time!"

Joe has a gas station in Alabama and was trying to increase his sales. So he put up a sign that read, "Free sex with Fill-Up."

Soon a local pulled in, filled his tank and asked for his free sex. The owner told him to pick a number from 1 to 10. If he guessed correctly he would get his free sex. The guy guessed 8, and Joe said, "You were close. The number was 7. Sorry. No sex this time."

A week later, the same chap, along with his buddy Jerry Lee, pulled in for another fill-up. Again he asked for his free sex. Joe again asked him to guess the correct number. He guessed 2 this time. Joe said, "Sorry, it was 3. You were close, but no free sex this time."

As they were driving away, the chap said to his buddy Billy Bob, "I think that game is rigged and he doesn't really give away free sex." Jerry Lee replied, "Noooo, it ain't rigged. My wife won twice last week.

The bride-to-be and her best friend were discussing her impending wedding.

"If you want an unforgettable wedding night," her friend said, "get him to eat a dozen oysters after the ceremony."

A week after, the new bride thanked her friend but said plaintively,

"Only eight of the oysters worked."

NEVER SAY TO A COP

1. I can't reach my license unless you hold my beer. (OK in Texas)

2. Sorry, Officer, I didn't realize my radar detector wasn't plugged in.

3. Aren't you the guy from the Village People?

4. Hey, you must've been doin' about 125 mph to keep up with me. Good job!

5. Are You Andy or Barney?

6. I thought you had to be in relatively good physical condition to be a police officer.

7. You're not gonna check the trunk, are you?

8. I pay your salary!

9. Gee, Officer! That's terrific. The last officer only gave me a warning, too!

10. Do you know why you pulled me over? Okay, just so one of us does.

11. I was trying to keep up with traffic. Yes, I know there are no other cars around. That's how far ahead of me they are.

12. When the Officer says "Gee Son. . . . Your eyes look red, have you been drinking?" You probably shouldn't respond with, "Gee Officer your eyes! look glazed, have you been eating doughnuts?"

A blonde, wanting to earn some extra money, decided to hire herself out as a "handywoman" and started canvassing a nearby well-to-do neighborhood.

She went to the front door of the first house, and asked the owner if he had any odd jobs for her to do.

"Well, I guess I could use somebody to paint my porch," he said, "How much will you charge me?"

"The blonde quickly responded, "How about $50?"

The man agreed and told her that the paint and everything she would need was in the garage

The man's wife, hearing the conversation, said to her husband, "Does she realize that our porch goes all the way around the house?"

He responded, "That's a bit cynical, isn't it?"

The wife replied, "You're right, I guess I'm starting to believe all those 'dumb blonde' jokes we've been getting by e-mail lately."

A short time later, the blonde came to the door to collect her money.

"You're finished already?" the husband asked.

"Yes," the blonde replied, "And I had paint leftover, so I gave it two coats."

Impressed, the man reached into his pocket for the $50 and handed it to her.

"And by the way," the blonde added, "it's not a Porch, it's a Lexus".

A Polish immigrant went to the DMV to apply for a driver's license.

First, of course, he had to take an eye sight test The optician showed him a card with the letters 'C Z W I X N O S T A C Z.' 'Can you read this?' the optician asked.

'Read it?' the Polish guy replied, 'I know the guy.'

Mother Superior called all the nuns together and said to them, 'I must tell you all something. We have a case of gonorrhea in the convent.' 'Thank God,' said an elderly nun at the back. I'm so tired of chardonnay.'

A guy walks into Dunkin' Donuts. He says, "Excuse me, miss . . . how many cups of coffee do you think this thermos will hold?" She says, "I think it's a seven-cup thermos." He says, "All right . . . give me two black, three cream and sugar."

Two bowling teams charter a double-decker bus; they're going to Atlantic City for the weekend. One team is in the bottom of the bus, and the other team is in the top of the bus. The team down below is whooping it up when one of them realizes he doesn't hear anything from the top. He walks up the stairs, and here are all the guys from the second team clutching the seats in front of them with white knuckles, scared to death. He says, "What the heck's goin' on? We're down here havin' a grand old time." One of the guys from the second team says, 'Yeah, but you guys've got a *driver.*"

A pompous minister was seated next to a hillbilly on a flight across the country. After the plane was airborne, drink orders were taken. The hillbilly asked for a whisky and soda, which was brought and placed before him. The flight attendant then asked the minister if he would like a drink.

He replied in disgust, "I'd rather be savagely raped by brazen whores than let liquor touch these lips."

The hillbilly then handed his drink back to the flight attendant and said, "Hell, me, too! I didn't know we got a choice"

Three blondes died and found themselves standing before St. Peter. He told them that before they could enter the Kingdom, they had to tell him what Easter was. The first blonde said, "Easter is a holiday where they have a big feast and we give thanks and eat turkey."

St. Peter said, "Noooooo," and he banished her to hell. The second blonde said, "Easter is when we celebrate Jesus' birth and exchange gifts." St. Peter said, "Noooooo," and he banished her to hell.

The third blonde said, she knew what Easter is, and St. Peter said, "So, tell me." She said, "Easter is a Christian holiday that coincides with the Jewish festival of Passover. Jesus was having Passover feast with His disciples when he was betrayed by Judas, and the Romans arrested him. The Romans hung Him on the cross and eventually He died. Then they buried Him in a tomb behind a very large boulder . . ."

St. Peter said, "Verrrrrry good." Then the blonde continued, "Now every year the Jews roll away the boulder and Jesus comes out. If he sees his shadow, we have 6 more weeks of basketball."

A blonde goes into a restaurant and notices there's a "peel and win" sticker on her coffee cup. So she's peels it off and starts screaming, "I've won a motor home! I've won a motor home!"

The waitress says, "That's impossible. The biggest prize is a free lunch."

But the blonde keeps screaming, "I've won a motor home! I've won a motor home!"

Finally the manager comes over and says, "Ma'am, I'm sorry, but you're mistaken. You couldn't possibly have won a motor home because we didn't have that as a prize!" The blonde says, "No it's not a mistake. I've won a motor home as she hands the ticket to the manager and he reads. .

WIN A BAGEL

A blonde pilot decided she wanted to learn how to fly a helicopter.

She went to the airport, but the only one available was a solo-helicopter. The Instructor figured he could let her go up alone since she was already a pilot for small planes and he could instruct her via radio.

So up the blonde went. She reached 1,000 feet and everything was going smoothly. She reached 2,000 feet. The blonde and the Instructor kept talking via radio. Everything was running smoothly.

At 3,000 feet the helicopter suddenly came down quickly! It skimmed the top of some trees and crash landed in the woods.

The Instructor jumped into his jeep and rushed out to see if the blonde was okay.

As he reached the edge of the woods, the blonde was walking out.

"What happened?" the Instructor asked. "All was going so well until you reached 3,000 feet. What happened then?"

"Well," began the blonde, "I got cold. So I turned off the big fan."

A blonde lady motorist was about two hours from San Diego when she was flagged down by a man whose truck had broken down.

The man walked up to the car and asked, "Are you going to San Diego?"

"Sure," answered the blonde, "do you need a lift?"

"Not for me. I'll be spending the next three hours fixing my truck. My problem is I've got two chimpanzees in the back that have to be taken to the San Diego Zoo. They're a bit stressed already so I don't want to keep them on the road all day. Could you possibly take them to the zoo for me? I'll give you $100 for your trouble."

"I'd be happy to," said the blonde. So the two chimpanzees were ushered into the back seat of the blonde's car and carefully strapped into their seat belts. Off they went. Five hours later, the truck driver was driving through the heart of San Diego when suddenly he was horrified!! There was the blonde walking down the street and holding hands with the two chimps, much to the amusement of a big crowd. With a screech of brakes he pulled off the road and ran over to the blonde. "What the heck are you doing here?" he demanded, "I gave you $100 to take these chimpanzees to the zoo."

"Yes, I know you did," said the blonde, but we had money left over—so now we're going to Sea World."

A blonde reads in a magazine that if you bathe in milk, it makes your skin beautiful.

So the next morning she leaves a note for the milkman, "Leave me 115 quarts of milk."

The next morning milkman reads this and thinks I better double check on this. He rings the bell and here is this beautiful blond with great complexion and tiny waist, he asks her if this is right.

She replies, "Yes it's good to bathe in milk."

The milkman then asks her if she wants it pasteurized.

She answers, "Oh no, just past my boobs would be fine!"

The blonde reported for her university final examination which consists of "Yes/No" type questions. She takes her seat in the examination hall, stares at the question paper for five minutes, and then in a fit of inspiration takes her purse out, removes a coin and starts tossing the coin and marking the answer sheet—Yes for Heads and No for Tails.

Within half an hour she is all done whereas the rest of the class is sweating it out. During the last few minutes, she is seen desperately throwing the coin, swearing and sweating.

The moderator, alarmed, approaches her and asks what is going on.

"I finished the exam in half an hour. But I'm rechecking my answers."

A blonde with two red ears went to her doctor.

The doctor asked her what had happened to her ears and she answered, "I was ironing a shirt and the phone rang—but instead of picking up the phone I accidentally picked up the iron and stuck it to my ear."

"Oh Dear!" the doctor exclaimed in disbelief. "But . . . what happened to your other ear?"

"The jerk called back."

As a trucker stops for a red light, a blonde catches up. She jumps out of her car, runs up to his truck, and knocks on the door. The trucker lowers the window and she says, "Hi, my name is Heather and you are losing some of your load."

The trucker ignores her and proceeds down the street. When the truck stops for another red light, the girl catches up again.

She jumps out of her car, runs up and knocks on the door. Again, the trucker lowers the window. As if they've never spoken, the blonde says brightly, "Hi my name is Heather, and you are losing some of your load!"

Shaking his head, the trucker ignores her again and continues down the street.

At the third red light, the same thing happens again. All out of breath, the blonde gets out of her car, runs up, and knocks on the truck door. The trucker lowers the window. Again she says, "Hi, my name is Heather, and you are losing some of your load!

When the light turns green the trucker revs up and races to the next light. When he stops this time, he hurriedly gets out of the truck, and runs back to the blonde. He knocks on her window, and as she lowers it, he says, "Hi, my name is Kevin. It's winter in Pennsylvania and I'm driving the salt truck.

A businessman got on an elevator in an office building.

When he entered the elevator, there was a blonde already inside, and she greeted him by saying, "T-G-I-F".

He smiled at her and replied, "S-H-I-T".

She looked at him, puzzled, and said, "T-G-I-F" again.

He acknowledged her remark again by answering, "S-H-I-T."

The blond was trying to be friendly, so she smiled her biggest smile and said as sweetly as possibly "T-G-I-F" Another time.

The man smiled back to her and once again replied, "S-H-I-T."

The blond finally decided to explain things, and this time she said, "T-G-I-F' means 'Thank Goodness It's Friday,' Get it?"

The man answered, "S-H-I-T, Sorry, Honey, It's Thursday."

MISCELLANEOUS JOKES

A woman has a dog who snores in his sleep. She goes to the vet to see if he can help. The vet tells the woman to tie a ribbon around the dog's testicles and he will stop snoring. A few hours after going to bed the dog is snoring as usual. Finally, she goes to the closet and grabs a piece of ribbon, ties it around the dog's testicles, and sure enough the dog stops snoring.

The woman is amazed. Later that night her husband returns home drunk. He climbs into bed, falls asleep, and begins snoring very loudly. The woman thinks maybe the ribbon will work on him. She goes to the closet, grabs a piece of ribbon, and ties it around her husband's testicles. Amazingly it also works on him. The woman sleeps very soundly.

The next morning the husband wakes up very hung over. He stumbles into the bathroom to urinate. As he is standing in front of the toilet, he looks in the mirror and sees a blue ribbon attached to his scrotum. He is very confused. He walks back into the bedroom and sees a red ribbon attached to his dog's scrotum. He looks at the dog and says, "Boy, I don't remember what the hell happened last night, but wherever you and I were, we got first and second place."

Why do Italians hate Jehovah's Witnesses?
Because Italians hate all witnesses.

Do you know why most men from Italy are named Tony?

On the boat over to America they put a sticker on them that said—TO NY.

You know you're Italian when . . . You can bench press 325 pounds, shave twice a day and still cry when your mother yells at you.

You carry your lunch in a produce bag because you can't fit two cappicola sandwiches, 4 oranges, 2 bananas and a cantalope into a regular lunch bag.

Your mechanic, plumber, electrician, accountant, travel agent and lawyer are all your cousins.

You have at least 5 cousins living in the same town or on the same block.

All five or those cousins are named after your grandfather or grandmother.

You are on a first name basis with at least 8 banquet hall owners.

You only get one good shave from a disposable razor.

If someone in your family! grows beyond 5'9", it is presumed his Mother had an affair.

There were more than 28 people in your bridal party.

You netted more than $50,000 on your first communion.

And you REALLY, REALLY know you're Italian when . . .

Your grandfather had a fig tree.

You eat Sunday dinner at 2:00.

Christmas Eve . . . only fish.

Your mom's meatballs are the best.

You've been hit with a wooden spoon or had a shoe thrown at you.

Clear plastic covers on all the furniture.

You know how to pronounce "manicotti" and "mozzarella."

You fight over whether it's called "sauce" or "gravy."

You've called someone a "mamaluke."

And you understand "bada bing".

A Doctor who was addressing a large audience said "The material we put into our stomachs is enough to have killed most of us sitting here, years ago. Red meat is awful. Soft drinks corrode your stomach lining. Chinese food is loaded with MSG. High fat diets can be disastrous, and none of us realizes the long-term harm caused by the germs in our drinking water.

But there is one thing that is the most dangerous of all and we all have, or will, eat it. Can anyone here tell me what food it is that causes the most grief and suffering for years after eating it?"

After several seconds of quiet, a 75-year-old man in the front row raised his hand, and softly said, "Wedding Cake."

On the first day, God created the dog and said:

"Sit all day by the door of your house and bark at anyone who comes in or walks past. For this, I will give you a life span of twenty years."

The dog said: "That's a long time to be barking. How about only ten years and I'll give you back the other ten?"

So God agreed.

On the second day, God created the monkey and said:

"Entertain people, do tricks, and make them laugh. For this, I'll give you a twenty-year life span."

The monkey said: "Monkey tricks for twenty years? That's a pretty long time to perform. How about I give you back ten like the dog did?"

And God agreed.

On the third day, God created the cow and said:

"You must go into the field with the farmer all day long and suffer under the sun, have calves and give milk to support the farmer's family. For this, I will give you a life span of sixty years."

The cow said: "That's kind of a tough life you want me to live for sixty years. How about twenty and I'll give back the other forty?"

And God agreed again.

On the fourth day, God created man and said:

"Eat, sleep, play, marry and enjoy your life. For this, I'll give you twenty years."

But man said: "Only twenty years? Could you possibly give me my twenty, the forty the cow gave back, the ten the monkey gave back, and the ten the dog gave back; that makes eighty, okay?"

"Okay," said God, "you asked for it."

So that is why for our first twenty years we eat, sleep, play and enjoy ourselves. For the next forty years we slave in the sun to support our family. For the next ten years we do monkey tricks to entertain the grandchildren. And for the last ten years we sit on the front porch and bark at everyone.

Life has now been explained to you . . .

If you had purchased $1,000 of AIG stock one year ago, you would have $42 left. With Lehman, you would have $6.60 left. With Fannie or Freddie, you would have less than $5 left. But if you had purchased $1,000 worth of beer one year ago, drank all of the beer, then turned in the cans for the aluminum recycling REFUND, you would have had $214. Based on the above, the best current investment advice is to drink heavily and recycle. It's called the 401-Keg. . . .

An attorney arrived home late after a very tough day trying to get a stay of execution for a client who was due to be hanged for murder at midnight. His last minute plea for clemency to the governor had failed and he was feeling worn out and depressed. As soon as he walked through the door at home, his wife started on him about, "What time of night to be getting home is this? Where have you been? Dinner is cold and I'm not reheating it." And on and on and on.

Too shattered to play his usual role in this familiar ritual, he went and poured himself a shot of whiskey and headed off for a long hot soak in the bathtub, pursued by the predictable sarcastic remarks as he dragged himself up the stairs.

While he was in the bath, the phone rang. The wife answered and was told that her husband's client, James Wright, had been granted a stay of execution after all. Wright would not be hanged tonight. Finally realizing what a terrible day he must have had, she decided to go upstairs and give him the good news. As she opened the bathroom door, she was greeted by the sight of her husband, bent over naked, drying his legs and feet.

"They're not hanging Wright tonight," she said.

To which he whirled around and screamed, "FOR THE LOVE OF GOD, WOMAN, DON'T YOU EVER STOP?"

Anesthesiologist's business card: When you care enough to sleep with the very best.

Sign over a Gynecologist's office: "Dr. Jones, at your cervix."

In a Podiatrist's office: "Time wounds all heels."

On a Septic Tank truck: Yesterday's Meals on Wheels.

At a Proctologist's door: "To expedite your visit please back in."

On a Plumber's truck: We repair what your husband fixed."

On another Plumber's truck: "Don't sleep with a drip, call your plumber."

On a Church's billboard: "7 days without God makes one weak."

At a Tire Shop in Milwaukee: "Invite us to your next blowout."

At a Towing company: "We don't charge an arm and a leg. We want tows."

On an Electrician's truck: "Let us remove your shorts."

In a Nonsmoking Area: "If we see smoke, we will assume you are on fire and take appropriate action."

On a Maternity Room door: "Push. Push. Push."

At an Optometrist's office: "If you don't see what you're looking for, you've come to the right place."

On a Taxidermist's window: "We really know our stuff."

On a Fence: "Salesmen welcome! Dog food is expensive!"

At a Car Dealership: "The best way to get back on your feet—miss a car payment."

Outside a Muffler Shop: "No appointment necessary. We hear you coming."

In a Veterinarian's Waiting Room: "Be back in 5 minutes. Sit! Stay!"

At the Electric Company: "We would be delighted if you send in your payment. However, if you don't, you will be."

In a Restaurant window: "Don't stand there and be hungry, come on in and get fed up."

In the front yard of a Funeral Home: "Drive carefully. We'll wait."

At a Propane Filling Station: "Thank heaven for little grills."

And don't forget the sign at a Chicago Radiator Shop: "Best place in town to take a leak."

Two bored casino dealers were waiting at a craps table. A very attractive blonde woman arrived and bet twenty-thousand dollars on a single roll of the dice.

She said, "I hope you don't mind, but I feel much luckier when I'm completely nude."

With that she stripped from her neck down, rolled the dice and yelled, "Mama needs new clothes!"

Then she hollered . . . "YES! YES! I WON!" She jumped up and down and hugged each of the dealers. She then picked up all the money and clothes and quickly departed.

The dealers just stared at each other dumbfounded. Finally, one of them asked, "What did she roll?" The other answered, "I don't know I thought YOU were watching!"

A cabbie picks up a nun. She gets into the cab, and notices that the VERY handsome cab driver won't stop staring at her. She asks him why he is staring. He replies: "I have a question to ask you but I don't want to offend you." She answers, "My son, you cannot offend me. When you're as old as I am and have been a nun as long as I have, you get a chance to see and hear just about everything. I'm sure that there's nothing you could say or ask that I would find offensive."

"Well, I've always had a fantasy to have a nun kiss me." She responds, "Well, let's see what we can do about that: #1, you have to be single and #2, you must be Catholic." The cab driver is very excited and says, "Yes, I'm single and Catholic!" "OK" the nun says. "Pull into the next alley."

The nun fulfills his fantasy, with a kiss that would make a hooker blush. But when they get back on the road, the cab driver starts crying. "My dear child," says the nun, "why are you crying?" "Forgive me but I've sinned. I lied and I must confess, I'm married and I'm Jewish."

The nun says, "That's OK, my name is Kevin and I'm going to a Halloween party."

All eyes were on the radiant bride as her father escorted her down the aisle. They reached the altar and the waiting groom. The bride kissed her father and placed something in his hand. The guests in the front pews responded with ripples of laughter. Even the priest smiled broadly. As her father gave her away in marriage, the bride gave him back his credit card.

Three friends from the local congregation were asked, “When you’re in your casket, and friends and congregation members are mourning over you, what would you like them to say?”

Artie said: “I would like them to say I was a wonderful husband, a fine spiritual leader, and a great family man.”

Eugene commented: “I would like them to say I was a wonderful teacher and servant of God who made a huge difference in people’s lives.”

Al said: “I‘d like them to say, ‘Look, he’s moving!’ ”

Paddy and Mick were both laid off from their jobs in a clothing factory, so they went to the unemployment office.

When asked his occupation, Paddy answered, “Panty Stitcher—I sew da elastic onto ladies cotton panties.”

The clerk looked up panty stitcher on his computer and, finding it classified as unskilled labour, he gave him $80 a week unemployment pay.

Mick was next in and when asked his occupation replied, “Diesel fitter.” Since a diesel fitter was a skilled job, the clerk gave Mick $160 a week.

When Paddy found out he was furious. He stormed back into the office to find out why his friend and co-worker was collecting double his pay.

The clerk explained, “Panty Stitchers are unskilled labour and Diesel fitters are skilled labour.”

“What skill?” yelled Paddy? “I sew da elastic on da panties and then Mick puts ’em over his head and says: “Yep, diesel fitter.”

Actual School Absence Excuses from Parents (Supposedly)—Including Spelling.

My son is under a doctor's care today and should not take P.E. today. Please execute him.

Please excuse Lisa for being absent. She was sick and I had her shot.

Dear School: Please excuse John for being absent on Jan. 28, 29, 30, 31, 32, and also 33.

Please excuse Gloria from Jim today. She is administrating.

Please excuse Roland from P.E. for a few days. Yesterday, he fell out of a tree and misplaced his hip.

John has been absent because he had two teeth taken out of his face.

Carlos was absent yesterday because he was playing football. He was hurt in the growing part.

Megan could not come to school today because she has been bothered by very close veins.

Chris will not be in school because he has an acre in his side.

Please excuse Ray Friday from school. He has very loose vowels.

Please excuse Pedro from being absent yesterday. He had diahre, dyrea, direathe, the shits.

Please excuse Tommy for being absent yesterday. He had diarrhea and his boots leak.

Irving was absent yesterday because he missed his bust.

Please excuse Jim for being. It was his father's fault.

I kept Billie home because she had to go Christmas shopping because I don't know what size she wear.

Fifteen Things That It Took Over 50 Years To Learn

1. Never, under any circumstances, take a sleeping pill and a laxative on the same night.

2. If you had to identify, in one word, the reason why the human race has not achieved, and never will achieve, its full potential, that word would be "meetings."

3. There is a very fine line between "hobby" and "mental illness."

4. People who want to share their religious views with you almost never want you to share yours with them.

5. You should not confuse your career with your life.

6. Nobody cares if you can't dance well. Just get up and dance.

7. Never lick a steak knife.

8. The most destructive force in the universe is gossip.

9. You will never find anybody who can give you a clear and compelling reason why we observe daylight savings time.

10. You should never say anything to a woman that even remotely suggests that you think she's pregnant unless you can see an actual baby emerging from her at that moment.

11. There comes a time when you should stop expecting other people to make a big deal about your birthday. That time is age eleven.

12. The one thing that unites all human beings, regardless of age, gender, religion, economic status or ethnic background, is that, deep down inside, we ALL believe that we are above average drivers.

13. A person who is nice to you, but rude to the waiter, is not a nice person. (This is very important. Pay attention. it never fails.)

14. Your friends love you anyway.

15. Never be afraid to try something new. Remember that a lone amateur built the Ark. A large group of professionals built the Titanic.

FINAL thought for the day: Men are like a fine wine. They start out as grapes, and it's up to women to stomp the crap out of them until they turn into something acceptable to have dinner with.

You can tell you've had too much of the 21st Century when . . .

1. You try to enter your password on the microwave.

2. You haven't played solitaire with real cards in years.

3. You have a list of 15 phone numbers to reach your family of three.

4. You e-mail your work colleague at the desk next to you to ask "Wanna go for a drink?" and he replies, "Yeah, give me five minutes."

5. You chat several times a day with a stranger from South

America, but you haven't spoken to your next door neighbor yet this year.

6. You buy a computer and a week later it is out of date.

7. Your reason for not staying in touch with friends is that they do not have e-mail addresses.

8. You consider US Mail painfully slow and call it "snail mail."

9. Your idea of being organized is multiple colored post-it notes.

10. You hear all good jokes via e-mail instead of in person.

11. When you go home after a long day at work you still answer the phone with your company's name.

12. When you make phone calls from home, you accidentally dial "9" to get an outside line.

13. You've sat at the same desk for four years and worked for three different companies.

14. Your company welcome sign is attached with Velcro.

15. Your resume is on a disc in your pocket.

16. You really get excited about a 1.7% pay raise.

17. Your biggest loss from a system crash is that you lose all your best jokes.

18. Temps in your department outnumber permanent staff and are more likely to get long-service awards.

19. Board members salaries are higher than all the Third World countries annual budgets combined.

20. It's dark when you drive to and from work.

21. Free food left over from meetings is your staple diet.

22. The intern gets a brand-new state-of-the-art laptop with all the features, while you have time to go for lunch while yours powers up.

23. Being sick is defined as "you can't walk" or "you're in the hospital."

24. You're already late on the assignment you just got.

25. There's no money in the budget for the five permanent staff your department is short, but they can afford four full-time management consultants advising your boss's boss on strategy.

26. Your boss's favorite lines are: When you've got a few minutes . . . Could you fit this in? . . . In your spare time . . . When you're freed up . . . I know you're busy but . . . I have an opportunity for you.

27. Every week another brown collection envelope comes around because someone you didn't even know had started is leaving.

28. You wonder who's going to be left to put into your "leaving" collection.

29. Your relatives and family describe your job as "works with computers."

30. The only reason you recognize your kids is because their pictures are on your desk.

31. You've run out of family members' birthdays to use for all of the ATM and banking PINs, e-mail passwords, computer codes, and voice mail IDs you need to remember.

32. You read this entire list, kept nodding and smiling.

Law of Mechanical Repair:

After your hands become coated with grease, your nose will begin to itch or you'll have to pee.

Law of the Workshop

Any tool, when dropped, will roll to the least accessible corner.

Law of Probability

The probability of being watched is directly proportional to the stupidity of your act.

Law of the Telephone

If you dial a wrong number, you never get a busy signal.

Law of the Alibi

If you tell the boss you were late for work because you had a flat tire, the very next morning you will have a flat tire.

Variation Law

If you change lines (or traffic lanes), the one you were in will start to move faster than the one you are in now.

Law of the Bath

When the body is fully immersed in water, the telephone rings.

Law of Close Encounters
The probability of meeting someone you know increases dramatically when you are with someone you don't want to be seen with.

Law of the Result
When you try to prove to someone that a machine won't work, it will.

Law of Biomechanics
The severity of the itch is inversely proportional to the reach.

Law of the Theater
At any event, the people whose seats are furthest from the aisle arrive last.

Law of Coffee
As soon as you sit down to a cup of hot coffee, your boss will ask you to do something which will last until the coffee is cold.

Law of Lockers
If there are only two people in a locker room, they will have adjacent lockers.

Law of Carpets
The chances of an open-faced jelly sandwich landing face down on a floor covering are directly correlated to the newness and cost of the carpet.

Law of Location
No matter where you go, there you are.

Law of Logical Argument: Anything is possible if you don't know what you are talking about.

Brown's Law
If the shoe fits, it's ugly.

Oliver's Law
A closed mouth gathers no feet.

Wilson's Law

As soon as you find a product that you really like, they will stop making it.

Doctor Law

If you don't feel well, make an appointment to go to the doctor, by the time you get there, you'll feel better. Don't make an appointment, and you'll stay sick.

ITALIAN KIDS VS. AMERICAN KIDS

American Kids: Move out when they're 18 with the full support of their parents.

Italian Kids: Move out when they're 28, having saved enough money for a house, and are two weeks away from getting married . . . unless there's room in the basement for the newlyweds.

American Kids: When their Mom visits them, she brings a Bundt cake, and you sip coffee and chat.

Italian Kids: When their Mom visits them, she brings 3 days worth of food, begins to tidy up, dust, do the laundry, and rearrange the furniture.

American Kids: Their Dads always call before they come over to visit them, and it's usually only on special occasions.

Italian Kids: Are not at all fazed when their Dads show up, unannounced, on a Saturday morning at 8:00, and starts pruning the fruit trees. If there are no fruit trees, he'll plant some.

American Kids: Always pay retail, and look in the Yellow Pages when they need to have something done.

Italian Kids: Call their Dad or Uncle, and ask for another Dad's or Uncle's phone number to get it done . . . cash deal. Know what I mean?

American Kids: Will come over for cake and coffee, and get only cake and coffee. No more.

Italian Kids: Will come over for cake and coffee, and get antipasto, wine, a pasta dish, a choice of two meats, salad, bread, a cannoli, fruit, espresso, and a few after dinner drinks.

American Kids: Will greet you with "Hello" or "Hi".

Italian Kids: Will give you a big hug, a kiss on your cheek, and a pat on your back.

American Kids: Call your parents Mr. and Mrs.

Italian Kids: Call your parents Mom and Dad.

American Kids: Have never seen you cry.

Italian Kids: Cry with you.

American Kids: Borrow your stuff for a few days and then return it.

Italian Kids: Keep your stuff so long, they forget it's yours.

American Kids: Will eat at the dinner table and leave.

Italian Kids: Will spend hours there, talking, laughing, and just being together.

American Kids: Know few things about you.

Italian Kids: Could write a book with direct quotes from you.

American Kids: Eat peanut butter and jelly sandwiches on soft mushy white bread.

Italian Kids: Eat Genoa Salami and Provolone sandwiches on crusty Italian bread.

American Kids: Will leave you behind if that's what the crowd is doing.

Italian Kids: Will kick the whole crowds' ass who left you behind.

American Kids: Are for a while.

Italian Kids: Are for life.

American Kids: Like Rod Stewart and Steve Tyrell.

Italian Kids: Worship Tony Bennett and Sinatra.

American Kids: Think that being Italian is cool.

Italian Kids: Know that being Italian is cool.

American Kids: Will ignore this.

Italian Kids: Will forward it.

I drove by the fire department the other day, and they had a big public awareness sign that read, "Are your house numbers visible?"

I thought, "Who the hell cares? How about you just stop at the house that's on fire?!"

A man enters a barber shop for a shave. While the barber is foaming him up, he mentions the problems he has getting a close shave around the cheeks. "I have just the thing," says the barber, as he takes a small wooden ball from a nearby drawer. "Just place this between your cheek and gum."

The client places the ball in his mouth and the barber proceeds with the closest shave the man has ever experienced. After a few strokes the client says, "And what if I swallow it?"

"No problem," says the barber. "Just bring it back tomorrow like everyone else does!"

If you receive an e-mail entitled "Bedtimes" delete it IMMEDIATELY. Do not open it. Apparently this one is pretty nasty. It will not only erase everything on your hard drive, but it will also delete anything on disks within 20 feet of your computer. It demagnetizes the strips on ALL your credit cards. It re-programs your ATM access code, screws up the tracking on your VCR and uses subspace field harmonics to scratch any CD's you attempt to play. It will program your phone to auto Dial only 900 numbers.

This virus will mix antifreeze into your fish tank. It will cause your toilet to flush while you are showering. It will leave dirty underwear on the coffee table when you are expecting company. It will replace your shampoo with Nair and your Nair with Rogaine. If the "Bedtimes" message is opened in a Windows environment, it will leave the toilet seat up and leave your hair dryer plugged in dangerously close to a full bathtub. It will not only remove the forbidden tags from your mattresses and pillows, it will also refill your skim milk carton with whole milk.

The lovers had decided that a mutual parting of the ways was best for both of them . . .

However, on their way to the airport a rather heated debate started as to whose fault their break-up was.

At the crowded gate, she turned and said, "Thanks for nothing you cheap bastard."

As she went down the ramp with the other passengers, he shouted back: "Hey baby, don't be like that. If you ever work this town again, give me a call."

A recent bride called her mother one evening in tears. "Oh, Mom, I tried to make Grandmother's meat loaf for dinner tonight, and it's just awful! I followed the recipe exactly, and I know I have the recipe right because it's the one you gave me. But it just didn't come out right, and I'm so upset. I wanted this to be so special for George because he loves meat loaf. What could have gone wrong?"

Her mother replied soothingly, "Well, dear, let's go through the recipe. You read it out loud and tell me exactly what you did at each step, and together we'll figure it out."

"Ok," the bride sniffled. "Well, it starts out, 'Take fifty cents worth of ground beef' . . ."

A flight attendant was stationed at the departure gate to check tickets. As a man approached, she extended her hand for the ticket, and he opened his trench coat and flashed her. Without missing a beat she said, "Sir, I need to see your ticket, not your stub."

A lady was picking through the frozen turkeys at the grocery store, but couldn't find one big enough for her family. She asked a stock boy, "Do these turkeys get any bigger?" The stock boy replied, "No ma'am, they're dead."

In the beginning, God created the Heavens and the Earth and populated the Earth with broccoli, cauliflower and spinach, green and yellow and red vegetables of all kinds, so Man and Woman would live long and healthy lives.

Then using God's great gifts, Satan created Ben and Jerry's Ice Cream and Krispy Creme Donuts. And Satan said, "You want chocolate with that?"

And Man said, "Yes!" and Woman said, "And as long as you're at it, add some sprinkles." And they gained 10 pounds, and Satan smiled.

And God created the healthful yogurt that Woman might keep the figure that Man found so fair. And Satan brought forth white flour from the wheat, and sugar from the cane and combined them. And Woman went from size 6 to size 14.

So God said, "Try my fresh green salad." And Satan presented Thousand-Island Dressing, buttery croutons and garlic toast on the side.

And Man and Woman unfastened their belts following the repast.

God then said, "I have sent you heart healthy vegetables and olive oil in which to cook them." And Satan brought forth deep fried fish and chicken-fried steak so big it needed its own platter. And Man gained more weight and his cholesterol went through the roof.

God then created a light, fluffy white cake, named it "Angel Food Cake," and said, "It is good." Satan then created chocolate cake and named it "Devil's Food."

God then brought forth running shoes so that His children might lose those extra pounds. And Satan gave cable TV with a remote control so Man would not have to toil changing the channels. And Man and Woman laughed and cried before the flickering blue light and gained pounds.

Then God brought forth the potato, naturally low in fat and brimming with nutrition. And Satan peeled off the healthful skin and sliced the starchy center into chips and deep-fried them. And Man gained pounds.

God then gave lean beef so that Man might consume fewer calories and still satisfy his appetite. And Satan created McDonald's and its 99- cent double cheeseburger. Then said, "You want fries with that?" And Man replied, "Yes! And super-size them!" And Satan said, "It is good." And Man went into cardiac arrest.

God sighed and created quadruple bypass surgery. Then Satan created HMOs.

Food For Thought

If you take an Oriental person and spin him around several times, does he become disoriented?

If people from Poland are called Poles, why aren't people from Holland called Holes?

If you mixed vodka with orange juice and milk of magnesia, would you get a Philip's screwdriver?

If a pig loses its voice, is it disgruntled?

If love is blind, why is lingerie so popular?

When someone asks you, “A penny for your thoughts” and you put your two cents in, what happens to the other penny?

Why is the man who invests all your money called a broker?

Why do croutons come in airtight packages? It’s just stale bread to begin with.

When cheese gets its picture taken, what does it say?

Why is a person who plays the piano call a pianist, but a person who drives a race car not called a racist?

Why are a wise man and a wise guy opposite things?

If horrific means to make horrible, doesn’t terrific mean to make terrible?

Why isn’t 11 pronounced one-to-one?

“I am.” is reportedly the shortest sentence in the English language. Could it be that “I do.” Is the longest sentence?

If lawyers are disbarred and clergyman are defrocked, doesn’t it follow that electricians can be delighted, musicians denoted, cowboys deranged, models deposed, tree surgeons debarked and dry cleaners depressed?

Do Roman paramedics refer to IV’s as 4’s?

Why is it that if someone tells you that there are 1 billion stars in the universe you will believe them, but if they tell you a wall has wet paint, you will have to touch it to be sure?

One day this guy, who has been stranded on a desert island all alone for ten years, sees an unusual speck on the horizon. “It’s certainly not a ship,” he thinks to himself.

And as the speck gets closer and closer, he begins to rule out the possibilities of a small boat, then even a raft.

Suddenly, emerging from the surf comes this drop-dead gorgeous blonde woman wearing a wet suit and scuba gear.

She approaches the stunned guy and asks, “How long has it been since you’ve had a cigarette?”

“Ten years!” he says.

She reaches over and unzips a waterproof pocket on her left sleeve and pulls out a pocket of fresh cigarettes. He takes one, lights it, and takes a long drag, and says, "Man, oh man! Is that ever good!"

She then asks him, "How long has it been since you've had a sip of bourbon?"

Trembling, he replies, "Ten years!"

She reaches over, unzips her waterproof pocket on her right sleeve, pulls out a flask, and gives it to him. He opens the flask, takes a long swig, and says, "Wow, that's absolutely fantastic!"

Then she starts slowly unzipping the long zipper that runs down the front of her wet suit, looks at him seductively and asks, "And how long has it been since you've played around?"

The guy, with tears in his eyes, replies, "Oh sweet Lord God!" "Don't tell me you've got golf clubs in there!"

A bill collector came knocking at Dana's door; she had fallen behind on her bills.

"All right, lady," said the bill collector, "how about the next installment on that couch?"

Dana shrugged and said, "I guess that's better than having to give you money."

Stumpy and his wife Martha went to the state fair every year. Every year Stumpy would say, "Martha, I'd like to ride in that there airplane." And every year Martha would say, "I know Stumpy, but that airplane ride costs ten dollars, and ten dollars is ten dollars."

One year Stumpy and Martha went to the fair and Stumpy said, "Martha, I'm 71 years old. If I don't ride that airplane this year I may never get another chance." Martha replied, "Stumpy that there airplane ride costs ten dollars, and ten dollars is ten dollars."

The pilot overheard them and said, "Folks, I'll make you a deal. I'll take you both up for a ride. If you can stay quiet for the entire ride and not say one word, I won't charge you, but if you say one word it's ten dollars."

Stumpy and Martha agreed and up they go. The pilot does all

kinds of twists and turns, rolls and dives, but not a word is heard. He does all his tricks over again, but still not a word.

They land and the pilot turns to Stumpy. "By golly, I did everything I could think of to get you to yell out, but you didn't." Stumpy replied, "Well, I was gonna say something when Martha fell out, but ten dollars is ten dollars."

Jimmy and Kathy are newlyweds in the honeymoon suite on their wedding night, and Kathy's in the bathroom. As Jimmy's getting undressed he says to himself, "How am I going to tell her? How am I going to tell my new wife that I have the world's smelliest feet?" Then he throws his socks under the bed. Kathy walks out of the bathroom, and, too chicken to face her, Jimmy runs past her and he goes into the bathroom. Kathy sits on the edge of the bed and says to herself, "How am I going to tell him? How am I going to tell my new husband that I have the world's worst breath? I've got to tell him." Just then Jimmy walks out of the bathroom. Kathy runs up to him, gives him a huge wet kiss, pulls back and says, "Honey, I've got to tell you something." Jimmy says, "Yeah, I know. You just ate my socks."

Airhead Airlines, Flight 101, is coming in for a landing, and the pilot is freaking out. The sweat is jumping off his brow. (Plane landing and screeching to a halt.) RRRtttt! He turns to the co-pilot, and he says, "Man, that is the *shortest* runway I ever landed on." The co-pilot says, "Yeah, and so wide."

An eccentric philosophy professor gave a one question final exam after a semester dealing with a broad array of topics.

The class was already seated and ready to go when the professor picked up his chair, plopped it on his desk and wrote on the board: "Using everything we have learned this semester, prove that this chair does not exist."

Fingers flew, erasers erased, notebooks were filled in furious fashion. Some students wrote over 30 pages in one hour attempting to refute the existence of the chair. One member of the class, however, was up and finished in less than a minute.

Weeks later when the grades were posted, the rest of the group wondered how he could have gotten an "A" when he had barely written anything at all. His answer consisted of two words: "What chair?"

A motorist was mailed a picture of his car speeding through an automated radar camera. A $40 speeding ticket was included. Being cute, he sent the police department a picture of $40. The police responded with another mailed photo of handcuffs.

A young woman was pulled over for speeding. As the motorcycle officer walked to her car window, flipping open his ticket book, she said, "I bet you are going to sell me a ticket to the Highway Patrolmen's Ball."

He replied, "Highway patrolmen don't have balls."

There was a moment of silence while she smiled, and he realized what he'd just said. He then closed his book, got back on his motorcycle and left.

A pretty young blonde visiting her new doctor for the first time found herself alone in a small waiting room. She began undressing nervously, preparing herself for the upcoming examination. Just as she draped the last of her garments over the back of a chair, a light rap sounded on the door and a young doctor strode in.

Coming to an abrupt halt, the doctor looked his nude patient up and down carefully and with considerable appreciation.

"Miss Smith," he said finally, "it seems quite obvious to me that until today you have never undergone an eye examination."

Old Fred's hospital bed is surrounded by well-wishers, but it doesn't look good.

Suddenly, he motions frantically to the pastor for something to write on.

The pastor lovingly hands him a pen and a piece of paper, and Fred uses his last bit of energy to scribble a note, then dies. The pastor thinks it best not to look at the note right away, so he places it in his jacket pocket.

At Fred's funeral, as the pastor is finishing his eulogy, he realizes he's wearing the jacket he was wearing when Fred died.

"Fred handed me a note just before he died," he says. "I haven't looked at it, but knowing Fred, I'm sure there's a word of inspiration in it for us all." Opening the note, he reads aloud, "Help! You're standing on my oxygen hose."

Men are Like . . .

1. Men are like laxatives. They irritate the crap out of you.
2. Men are like bananas. The older they get, the less firm they are.
3. Men are like weather. Nothing can be done to change them.
4. Men are like blenders. You need one, but you're not quite sure why.
5. Men are like chocolate bars. Sweet, smooth, and they usually head right for your hips.
6. Men are like commercials. You can't believe a word they say.
7. Men are like department stores. Their clothes are always 1/2 off!
8. Men are like government bonds. They take sooooooo long to mature.
9. Men are like mascara. They usually run at the first sign of emotion.
10. Men are like popcorn. They satisfy you, but only for a little while.
11. Men are like snowstorms. You never know when they're coming, how many inches you'll get or how long it will last.
12. Men are like lava lamps. Fun to look at, but not very bright.
13. Men are like parking spots. All the good ones are taken, the rest are handicapped.

An elderly couple was attending church services. About halfway through she leans over and says to her husband, "I just let out a silent fart. What do you think I should do?"

He replies, "Put a new battery in your hearing aid."

A man, his wife, and mother-in-law went on vacation to the Holy Land.

While they were there the mother-in-law passed away.

The undertaker told them, "You can have her shipped home for $5,000, or you can bury her here in the Holy Land for $150.00."

The man thought about it and told him he would just have her shipped home.

The undertaker asked, "Why? Why would you spend $5,000 to ship your mother-in-law home, when it would be wonderful to be buried here and spend only $150.00?"

The man said, "A man died here 2000 years ago, he was buried here and three days later he rose from the dead. I just can't take that chance."

Dear Diary,

For my birthday this year, my wife (the dear) purchased a week of personal training at the local health club for me. Although I am still in great shape since playing on my college football team . . . . I decided it would be a good idea to go ahead and give it a try.

I called the club and made my reservation with a personal trainer named Belinda, who identified herself as a 26 yr. old aerobics instructor and model for athletic clothing and swimwear. My wife seemed pleased with my enthusiasm to get started! The club encouraged me to keep a diary to chart my progress for my cardiologist.

MONDAY:

Started my day at 6:00 a.m. Tough to get out of bed, but it was well worth it when I arrived at the health club to find Belinda waiting for me. She was something of a Greek goddess—with blonde hair, dancing eyes and a dazzling white smile. Woo Hoo!!!!!

She took my pulse after 5 minutes on the treadmill. She was

alarmed that my pulse was so fast, but I attributed it to standing next to her in her Lycra aerobics outfit. I enjoyed watching the skilful way in which she conducted her aerobics class after my workout today. Very inspiring, Belinda was encouraging as I did my sit-ups, although my gut was already aching from holding it in the whole time she was around. This is going to be a FANTASTIC week!!

TUESDAY:

I drank a whole pot of coffee, but I finally made it out the door. Belinda made me lie on my back and push a heavy iron bar into the air, and then she put weights on it! My legs were a little wobbly on the treadmill, but I made the full mile. Belinda's rewarding smile made it all worthwhile. I feel GREAT!! It's a whole new life for me.

WEDNESDAY:

The only way I can brush my teeth is by lying on the toothbrush on the counter and moving my mouth back and forth over it. I believe I have a hernia in both pectorals. Driving was OK as long as I didn't try to steer or stop. I parked on top of a GEO in the club parking lot. Belinda was impatient with me, insisting that my screams bothered the other club members. Her voice is a little too perky for early in the morning and when she scolds, she gets this nasally whine that is VERY annoying. My chest hurt when I got on the treadmill, so Belinda put me on the "stairmonster". Why the hell would anyone invent a machine to simulate an activity rendered obsolete by elevators? Belinda told me it would help me get in shape and enjoy life. She said some other stuff too.

THURSDAY:

Her thin, cruel lips were pulled back in a full snarl. I couldn't help being a half an hour late; it took me that long to tie my shoes. Belinda took me to work out with dumbbells. When she was not looking, I ran and hid in the men's room. She sent Lars to find me, then, as punishment, put me on the rowing machine which I sank.

FRIDAY:

I hate that bitch Belinda more than any human being has ever hated any other human being in the history of the world. Stupid, skinny, anemic little cheerleading bitch. If there were part of my body I could move without unbearable pain, I would beat her with it. Belinda wanted me to work on my triceps. I don't have any triceps! And if you don't want dents in the floor, don't hand me the *&%#(#&** barbells or anything that weighs more than a sandwich. The treadmill flung me off and I landed on a health and nutrition teacher. Why couldn't it have been someone softer, like the drama coach or the choir director?

SATURDAY:

Belinda left a message on my answering machine in her grating, shrilly voice wondering why I did not show up today. Just hearing her made me want to smash the machine with my planner. However, I lacked the strength to even use the TV remote and ended up catching eleven straight hours of the Weather Channel.

SUNDAY:

I'm having the Church van pick me up for services today so I can go and thank GOD that this week is over. I will also pray that next year, my wife will choose a gift for me that is fun—like a root canal or a heart transplant . . .

Here's the final word on nutrition and health. It's a relief to know the truth after all those conflicting medical studies:

1. The Japanese eat very little fat and suffer fewer heart attacks than the Americans.
2. The Mexicans eat a lot of fat and suffer fewer heart attacks than the Americans.
3. The Japanese drink very little red wine and suffer fewer heart attacks than the Americans.
4. The Italians drink excessive amounts of red wine and suffer fewer heart attacks than the Americans.
5. The Germans drink a lot of beers and eat lots of sausages and fats and suffer fewer heart attacks than the Americans.

CONCLUSION:

Eat and drink what you like. Speaking English is apparently what kills you.

At a recent U2 concert in Ireland, Bono (the lead singer) asks the audience for some quiet. Then he starts to slowly clap his hands. Holding the audience in total silence, he says into the microphone . . .

"I want you to think about something. Every time I clap my hands, a child in Africa dies."

A voice from the front of the audience yells out . . . "Then stop clapping, ya dummy."

A soldier ran up to a nun. Out of breath he asked, "Please, may I hide under your skirt. I'll explain later."

The nun agreed. A moment later two military policemen ran up and asked, "Sister, have you seen a soldier?"

The nun replied, "He went that way."

After the MP's ran off, the soldier crawled out from under her skirt and said, "I can't thank you enough Sister. You see, I don't want to go to Iraq."

The nun said, "I understand completely."

The soldier added, "I hope I'm not rude, but you have a great pair of legs!"

The nun replied, "If you had looked a little higher, you would have seen a great pair of balls . . . I don't want to go to Iraq either."

I ended up with an older woman at a club last night. She looked pretty good for a 60-year-old.

In fact, she wasn't too bad at all, and I found myself thinking that she probably had a hot daughter.

We drank a bit, and had a bit of a snuggle, and she asked if I'd ever had a Sportsman's Double.

"What's that?" I asked.

"It's a mother and daughter threesome," she said.

I said, "No." We drank a bit more, then she said that tonight was "my lucky night." I went back to her place.

She put on the hall light and shouted upstairs: "Mom, you still awake"?

10 Things Black and Latin People Know, But White People Won't Admit:

1. Elvis is dead.

2. Having your children curse you out in public is not normal.
3. Jesus was not White.
4. Skinny does not equal sexy.
5. A 5 year child is too big for a stroller.
6. N'SYNC will never hold a candle to the Jackson 5.
7. Thomas Jefferson had black children.
8. An occasional butt whupping helps a child stay in line.
9. Kissing your pet is not cute.
10. Rap music is here to stay.

10 Things White and Black People Know, but Latin People Won't Admit:

1. Chicken is food, not a roommate.
2. "Jump out and run" is not in any insurance policies.
3. Your country's flag is not a car decoration.
4. Hickey's are unattractive.
5. Mami and Papi can't possibly be the nickname of every person in your family.
6. Buttoning just the top button of your shirt is a bad fashion statement.
7. 10 people to a car or home is considered too many.
8. Jesus is not a name for your son.
9. Maria is a name but not for every other daughter.
10. Letting your children run wildly through the store can get your butt whupped (or theirs).

10 Things White and Latin People Know, But Black People Won't Admit:

1. Tupac is dead.
2. Crown Royal bags are meant to be thrown away.
3. Having a ring on every finger is too much.
4. O.J. did it.
5. Teeth should not be decorated.
6. Breaks are usually only 15 minutes.
7. Jesse Jackson will never be President.

8. Red is not a Kool-aid flavor (it's a color).
9. Your rims and sound system should not be worth more than your car.
10. Your pastor doesn't know everything.

A man goes into a lawyer's office and says, "I heard people have sued the tobacco companies for giving them lung cancer, and McDonald's for making them fat."

The lawyer says, "Yes, that's true."

The man says, "Well, I'm interested in suing too."

The lawyer says, "Okay, McDonald's or the tobacco companies?"

The man says, "Neither, I'm suing Budweiser for all the ugly women I've slept with."

For centuries, Hindu women have worn a red spot on their foreheads. We have naively thought it had something to do with their religion. The true story has just been revealed by the Indian Embassy in Washington.

When one of these women gets married, on her wedding night, the husband scratches off the red spot to see if he has won a convenience store, a gas station, or a hotel in Florida.

A woman went down to the Welfare Office to get aid.

The office worker asked her, "How many children do you have?"

"Ten," she replied.

"What are their names?" he asked.

"David, David, David, David, David, David, David, David, David and David," she answered.

"They're all named David?" he asked. "What if you want them to come in from playing outside?"

"Oh, that's easy," she said. "I just call 'David,' and they all come running in."

"And, if you want them to come to the table for dinner?"

"I just say, 'David, come eat your dinner,' " she answered.

"But what if you just want ONE of them to do something?" he asked.

"Oh, that's easy," she said. "I just use their last name!"

At a recent computer expo, Bill Gates reportedly compared the computer industry with the auto industry and stated,

"If GM had kept up with technology like the computer industry has, we would all be driving $25.00 cars that got 1,000 miles to the gallon."

In response to Bill's comments, General Motors issued a press release stating:

If GM had developed technology like Microsoft, we would all be driving cars with the following characteristics:

1. For no reason whatsoever, your car would crash . . . twice a day.

2. Every time they repainted the lines in the road, you would have to buy a new car.

3. Occasionally your car would die on the freeway for no reason. You would have to pull to the side of the road, close all the windows, shut off the car, restart it, and reopen the windows before you could continue. For some reason you would simply accept this.

4. Occasionally, executing a maneuver such as a left turn would cause your car to shut down and refuse to restart, in which case you would have to reinstall the engine.

5. Macintosh would make a car that was powered by the sun, was reliable, five times as fast and twice as easy to drive—but would run on only five percent of the roads.

6. The oil, water temperature, and alternator warning lights would all be replaced by a single "This Car Has Performed An Illegal Operation" warning light.

7. The airbag system would ask, "Are you sure?" before deploying.

8. Occasionally, for no reason whatsoever, your car would lock you out and refuse to let you in until you simultaneously lifted the door handle, turned the key and grabbed hold of the radio antenna.

9. Every time a new car was introduced, car buyers would have

to learn how to drive all over again because none of the controls would operate in the same manner as the old car.

10. You'd have to press the "Start" button to turn the engine off.

The plane was encountering severe problems on a transatlantic flight.

Then it got really rough.

Finally the pilot—a "good 'ol southern boy" announced in a pronounced drawl: "Folks . . . y'all can tell we're havin' trouble. We can't maintain altitude. So throw all the luggage off the plane, we'll lighten the load and get outta this mess."

The luggage went out but it wasn't much better. The pilot then announced: "We're in real trouble here. We're still too heavy. We're gonna have to lose a few people to save all the rest of us. The only thing I can think of is to do this . . . in alphabetical order. So here goes, starting with 'A'."

"Will all the African-Americans please stand up." Nobody moved.

"Will all the Blacks please stand up." Still nobody moved.

"Will all the Colored's please stand up." Again, nobody moved.

A young Black child turned to her mother: "Mom, aren't we all of those things?"

Her mother replied: "Nope. Today, we are Schvartzes."

Learn Chinese

1. That's not right .... Sum Ting Wong
2. Are you harboring a fugitive .... Hu Yu Hai Ding
3. See me ASAP .... Kum Hia Nao
4. Small Horse .... Tai Ni Po Ni
5. Did you go to the beach? .... Wai Yu So Tan
6. I think you need a face lift .... Chin Tu Fat
7. It's very dark in here .... Wao So Dim
8. I thought you were on a diet .... Wai Yu Mun Ching
9. This is a tow away zone .... No Pah King
10. Our meeting is tomorrow .... Wai Yu Kum Nao
11. Staying out of sight .... Lei Ying Lo

12. He's cleaning his automobile......... Wa Shing Ka
13. Your body odor is offensive............ Yu Stin Ki Pu
14. Great.. Fa Kin Su Pah

Three little pigs went out to dinner one night. The waiter came and took their drink order.

"I would like a Sprite," said the first little piggy.

"I would like a Coke," said the second little piggy.

"I want beer, lots and lots of beer," said the third little piggy.

The drinks were brought out and the waiter took their orders for dinner.

"I want a nice big steak," said the first piggy.

"I would like the salad plate," said the second piggy.

"I want beer, lots and lots of beer," said the third little piggy.

The meals were brought out and a while later the waiter approached the table and asked if the piggies would like any dessert.

"I want a banana split," said the first piggy.

"I want a root beer float," said the second piggy.

"I want beer, lots and lots of beer," exclaimed the third little piggy.

"Pardon me for asking," said the waiter to the third little piggy, "but why have you only ordered beer all evening?"

The third piggy says—

"Well, somebody has to go 'Wee, wee, wee, all the way home!"

Three women, two younger, and one senior citizen, were sitting naked in a sauna. Suddenly there was a beeping sound. The first young woman pressed her forearm and the beep stopped. The others looked at her questioningly. That was my pager," she said. "I have a microchip under the skin of my arm."

A few minutes later, a phone rang. The second young woman lifted her palm to her ear. When she finished, she explained, "That was my mobile phone. I have a microchip in my hand."

The older woman felt very low tech. However, not to be outdone, she decided she had to do something just as impressive.

She stepped out of the sauna, went to the bathroom. She returned with a piece of toilet paper hanging from her rear end. The others raised their eyebrows and stared at her. The older woman finally said . . . "Well, will you look at that . . . I'm getting a fax!!"

A California highway patrolman pulled a car over and told the driver that because he had been wearing his seat belt, he had just won $5,000 in the statewide safety competition.

"What are you going to do with the money?" asked the policeman.

"Well, I guess I'm going to get a driver's license," he answered.

"Oh, don't listen to him," yelled a woman in the passenger seat. "He's a smart-aleck when he's drunk."

This woke up the guy in the back seat who took one look at the cop and moaned, "I knew we wouldn't get far in a stolen car."

At that moment, there was a knock from the trunk and a voice said, in Spanish, "Are we over the border yet?"

A couple attending an art exhibition at the National Gallery were staring at a portrait that had them completely confused.

The painting depicted three very black and totally naked men sitting on a park bench. Two of the figures had black weenies, but the one in the middle had a pink weenie.

The curator of the gallery realized that they were having trouble interpreting the painting and offered his assessment.

He went on for nearly half an hour explaining how it depicted the sexual de-masculation of African Americans in a predominantly white, patriarchal society.

"In fact," he pointed out, "some serious critics believe that the pink weenie also reflects the cultural and sociological oppression experienced by gay men in contemporary society."

After the curator left, a young man in a Kentucky T-shirt approached the couple and said, "Would you like to know what the painting is really about?"

"Now why would you claim to be more of an expert than the curator of the gallery?" asked the couple.

"Because I'm the guy who painted it," he replied. "In fact, there are no African-Americans depicted at all. They're just three Kentucky coal miners, and the guy in the middle went home for lunch."

A Texas Air Traffic Control Conversation:

Dallas ATC: "Tower to Saudi Air 911—You are cleared to land eastbound on runway 9R."

Saudi Air: "Thank you Dallas ATC. Acknowledge cleared to land on infidel's runway 9R—Allah be Praised!!"

Dallas ATC: "Tower to Iran Air 7441—You are cleared to land westbound on runway 9R."

Iran Air: "Thank you Dallas ATC. We are cleared to land on infidel's runway 9R—Allah is Great!!"

Pause: Static . . .

Saudi Air: "DALLAS ATC! DALLAS ATC!"

Dallas ATC: "Go ahead Saudi Air 911?"

Saudi Air: "YOU HAVE CLEARED BOTH OUR AIRCRAFT FOR THE SAME RUNWAY—GOING IN OPPOSITE DIRECTIONS!!!

WE ARE ON A COLLISION COURSE!!! INSTRUCTIONS PLEASE!!!"

Dallas ATC: "Well bless your hearts. Y'all be careful now and tell Allah 'hey' for us—ya hear?

A redneck is driving down a back road in South Carolina.

A sign in front of a restaurant reads: Happy Hour Special. Lobster Tail and Beer.

"Lord almighty," he says to himself, "my three favorite things!!"

A redneck from Georgia decides to travel across the south to Virginia to see God's country.

When he gets to Franklin, he likes the place so much that he decides to stay. But first he must find a job!!!!

He walks into the International Paper Company office and fills out an application as an experienced log inspector. It's his lucky day!!! They just happen to be looking for someone. But first, the log foreman takes him for a ride into the forest in the company pickup truck to see how much he knows.

The foreman stops the truck on the side of the road and points at a tree. "See that tree over there? I want you to tell me what species it is and how many board feet of lumber it contains."

The redneck promptly answers, "That thar's a whitepine, 383 board feet of lumber in 'er."

The foreman is impressed!!! He puts the truck in motion and stops about a mile down the road. He points at another tree through the passenger window and asks the same question. This time, it's a bigger tree of a different class.

"That's a loblolly pine and she's got about 456 clear board feet." The foreman is really impressed with the good ol' boy. He has been quick and got the answers right without using a calculator!!! One more test. They drive a little further down the road, and the foreman stops again. This time, he points across the road through his driver side window and says, "And what about that one?" Before the foreman finishes pointing, the redneck says, "White Oak, 242 board feet at best." The foreman spins the truck around and heads back to the office a little ticked off because he thinks the red neck is smarter than he is. As they near the office, the foreman stops the truck and ask Bubba to step outside.

He hands him a piece of chalk and tells him, "See that tree over there?" I want you to mark an X on the front of that tree!!"

The foreman thinks to himself, "Idiot, how would he know which is the front of the tree?" When Bubba reaches the tree, he goes around it in a circle while looking at the ground. He then reaches up and places a white X on the trunk. He walks back to the foreman and hands him the chalk. "That thar's the front," the redneck says.

The foreman laughs to himself and asks sarcastically, "How in the hell do you know that's the front of the tree?"

The good ol' boy looks down at his feet, while rubbing the toe of his left boot, cleaning it in the gravel and replies, "Cuz somebody did number 2 behind it!"

He got the job and is now the foreman!!!!!

A couple of good friends—a Kiwi and an Aussie—were sitting around talking one afternoon over a cold beer. After a while the Kiwi said to the Aussie.

"If I was to sneak over to your place and shag your wife while you were off fishing, and she got pregnant and had a baby, would that make us related?"

The Aussie crooked his head sideways for a minute, scratched his head, and squinted his eyes thinking real hard about the question.

Finally, he said, "I don't know about being related . . . but it would make us even."

Ahkmed the Arab came to the United States from the Middle East and he was only here a few months when he became ill. He went to doctor after doctor, but none of them could help him. Finally, he went to an Arab doctor who said: "Take dees bocket, go into de odder room, poop in de bocket, pee pee on de poop, and den put your head down over de bocket ahn breathe in de fumes for ten minutes." Ahkmed took the bucket, went into the other room, pooped in the bucket, peed on the poop, and bent over and breathed in the fumes for ten minutes. Coming back to the doctor, he said, "It worked. I feel terrific! What was wrong with me?" The doctor said, "You were homesick."

After three weeks in the Garden of Eden, God came to visit Eve. "So, how is everything going?" inquired God.

"It is all so beautiful, God," she replied. "The sunrises and sunsets are breathtaking, the smells, the sights, everything is wonderful, but I have just one problem.

It's these breasts you have given me. The middle one pushes the other two out and I am constantly knocking them with my arms, catching them on branches and snagging them on bushes. They're a real pain," reported Eve. And Eve went on to tell God that since many other parts of her body came in pairs, such as her limbs, eyes, ears, etc. . . . she felt that having only two breasts might leave her body more "symmetrically balanced".

"That's a fair point," replied God. "But it was my first shot at this, you know. I gave the animals six breasts, so I figured that you needed only half of those, but I see that you are right. I will fix it up right away."

And God reached down, removed the middle breast and tossed it into the bushes.

Three weeks passed and God once again visited Eve in the Garden of Eden.

"Well, Eve, how is my favorite creation?"

"Just fantastic," she replied, "But for one oversight. You see, all the animals are paired off. The ewe has a ram and the cow has her bull. All the animals have a mate except me. I feel so alone."

God thought for a moment and said, "You know, Eve, you are right. How could I have overlooked this? You do need a mate and I will immediately create a man from a part of you. Let's see . . . where did I put the useless boob?"

Now doesn't THAT make more sense than the crap about the rib?

Three rednecks were working up on a cell phone tower: Cooter, Ronnie and Donnie. As they start their descent Cooter slips, falls off the tower and is killed instantly. As the ambulance takes the body away, Ronnie says, "Well, damn, someone should go and tell his wife."

Donnie says, "OK, I'm pretty good at that sensitive stuff, I'll do it."

Two hours later, he comes back carrying a case of Budweiser.

Ronnie says, "Where did you get that beer, Donnie?"

"Cooter's wife gave it to me," Ronnie replies.

"That's unbelievable, you told the lady her husband was dead and she gave you a case of beer?"

"Well, not exactly," Donnie says. "When she answered the door, I said to her, You must be Cooter's widow. She said, 'You must be mistaken, I'm not a widow.' Then I said, 'I'll bet you a case of Budweiser you are.' "

Rednecks Are Good At This Sensitive Stuff

A man who just died is delivered to a local mortuary wearing an expensive, expertly tailored black suit. The mortician asks the deceased's wife how she would like the body dressed. She points out that the man does look good in the black suit he is already wearing. The widow, however, says that she always thought her husband looked his best in blue, and that she wants him in a blue suit. She gives the mortician a blank check and says, "I don't care what it costs, but please have my husband in a blue suit for the viewing."

The woman returns the next day for the wake. To her delight, she finds her husband dressed in a gorgeous blue suit with a subtle chalk stripe; the suit fits him perfectly.

She says to the mortician, "Whatever this cost, I'm very satisfied. You did an excellent job and I'm very grateful. How much did you spend?" To her astonishment, the mortician presents her with the blank check.

"There's no charge," he says.

"No, really, I must compensate you for the cost of that exquisite blue suit!" she says.

"Honestly, ma'am," the mortician says, "it cost nothing. You see, a deceased gentleman of about your husband's size was brought in shortly after you left yesterday, and he was wearing an attractive blue suit. I asked his wife if she minded him going to his grave wearing a black suit instead, and she said it made no difference as long as he looked nice.'

"So I just switched the heads."

An old Italian lived alone in New Jersey. He wanted to plant his annual tomato garden, but it was very difficult work, as the ground was hard. His only son, Vincent, who used to help him, was in prison. The old man wrote a letter to his son and described his predicament:

Dear Vincent,

I am feeling pretty sad because it looks like I won't be able to plant my tomato garden this year. I'm just getting too old to be digging up a garden plot. I know if you were here my troubles would be over. I know you would be happy to dig the plot for me, like in the old days.

Love, Papa

A few days later he received a letter from his son.

Dear Pop,

Don't dig up that garden. That's where the bodies are buried.

Love, Vinnie

At 4 a.m. the next morning, FBI agents and local police arrived and dug up the entire area without finding any bodies. They apologized to the old man and left. Later, that same day the old man received a telegram from his son.

Dear Pop,

Go ahead and plant the tomatoes now. That's the best I could do under the circumstances.

Love you,

Vinnie

A woman scanned the guests at a party and spotted an attractive man standing alone. She approached him. "Hello," she said. "My name is Carmen Gold."

"That's a beautiful name," he said. "Is it a family name?"

"No", she replied. "I gave it to myself. It reflects the things I like most in life—cars, men, and fine jewelry."

"What's your name?" she asked.

He replied, "B. J. Titsengolf."

A man boarded a plane with 6 kids.

After they got settled in their seats, a woman sitting across the aisle from him leaned over to him and asked, "Are all of those kids yours?"

He replied,

"No. I work for a condom company. These are customer complaints."

A lady is having a bad day at the tables in Vegas. Down to her last $100, completely exasperated, she cries, "What rotten luck! What in the world should I do now?"

A gent next to her, trying to calm her down a bit, calmly suggests, "I don't know . . . why don't you play your age?"

He walks away. Moments later, he is intrigued to hear a great commotion at the roulette table. Maybe, she won!

Rushing back to the table and pushing his way through the crowd, he is stunned to see the lady lying limp on the floor, with the table operator kneeling over her.

He asks, "What happened? Is she all right?"

The operator replies, "I don't know, buddy . . . She put all her money on 29. When 36 came up, she fainted!"

A man was walking past the mental hospital the other day, and all the patients were shouting, "13 . . . 13 . . . 13."

The fence was too high to see over, but he saw a little gap in the planks, so he looked through to see what was going on . . .

Some bastard poked him in the eye with a stick!

Then they all started shouting, "14 . . . 14 . . . 14".

John was a salesman's delight when it came to any kind of unusual gimmick. His wife, Marsha had long ago given up trying to get him to change.

One day, John came home with another one of his unusual purchases. It was a robot that John claimed was actually an infallible lie detector.

It was just about 5:30 that afternoon when Tommy, their 11 year old son returned home from school. Tommy was over 2 hours late.

"Where have you been? Why are you over 2 hours late getting home?", they asked.

"Several of us went to the library to work on an extra credit project", said Tommy.

The robot then walked around the table and slapped Tommy, knocking him complete out of his chair.

"Son, this robot is a lie detector, now tell us where you went after school."

"We went to Bobby's house and watched a movie."

"What did you watch?" asked Marsha.

"The Ten Commandments." answered Tommy.

The Robot went around to Tommy and once again slapped him, knocking him off his chair.

With lip quivering, Tommy got up, sat down and said, "I am sorry I lied. We really watched a tape called Sex Queen."

"I am ashamed of you Son," said John. "When I was your age, I never lied to my parents."

The robot then walked around to John and delivered a roundhouse right that nearly knocked him out of his chair.

Marsha was bent double laughing, almost in tears. "Boy, did you ever ask for that one. So you can't be too mad with Tommy. After all, he is your son!"

The robot immediately walked around to Marsha and slapped her three times!

A young couple met with their pastor to set a date for their wedding. When he asked whether they preferred a contemporary or a traditional service, they opted for the contemporary. On the big day, a major storm forced the groom to take an alternate route to the church. The streets were flooded, so he rolled up his pants legs to keep his trousers dry. When he finally reached the church, his best man rushed him into the sanctuary and up to the altar, just as the ceremony was starting.

"Pull down your pants," whispered the pastor.

"Uh, Reverend, I've changed my mind," the groom responded. "I think I would prefer the traditional service."

Romance Mathematics
Smart Man + Smart Woman = Romance
Smart Man + Dumb Woman = Affair
Dumb Man + Smart Woman = Marriage
Dumb Man + Dumb Woman = Pregnancy

Office Arithmetic
Smart Boss + Smart Employee = Profit
Smart Boss + Dumb Employee = Production

Dumb Boss + Smart Employee = Promotion
Dumb Boss + Dumb Employee = Overtime

Shopping Math

A man will pay $20 for a $10 item he needs.

A woman will pay $10 for a $20 item that she doesn't need.

General Equations and Statistics

A woman worries about the future until she gets a husband.

A man never worries about the future until he gets a wife.

A successful man is one who makes more money than his wife can spend.

A successful woman is one who can find such a man.

Happiness

To be happy with a man, you must understand him a lot and love him a little.

To be happy with a woman, you must love her a lot and not try to understand her at all.

Longevity

Married men live longer than single men do, but married men are a lot more willing to die.

Propensity to Change

A woman marries a man expecting he will change, but he doesn't.

A man marries a woman expecting that she won't change, and she does.

Discussion Technique

A woman has the last word in any argument.

Anything a man says after that is the beginning of a new argument.

How to Stop People From Bugging You About Getting Married

Old aunts used to come up to me at weddings, poking me in the ribs and cackling, telling me, "You're next." They stopped after I started doing the same thing to them at funerals.

Reverend Boudreaux was the part-time pastor of the local Cajun Baptist Church, and Pastor Thibodaux was the minister of the Covenant Church across the road. They were both standing by the road, pounding a sign into the ground, that read:

"Da End is Near! Turn You Self Around Now! Before It's Too Late!"

As a car sped past them, the driver leaned out his window and yelled, "You religious nuts!"

From the curve they heard screeching tires and a big splash . . . Bordeaux turns to Thibodaux and asks, "Do ya tink maybe da sign should jus say 'Bridge Out'?"

When the priest slid open the panel in the confessional, the woman said, "Father . . . During World War II, a handsome young man knocked on my door and asked me to hide him from the enemy. So I hid him in the attic."

The priest replied, "That was a wonderful thing you did! You have no need to confess that."

"It's worse than that, Father. He started to repay me with sexual favors."

The priest said, "By doing that, you were both in great danger. However, two young people under those circumstances can be very tempted to act that way. But if you are truly sorry for your actions, you are indeed forgiven."

"Thank you, Father. That's a great load off my mind. But I do have one more question."

"And what is that?" asked the priest.

"Should I tell him the war is over?"

It was a small town and the patrolman was making his evening rounds. As he was checking a used car lot, he came upon two little old ladies sitting in a used car. He stopped and asked them why they were sitting there in the car. Were they trying to steal it?

"Heavens no, we bought it."

"Then why don't you drive it away."

"We can't drive."

"Then why did you buy it?"

"We were told that if we bought a used car here we'd get screwed . . . we're just waiting."

Two families moved from Pakistan to the USA. When they arrived the two fathers made a bet—in a year's time whichever family had become more American would win.

A year later, they met again. The first man said, "My son is playing baseball, I had McDonalds for breakfast and I'm on my way to pick up a case of Bud. How about you?"

The second man replied, "Screw you, towel head."

One day, in line at the company cafeteria, Joe says to Mike behind him, "My elbow hurts like hell. I guess I'd better see a doctor."

"Listen, you don't have to spend that kind of money," Mike replies.

"There's a diagnostic computer down at Wal-Mart. Just give it a urine sample and the computer will tell you what's wrong and what to do about it.

It takes ten seconds and costs ten dollars . . . a lot cheaper than a doctor . . ."

So, Joe deposits a urine sample in a small jar and takes it to Wal-Mart. He deposits ten dollars, and the computer lights up and asks for the urine sample. He pours the sample into the slot and waits.

Ten seconds later, the computer ejects a printout:

"You have tennis elbow. Soak your arm in warm water and avoid heavy activity. It will improve in two weeks. Thank you for shopping at Wal-Mart."

That evening, while thinking how amazing this new technology was, Joe began wondering if the computer could be fooled.

He mixed some tap water, a stool sample from his dog, urine samples from his wife and daughter, and a sperm sample for good measure.

Joe hurries back to Wal-Mart, eager to check the result. He deposits ten dollars, pours in his concoction, and awaits the results.

The computer prints the following:

1. Your tap water is too hard. Get a water softener. (Aisle 9)
2. Your dog has ringworm. Bathe him with anti-fungal shampoo. (Aisle 7)
3. Your daughter has a cocaine habit. Get her into rehab.

4. Your wife is pregnant. Twins. They aren't yours. Get a lawyer.

5. If you don't stop playing with yourself, your elbow will never get better!

Thank you for shopping at Wal-Mart.

A guy goes to the supermarket and notices an attractive woman waving at him. She says hello. He's rather taken aback because he can't place where he knows her from. So he says, "Do you know me?" To which she replies, "I think you're the father of one of my kids."

Now his mind travels back to the only time he has ever been unfaithful to his wife and says, "My God, are you the stripper from my bachelor party that I made love to on the pool table with all my buddies watching.

She looks into his eyes and says calmly, "No, I'm your son's teacher."

You may have missed the passing of a great American legend. Here's the full obituary for those of you who may have missed it:

Please join me in remembering a great icon of the entertainment community. The Pillsbury Doughboy died yesterday of a yeast infection and trauma complications from repeated pokes in the belly. He was 71.

Doughboy was buried in a lightly greased coffin. Dozens of celebrities turned out to pay their respects, including Mrs. Butterworth, Hungry Jack, the California Raisins, Betty Crocker, the Hostess Twinkies, and Captain Crunch. The grave site was piled high with flours.

Aunt Jemima delivered the eulogy and lovingly described Doughboy as a man who never knew how much he was kneaded. Doughboy rose quickly in show business, but his later life was filled with turnovers. He was not considered a very smart cookie, wasting much of his dough on half-baked schemes. Despite being a little flaky at times, he still was a crusty old man and was considered a positive roll model for millions.

Doughboy is survived by his wife Play Dough, three children: John Dough, Jane Dough and Dosey Dough, plus they had one in the oven. He is also survived by his elderly father, Pop Tart. The funeral was held at 3:50 for about 20 minutes.

Sherlock Holmes and Dr. Watson went on a camping trip. After a good meal and a bottle of wine they lay down for the night, and went to sleep.

Some hours later, Holmes awoke and nudged his faithful friend.

"Watson, look up at the sky and tell me what you see."

Watson replied, "I see millions and millions of stars."

"What does that tell you?"

Watson pondered for a minute.

"Astronomically, it tells me that there are millions of galaxies and potentially billions of planets. Astrologically, I observe that Saturn is in Leo. Horologically, I deduce that the time is approximately a quarter past three.

"Theologically, I can see that God is all powerful and that we are small and insignificant.

"Meteorologically, I suspect that we will have a beautiful day tomorrow. What does it tell you?"

Holmes was silent for a minute, then spoke.

"Watson, you dummy. Someone has stolen our tent."

You live in California when . . .

1. You make over $250,000 and you still can't afford to buy a house.
2. The high school quarterback calls a time-out to answer his cell phone.
3. The fastest part of your commute is going down your driveway.
4. You know how to eat an artichoke.
5. You drive to your neighborhood block party.

You live in New York when . . .

1. You say "the city" and expect everyone to know you mean Manhattan.

2. You have never been to the Statue of Liberty.

3. You can get into a 4-hour argument about how to get from Columbus Circle to Battery Park, but can't find Wisconsin on a map.

4. You think Central Park is "nature."

5. You believe that being able to swear at people in their own language makes you multilingual.

6. You've worn out a car horn.

7. You think eye contact is an act of aggression.

You live in Alaska when . . .

1. You only have four spices: salt, pepper, ketchup and Tabasco.

2. Halloween costumes fit over parkas.

3. You have more than one recipe for moose.

4. Sexy lingerie is anything flannel with less than eight buttons.

5. The four seasons are: winter, still winter, almost winter, and construction.

You live in the Deep South when . . .

1. You get a movie and bait in the same store.

2. "Ya'll" is singular and "all ya'll" is plural.

3. After fifteen years you still hear, "You ain't from 'round here, are ya?"

4. "He needed killin' " is a valid defense.

5. Everyone has 2 first names.

You live in Colorado when . . .

1. You carry your $3,000 mountain bike atop your $500 car.

2. You tell your husband to pick up Granola on his way home, and he stops at the Day Care Center.

3. A pass does not involve a football or dating.

4. The top of your head is bald, but you still have a ponytail.

You live in the Midwest when . . .

1. You've never met any celebrities, but the mayor knows your name.

2. Your idea of a traffic jam is ten cars waiting to pass a tractor.

3. You have had to switch from "heat" to "A/C" on the same day.

4. You end sentences with a preposition: "Where's my coat at?"
5. When asked how your trip was to any exotic place, you say, "It was different!"

You live in Florida when . . .

1. You eat dinner at 3:15 in the afternoon.
2. All purchases include a coupon of some kind—even houses and cars.
3. Everyone can recommend an excellent dermatologist.
4. Road construction never ends anywhere in the state.
5. Cars in front of you are often driven by headless people.
6. You don't know how to vote

You live in New Mexico when . . .

1. You can correctly pronounce Tesuque, Cerrillos, and Pojoaque.
2. You expect to pay more if your house is made of mud.
3. You can order a Big Mac with green chile.
4. You are still using the paper license tag that came with your car five years ago.
5. Your Christmas decorations include a "yard of sand and 200 paper bags".
6. Most restaurants you go to begin with "El" or "Los".
7. The tires on your roof have more tread than the ones on your car.
8. You price shop for tortillas.
9. You think a red light is merely a suggestion.
10. You have an extra freezer just for green chile.
11. You believe that using a turn signal is a sign of weakness.
12. You think six tons of crushed rock makes a beautiful front lawn.
13. There is a piece of UFO displayed in your home.
14. You just got your fifth DWI and got elected to the state legislature in the same week.
15. Your swamp cooler got knocked off your roof by a dust devil.
16. You think that Las Vegas is a town in the northeastern part of the state.
17. You iron your jeans to "dress up."

18. You don't see anything wrong with drive-up window liquor sales.

19. Your other vehicle is also a pick-up truck.

20. Two of your cousins are in Santa Fe, one in the legislature, the other in the state pen.

21. You know the punch line to at least one Espanola joke.

22. You have driven to an Indian Casino at 3 am because you were hungry.

23. You think the UNM Lobos fight song is "Louie, Louie."

24. You know whether you want "red or green."

25. You see nothing odd when, in conversations of the people in line around you at the store, every other word of each sentence alternates between Spanish and English.

26. You know you will run into at least 3 cousins whenever you shop at WalMart, Sams or Home Depot.

27. Someone asks you how far away something is, you tell them how long it will take to get there rather than how many miles away it is.

How to Identify Where a Driver is From

1. One hand on wheel, one hand on horn: Chicago.

2. One hand on wheel, one finger out window: New York.

3. One hand on wheel, one finger out window, cutting across all lanes of traffic: New Jersey.

4. One hand on wheel, one hand on newspaper, foot solidly on accelerator: Boston.

5. One hand on wheel, one hand on nonfat double decaf cappuccino, cradling cell phone, brick on accelerator, with gun in lap: Los Angeles.

6. Both hands on wheel, eyes shut, both feet on brake, quivering in terror: Ohio, but driving in California.

7. Both hands in air, gesturing' both feet on accelerator, head turned to talk to someone in back seat: Italy.

8. One hand on latte, one knee on wheel, cradling cell phone, foot on brake, mind on radio game: Seattle.

9. One hand on wheel, one hand on hunting rifle, alternating between both feet being on the accelerator and both feet on brake, throwing McDonald's bag out the window: Texas.

10. Four-wheel drive pick-up truck, shotgun mounted in rear

window, beer cans on floor, squirrel tails attached to antenna: West Virginia.

11. Two hands gripping wheel, blue hair barely visible above the steering wheel, driving in the left lane at 35 MPH on the Interstate with the left blinker on: Florida.

During a visit to the mental asylum, a visitor asked the Director how do you determine whether or not an individual should be institutionalized.

"Well," said the Director, "we fill up a bathtub, then we offer a teaspoon, a teacup and a bucket to the patient and ask him or her to empty the bathtub."

"Oh, I understand," said the visitor. "A normal person would use the bucket because it's bigger than the spoon or the teacup."

"No," said the Director. "A normal person would pull the plug. Do you want a bed near the window?"

The following ad appeared in a newspaper.

SBF Seeks Male companionship, ethnicity unimportant. I'm a svelte good looking girl who LOVES to play. I love long walks in the woods. Riding in your pickup truck. Hunting, Camping, Fishing trips. Cozy winter nights spent lying by the fire. Candlelight dinners will have me eating out of your hand. Rub me the right way and watch me respond. I'll be at the front door when you get home from work, wearing only what nature gave me. Kiss me and I'm yours. Call 555-XXXX and ask for Daisy.

(The phone number was the Humane Society and Daisy was an eight week old black Labrador Retriever.)

Jack has a girl friend he takes to a hotel for a night of pleasure. Lying in bed the following morning he's getting heartburn from worrying about the possible unpleasant consequences that could result from his indiscretion. He asks his companion: "What would you do if you found out you were pregnant?"

"I'd jump out of this tenth-story window!", she tells him.

Jack, with a great sigh of relief, looks at her admiringly and says, "Such a doll."

The success of the "Wonder Bra" for under-endowed women has encouraged the designers to come out with a bra for over-endowed women.

It's called the "Sheep Dog Bra" . . . It rounds them up and points them in the right direction.

The bar room was crowded. All of a sudden, the cute little thing on the stool began to cry.

The barkeep asked, "What's the trouble, Sweetie?"

She sobbed, "I'm a virgin, and my boyfriend won't have anything to do with me because I'm inexperienced. What should I do?"

Three men and a lesbian were killed in the rush.

Mujibar was trying to get a job in India.

The Personnel Manager said, "Mujibar, you have passed all the tests, except one. You must pass it to qualify for this job."

Mujibar said, "I am ready."

The manager said, "Make a sentence using the words Yellow, Pink and Green."

Mujibar thought for a few minutes and said, "Mister manager, I am ready."

The manager said, "Go ahead."

Mujibar said, "The telephone goes green, green, green, and I pink it up, and say, 'Yellow, this is Mujibar.' "

Mujibar now works as a technician at a call center for computer problems.

Scientists at NASA built a gun specifically to launch dead chickens at the windshields of airliners, military jets and the space shuttle, all traveling at maximum velocity. The idea is to stimulate the frequent incidents of collisions with airborne fowl to test the strength of the windshields.

British engineers heard about the gun and were eager to test it on the windshields of their new high speed trains. Arrangements were made, and a gun was sent to the British engineers.

When the gun was fired, the engineers stood shocked as the chicken hurtled out of the barrel, crashed into the shatterproof shield, smashed it to smithereens, blasted through the control console, snapped the engineer's backrest in two and embedded itself in the back wall of the cabin, like an arrow shot from a bow. The horrified Britons sent NASA the disastrous results of the experiment, along with the designs of the windshield, and begged the U.S. scientists for suggestions. NASA responded with a one-line memo: "Thaw the chicken."

Two guys are in a locker room after their racquetball game when one guy notices the other has a cork in his ass.

"If you don't mind me saying," said the second, "the cork looks terribly uncomfortable. Why don't you take it out?"

"I can't," lamented the first man. "It's permanent."

"I don't understand," said the other.

The first guy says, "I was walking along the beach and I tripped over an oil lamp. There was a puff of smoke, and then a huge man in a turban came oozing out. He said, "I am Hasan the Genie. I can grant you one wish. And I said, 'No shit.' "

Morris and Harry were both fanatics about deep sea fishing. Each would come back from fishing trips, and tell the other big lies about the number, and the sizes of the fish they caught.

So Morris comes back from his latest fishing trip, and tells Harry, "You wouldn't believe, but in the Bahamas I caught a 500 pound herring."

Harry says, "That's nothing, last time I fished in the Bahamas, I pulled up an old lantern from a sunken Spanish ship and the candle was still burning!"

They both looked at each other, knowing that the other was lying.

Finally, Harry said to Morris, "Look Morris, if you take 450 pounds from off your herring . . . I'll blow out my candle!"

David and Sue went out to dinner at a great seafood restaurant, and David indulged himself in a dozen fresh oysters.

Later that night, when they went to bed, David took out a book, propped himself up on some pillows and began to read. He felt the stare of Sue upon him, turned to look at her, and asked, "What?"

Sue smiled and said, "I'm just waiting to see if those oysters are going to kick in."

An Amish farmer walking through his field, notices a man drinking from his pond, with his hand.

The Amish man shouts: "Trink das wasser nicht. Die kuhen haben dahin geheissen."

Which means: "Don't drink the water, the cows have shit in it."

The man shouts back: "I'm a Muslim, I don't understand. Please speak in English."

The Amish man says:

"Use two hands. You'll get more."

In a tiny village on the Irish coast lived an old lady, a virgin and very proud of it. Sensing that her final days were rapidly approaching, and desiring to make sure everything was in proper order when she died, she went to the town's undertaker (who also happened to be the local postal clerk) to make the proper "final" arrangements. As a last wish, she informed the undertaker that she wanted the following inscription engraved on her tombstone:

"BORN A VIRGIN, LIVED AS A VIRGIN, DIED A VIRGIN"

Not long after, the old maid died peacefully. A few days after the funeral, as the undertaker/postal clerk went to prepare the tombstone that the lady had requested, it became quite apparent that the tombstone that she had selected was much too small for the wording that she had chosen. He thought long and hard about how he could fulfill the old maid's final request, considering the very limited space available on the small piece of stone. For days, he agonized over the dilemma. But finally his experience as a postal worker allowed him to come up with what he thought was the appropriate solution to the problem.

The virgin's tombstone was finally completed and duly engraved, and it read as follows:

"RETURNED UNOPENED."

The girl was supposed to write a short story in as few words as possible for her college class and the instructions were that it had to discuss Religion, Sexuality and Mystery. She was the only one who received an A+ and this is what she wrote:

Good God, I'm pregnant, I wonder who the father is?

The Lone Ranger and Tonto walked into a bar and sat down to drink a beer. After a few minutes, a big tall cowboy walked in and said, "Who owns the big white horse outside?"

The Lone Ranger said, "I do, why?"

The cowboy said, "I just thought you'd like to know that your horse is about dead outside!"

The Lone Ranger and Tonto rushed outside and sure enough Silver was about to die from heat exhaustion. The Lone Ranger got water and soon Silver was starting to feel a little better. The Lone Ranger turns to Tonto and said, "I want you to run around Silver and see if you can create enough of a breeze to help cool him down."

Tonto said, "Sure, Kemosabe," and he begins running circles around Silver.

Unable to do anything except wait, the Lone Ranger returns to the bar to finish his drink.

A few minutes later, another cowboy struts into the bar and asks, "Who owns that big white horse outside?"

The Lone Ranger stands and says, "I do, what's wrong with him this time?"

The cowboy looks him in the eye and says . . . "Nothing, but you left your Injun running."

This may come as a surprise to those of you not living in Las Vegas, but there are more Catholic churches there than casinos. Not surprisingly, some worshippers at Sunday services will give casino chips rather than cash when the basket is passed.

Since they get chips from so many different casinos, the churches have devised a method to collect the offerings. The churches send all their collected chips to a nearby Franciscan Monastery for sorting and then the chips are taken to the casinos of origin and cashed in.

This is done by the chip monks.

One day a father gets out of work and on his way home he remembers that it's his daughter's birthday. He pulls over to a toy store and asks the salesperson, "How much is the Barbie on the display window?"

The salesperson answers, "Which one? We have:

Work-out Barbie for $19.95

Shopping Barbie for $19.95

Beach Barbie for $19.95

Disco Barbie for $19.95

Divorced Barbie for $265.95."

The amazed father asks, "What? Why is the Divorced Barbie $265.95 and the others only $19.95?"

The salesperson answers: "Sir . . . , Divorced Barbie comes with:

Ken's Car.

Ken's House.

Ken's Boat.

Ken's Furniture.

and . . .

One of Ken's Friends."

A young cowboy from Wyoming goes off to college, but half way through the semester, he has foolishly squandered all his money. He calls home, "Dad," he says, "You won't believe what modern education is developing! They actually have a program here in Laramie that will teach our dog, Ol' Blue how to talk!"

"That's amazing," his Dad says. "How do I get Ol' Blue in that program?"

"Just send him down here with $1,000" the young cowboy says. "I'll get him in the course."

So his father sends the dog and $1,000.

About two-thirds through the semester, the money again runs out. The boy calls home.

"So how's Ol' Blue doing, son?" his father asks.

"Awesome, Dad, he's talking up a storm," he says, "but you just won't believe this. They've had such good results they have started to teach the animals how to read!"

"Read!" says his father, "No kidding! How do we get Ol' Blue in that program?"

"Just send $2,500, and I'll get him in the class."

The money promptly arrives.

But our hero has a problem. At the end of the year, his father will find out the dog can neither talk, nor read.

So he shoots the dog.

When he arrives home at the end of the year, his father is all excited.

"Where's Ol' Blue? I just can't wait to see him read something and talk!"

"Dad," the boy says, "I have some grim news. Yesterday morning, just before we left to drive home, Ol' Blue was in the living room, kicked back in the recliner, reading the Wall Street Journal, like he usually does.

Then he turned to me and asked, 'So, is your daddy still messing' around with that little redhead who lives in town?"

The father exclaimed, "I hope you shot that son of a bitch before he talks to your Mother!"

"I sure did, Dad!"

"That's my boy!"

The kid went on to be a successful lawyer.

Mike and Sam had not seen each other in many years. Now they had a long talk trying to fill in the gap of those years by telling about their lives. Finally, Mike invited Sam to visit him in his new apartment.

"I got a wife and three kids and I'd love to have you visit us."

"Great. Where do you live?"

"Here's the address. And there's plenty of parking behind the apartment. Park and come around to the front door, kick it open with your foot, go to the elevator and press the button with your left elbow, then enter! When you reach the sixth floor, go down the hall until you see my name on the door. Then press the doorbell with your right elbow and I'll let you in."

"Good. But tell me . . . what is all this business of kicking the front door open, then pressing elevator buttons with my right, then my left elbow?"

"Surely, you're not coming empty-handed?"

An elderly man in Miami calls his son in New York and says, "I hate to ruin your day, but I have to tell you that your mother and I are divorcing. Forty-five years of misery is enough."

"Pop, what are you talking about?" the son screams.

"We can't stand the sight of each other any longer," the old man says. "We're sick of each other, and I'm sick of talking about this, so you call your sister in Chicago and tell her," and he hangs up.

Frantic, the son calls his sister, who explodes on the phone, "Like heck they're getting divorced," she shouts, "I'll take care of this."

She calls her father immediately and screams at the old man, "You are NOT getting divorced! Don't do a single thing until I get there. I'm calling my brother back, and we'll both be there tomorrow. Until then, don't do a thing, DO YOU HEAR ME?" and hangs up.

The old man hangs up his phone and turns to his wife. "Okay," he says, "they're coming for Passover and paying their own airfares."

A couple made a deal that whoever died first would come back and inform the other of the afterlife. Their biggest fear was that there was no afterlife.

After a long life together, the husband was the first to die. True to his word, he made the first contact, "Elizabeth . . ."

"Is that you, Steve?"

"Yes, I've come back like we agreed."

"That's wonderful! What's it like?"

"Well, I get up in the morning, I have sex. I have breakfast and then it's off to the golf course. I have sex again, bathe in the warm sun and then have sex a couple of more times. Then I have lunch (you'd be proud—lots of greens) another romp around the golf course, then pretty much have sex the rest of the afternoon. After supper, it's back to the golf course again. Then it's more sex until late at night. I catch some much needed sleep and then the next day it starts all over again."

"Oh, Steve, you surely must be in heaven!"

"Not exactly . . . I'm a rabbit on a golf course in Arizona."

Three guys are convicted of a very serious crime, and they're all sentenced to twenty years in solitary confinement. They're each allowed one thing to bring into the cell with them. The first guy asks for a big stack of books. The second guy asks for his wife. And the third guy asks for two hundred cartons of cigarettes. At the end of the twenty years, they open up the first guy's cell. He comes out and says, "I studied so hard, I'm so bright now, I could be a lawyer. It was terrific." They open up the second guy's door. He comes out with his wife, and they've got five new kids. He says, "It was the greatest thing of my life. My wife and I have never been so close. I have a beautiful new family. I love it." They open up the third guy's door, and he's slapping at his pockets, going. "Anybody got a match?"

Two guys are out hiking. All of a sudden, a bear starts chasing them. They climb a tree, but the bear starts climbing up the tree after them. The first guy gets his sneakers out of his knapsack and starts putting them on. The second guy says, "What are you doing?" He says, "I figure when the bear gets close to us, we'll jump down and make a run for it." The second guy says, "Are you crazy? You can't outrun a bear." The first guy says, "I don't have to outrun the bear . . . I only have to outrun you."

It's Christmas Eve. Kelly walks into a bar and orders beer and a shot of whiskey. The bartender gives him a beer and a shot of whiskey. Kelly drinks his beer and pours the shot of whiskey into his shirt pocket. Kelly orders another beer and another shot of whiskey. Kelly drinks the beer and pours the shot of whiskey into his pocket. The bartender says, "Look, Mac, it's Christmas Eve, and I know we're both depressed, and I certainly don't mean to bug you, but my curiosity is killing me. Why do you keep pouring the shots in your pocket?" Kelly says, "It's none of your damn business! And if you be givin' me a hard time, I'll be breakin yer face!" A mouse pops out of Kelly's shirt pocket and says, "And that goes for your stupid cat, too!"

A little old man is walking down the street one afternoon when he sees a woman with perfect breasts. He says to her, "Hey miss, would you let me bite your breasts for $100?"

"Are you nuts?!!!" she replies, and keeps walking away. He turns around, runs around the block and gets to the corner before she does.

"Would you let me bite your breasts for $1,000 dollars?" he asks again.

"Listen you; I'm not that kind of woman! Got it?"

So the little old man runs around the next block and faces her again; "Would you let me bite your breasts just once for $10,000 dollars?"

She thinks about it for a while and says, "Hmmm, $10,000 dollars . . . Ok, just once, but not here. Let's go to that dark alley over there." So they go into the alley, where she takes off her blouse to reveal the most perfect breasts in the world. As soon as he sees them, he grabs them and starts caressing them, fondling them slowly, kissing them, licking them, burying his face in them, but not biting them. The woman finally gets annoyed and asks, "Well? Are you gonna bite them or not?"

"Nah," says the little old man . . . "Costs too much . . ."

The cruise ship went down and the following people were stranded on a chain of deserted islands in the South Pacific:

Two Italian men and one Italian woman.

Two French men and one French woman.

Two German men and one German woman.

Two Greek men and one Greek woman.

Two British men and one British woman.

Two Bulgarian men and one Bulgarian woman.

Two Japanese men and one Japanese woman.

Two Chinese men and one Chinese woman.

Two Irish men and one Irish woman.

Two American men and one American woman.

One month later.

One Italian man killed the other Italian man for the Italian woman.

The two French men and the French woman are living happily together in a ménage a trois.

The two German men have a strict weekly schedule of alternating visits with the German woman.

The two Greek men are sleeping together and the Greek woman is cooking and cleaning for them.

The two British men are waiting for someone to introduce them to the British woman.

The two Bulgarian men took one look at the Bulgarian woman and started swimming to another island.

The two Japanese have faxed Tokyo and are awaiting instructions.

The two Chinese men have set up a pharmacy, liquor store, restaurant, and laundry, and have got the woman pregnant in order to supply more employees for their stores.

The two Irish men divided the island into north and south and set up a distillery. They do not remember if sex is in the picture because it gets somewhat foggy after a few pints of coconut whisky. However, they're satisfied because the British aren't having any fun.

The two American men are contemplating suicide because the American woman will not shut up and complains relentlessly about her body, the true nature of feminism, what the sun is doing to her skin, how she can do anything they can do, the necessity of fulfillment, the equal division of household chores, how sand and palm trees make her look fat, how her last boyfriend respected her opinion and treated her nicer than they do, and how her relationship with her mother is the root cause of all her problems, and why didn't they bring a damn cell phone so they could call 911 and get them all rescued off this forsaken deserted island in the middle of freaking nowhere so she can get her nails done and go shopping.

Guy goes in an adult store and asks for an inflatable doll.
Guy behind the counter says, "Male or female?"
Customer says, "Female."
Counter guy says, "Black or white?"
Customer says, "White."
Counter guy asks, "Christian or Muslim?"
Customer says, "What the hell does religion have to do with it?"
Counter guy says, "The Muslim one blows itself up."

A walker noticed an old lady sitting on her front step, so he walked up to her and said, "I couldn't help noticing how happy you look! What is your secret?"

"I smoke ten cigars a day," she said. "Before I go to bed, I smoke a nice big joint.

Apart from that, I drink a whole bottle of Jack Daniels every week, and eat only junk food. On week-ends, I pop pills and do no exercise at all."

"That is absolutely amazing! How old are you?"

"24" she replied.

Not long after the marriage, Jack and his father met for lunch.

"Well son," asked the dad, "how is married life treating you?"

"Not very well, I'm afraid. It seems that I married a nun."

"A nun??" his father exclaimed.

"That's right. None in the morning, none at night and none unless I beg."

The father nodded knowingly, and patted his son on the back. "Why don't we all get together for a nice talk tonight?"

Tom's face brightened, "Say Dad, that's a great idea."

"Fine. I'll call and tell Mother Superior to set two extra plates."

My father always loved fast cars. Taking advantage of the empty roads one morning, he accelerated down a wide-open stretch. Unfortunately, a young police officer was waiting at the other end, and Dad was flagged down. He greeted the officer with a cheery "Good morning."

"And a good morning to you, Wing Commander," replied the officer. "Having trouble taking off?"

A man was telling a friend about a nudist party he'd been invited to.

"I rang the bell, and the nudist butler opened the door," he started.

His friend interrupted, "How did you know he was a butler?"

"Well," he answered smoothly, "I could tell right away that it wasn't the maid . . ."

The inveterate horseplayer paused before taking his place at the betting window, and offered up a fervent prayer to his Maker.

"Blessed Lord," he murmured with mountain-moving sincerity, "I know you don't approve of my gambling, but just this once, Lord, just this once, please let me break even. I need the money so badly."

A strong young man at the construction site was bragging that he could outdo anyone in a feat of strength. He made a special case of making fun of one of the older workmen. After several minutes, the older worker had enough.

"Why don't you put your money where your mouth is," he said. "I will bet you a week's wages that I can haul something in a wheelbarrow over to that building that you won't be able to wheel back."

"You're on, old man," the braggart replied. "Let's see what you got." The old man reached out and grabbed the wheelbarrow by the handles. Then, nodding to the young man, he said, "All right, Dumb Ass, get in."

A little guy is sitting at the bar just staring at his drink for half an hour when a big trouble-making biker steps next to him, grabs the drink, and gulps it down in one swig.

The poor little guy starts crying.

"Come on man, I was just giving you a hard time," the biker says. "I didn't think you'd CRY. I can't stand to see a man crying."

"This is the worst day of my life," the little guy blurts out between sobs. "I can't do anything right.

"I overslept and was late to an important meeting, so my boss fired me. When I went to the parking lot, I found my car was stolen, and I don't have gap insurance. I left my wallet in the cab I took home. I found my wife in bed with the gardener, and my dog bit me.

"So I came to this bar trying to work up the courage to put an end to my life, and then you show up and drink the damn poison."

A psychiatrist was conducting group therapy with 4 young moms and their small children.

"You all have obsessions," he observed.

To the first mother, he said, "You are obsessed with eating. You've even named your daughter Candy." He turned to the second mother, "Your obsession is with money. Again, it manifests itself in your child's name, Penny." He turns to the third mother. "Your obsession is alcohol. This manifests itself in your child's name,

Brandy." At this point, the fourth mother gets up, takes her little boy by the hand and whispers, "Come on, Dick, we're leaving!"

"Mary," asked Dawn thoughtfully one day, "what would you do if you caught your husband with another woman?"

"Another woman with MY husband?" Mary thought it over. "Let's see; I'd break her cane, shoot her guide dog, and call a cab to take her back to the institution she escaped from."

A trucker who has been out on the road for three weeks stops into a brothel outside Vegas. He walks straight up to the Madam, drops down $500 and says, "I want your ugliest woman and a bologna sandwich!!!"

The Madam is astonished. "But sir, for that kind of money you could have one of my finest ladies and a three-course meal."

The trucker replies, "Listen sweetheart, I ain't looking for great sex, I'm homesick."

Two ministers were discussing the decline in morals in the modern world. "I didn't sleep with my wife before I was married," said one clergyman self-righteously. "Did you?"

"I don't know," said the other. "What was her maiden name?"

It costs a lot of money to date. I took a girl out to dinner the other night. I said "What'll you have?" She said "Well, I guess I'll have the steak and lobster." I said "Well, guess again . . ."

A man has to take a business trip overseas so he entrusts his best friend with the job of keeping an eye on his wife. If anything out of the ordinary should occur, his friend was to notify him immediately. After about a week with no contact, the businessman received a telegram containing only one sentence.

"The man who comes to visit your wife every night didn't show up yesterday."

Two guys were discussing life in general over drinks one night.

"My grandfather lived to be 96."

"Ninety-six? What finally got him???"

"Liquor and women."

"Well, that just goes to show ya," snickered the one guy, "both'll get you in the end."

"Well actually, no, it's not what ya think. Towards the end, Grandpa couldn't get either one, so he just laid down and died."

A farmer was munching on a cookie as he watches the rooster chase a hen around.

Playfully, the farmer threw a piece of cookie to the ground. Seeing it, the rooster stopped chasing the hen and ran to the piece of cookie.

The farmer shook his head slowly and said, "Gosh, I hope I never get that hungry."

In the smoking-car the conversation turned to the merits and demerits of various ways of preserving health. One stout, florid man held forth with great eloquence on the subject.

"Look at me!" he said. "Never a day's sickness in my life, and all due to simple food. Why, gentlemen," he continued, "from the age of twenty to that of forty I lived an absolutely simple regular life—no effeminate delicacies, no late hours, no extravagances. Every day, in fact, summer and winter, I was in bed regularly at nine o'clock and up again at five in the morning. I worked from eight to one, then had dinner—a plain dinner, mark my words: after that, an hour's exercise; then . . ."

"Excuse me, sir," interrupted the sarcastic stranger in the corner, "but what were you in prison for?"

Two youngsters were closely examining bathroom scales on display at the department store. "What's it for?" one asked.

"I don't know," the other replied. "I think you stand on it and it makes you mad. At least it does that for my Mom and Dad."

A man and his wife were sitting in a bar. Dave came in and sat down next to the woman. As he sipped his drink, Dave ogled the woman until her husband, incensed, demanded that Dave stop looking at his wife, and that he wipe those filthy thoughts out of his mind.

Dave said, "Hey man, I wasn't ogling your wife; I wasn't thinking any filthy thoughts . . . back off buddy. I just came in here for a piece of beer."

Mary was out driving her car and while stopped at a red light, the car just died. It was a busy intersection and the traffic behind her starting growing. The guy in the car directly behind her started honking his horn continuously as Mary continued to try getting the car to start up again. Finally Mary got out of her car and approached the guy in the car behind her.

"I can't seem to get my car started," Mary said, smiling. "Would you be a sweetheart and go and see if you can get it started for me. I'll stay here in your car and lean on your horn for you."

Mary had to grab a cab to get to a meeting uptown. She hailed one, got in and told the cabbie the address to go to. The cabbie turned out to be a lunatic driver and Mary sat in the backseat clutching the door handle wondering if she could expect to survive this trip. The cabdriver sped through the crowded NYC streets, weaving in and out of traffic. Mary watched as one pedestrian after another leapt aside to avoid being run down by her lunatic driver.

Mary looked ahead and saw a truck double parked on the narrow street. Not only did the driver fail to slow down, he actually accelerated as he approached the truck. He slipped his cab through the available space with an inch or two to spare on either side.

"Driver," Mary screamed, "Are you crazy??? Are you trying to get us both killed?"

"Relax lady," the cabbie said. "Just do what I do. Close your eyes."

Mary goes to her first show at an art gallery and is looking at the paintings. One is a huge canvas that has black with yellow blobs of paint splattered all over it. The next painting is a murky gray color that has drips of purple paint streaked across it.

Mary walks over to the artist and says, "I don't understand your paintings."

"I paint what I feel inside me," explains the artist.

"Have you ever tried Alka-Seltzer?"

Three guys were sailing, when a storm blew up, and capsized their boat. Luckily, they were right near an island, so they quickly swam towards it. On the shore, there was a giant throne with a giant man on top of it. He was surrounded by wolves.

"If you go into the forest, and find 10 of one kind of fruit, I will tell my wolves not to eat you." So the three guys ran in to the forest to find some fruit. The first guy came back with 10 apples.

"Now you must stuff all 10 up your butt without wincing, or making a sound!" The guy started. He got 1, 2, 3—but then started crying. The wolves ate him.

The second guy came back with 10 berries. He was told to do the same thing. He got 1, 2, 3, 4, 5, 6, 7, 8—But then burst out laughing. The wolves ate him, too. The first guy and the second guy met up in heaven.

"Why'd you laugh? You were almost there!" the first guy asked.
"I saw the third guy coming with an armload of watermelons!"

The call came into the firehouse just as the crew sat down for dinner.

"Help!" shouted the caller, "you've got to come to 60 Rose Street! There's a fire in my basement!"

"Did you try throwing water on it?" asked the fireman.

"Of course I did!"

The fireman replied, "Well then there's no point in us going anywhere, that's all we do!"

When four of Santa's elves got sick, and the trainee elves did not produce the toys as fast as the regular ones, Santa was beginning to feel the pressure of being behind schedule. Then Mrs. Claus told Santa that her Mom was coming to visit. This stressed Santa even more. When he went to harness the reindeer, he found that three of them were about to give birth and two had jumped the fence and were out, heaven knows where. More stress. Then when he began to load the sleigh one of the boards cracked, and the toy bag fell to the ground and scattered the toys.

So, frustrated, Santa went into the house for a cup of apple cider and a shot of rum. When he went to the cupboard, he discovered that the elves had hidden the liquor, and there was nothing to drink. In his frustration, he accidentally dropped the cider pot, and it broke into hundreds of little pieces all over the kitchen floor. He went to get the broom and found that mice had eaten the straw end of the broom. Just then the doorbell rang, and a very irritable Santa trudged to the door. He opened the door, and there was a little angel with a great big Christmas tree. The angel said, very cheerfully, "Merry Christmas, Santa. Isn't it a lovely day? I have a beautiful tree for you. Where would you like me to put it?"

And so began the tradition of the little angel on top of the Christmas tree!

Religions of the World

Taoism	Shit happens.
Confucianism	Confucius says: “Shit happens.”
Buddhism	If shit happens, it isn’t really shit.
Zen	What is the sound of shit happening?
Hinduism	That shit happened before.
Islam	If shit happens, it is the will of Allah.
Protestantism	Let shit happen to someone else.
Catholicism	If shit happens, you deserve it.
Born Again	Same old shit, new cover.
Mormon	If shit happens, it is eternal.
Judaism	Why does this shit always happen to us?
Polytheism	Who did this shit?
Monotheism	I’ve narrowed this shit down to one.
Satanism	We make shit fly.
Agnosticism	What is this shit?
Atheism	I don’t believe this shit.
Rastafarianism	Let’s smoke this shit.

You Know You’re Trailer Trash When . . .

1. The Halloween pumpkin on your porch has more teeth than your spouse.
2. You let your twelve-year-old daughter smoke at the dinner table in front of her kids.
3. You’ve been married three times and still have the same in-laws.
4. You think a woman who is “out of your league” bowls on a different night.
5. Jack Daniel’s makes your list of “most admired people.”
6. You wonder how service stations keep their restrooms so clean.
7. Someone in your family died right after saying, “Hey, watch this.”
8. You think Dom Perignon is a Mafia leader.
9. Your wife’s hairdo was once ruined by a ceiling fan.
10. Your junior prom had a daycare.
11. You think the last words of the Star Spangled Banner are, “Gentlemen, start your engines.”

12. You lit a match in the bathroom and your house exploded right off its wheels.

13. The bluebook value of your truck goes up and down, depending on how much gas is in it.

14. You have to go outside to get something from the fridge.

15. One of your kids was born on a pool table.

16. You need one more hole punched in your card to get a freebie at the House of Tattoos.

17. You can't get married to your sweetheart because there's a law against it.

18. You think loading a dishwasher means getting your wife drunk.

19. Your toilet paper has page numbers on it.

20. Your front porch collapses and kills more than five dogs.

Two women came before wise King Solomon, dragging between them a young man in a three-piece suit.

"This young lawyer agreed to marry my daughter," said one.

"No! He agreed to marry MY daughter," said the other.

And so they haggled before the King until he called for silence.

"Bring me my biggest sword," said Solomon, "and I shall hew the young attorney in half. Each of you shall receive a half."

"Sounds good to me," said the first lady.

But the other woman said, "Oh Sire, do not spill innocent blood. Let the other woman's daughter marry him."

The wise king did not hesitate a moment. He proclaimed, "The attorney must marry the first lady's daughter."

"But she was willing to hew him in two!" exclaimed the King's court.

"Indeed," said the wise King Solomon. "That shows she is the TRUE mother-in-law."

A lady about 8 months pregnant got on a bus. She noticed the man opposite her was smiling at her. She immediately moved to another seat. This time the smile turned into a grin, so she moved again. The man seemed more amused. When on the fourth move, the man burst out laughing, she complained to the driver and he had the man arrested.

The case came up in court. The judge asked the man (about 20 years old) what he had to say for himself. The man replied, "Well Your Honor, it was like this: When the lady got on the bus, I couldn't help but notice her condition. She sat down under a sign that said, 'The Double Mint Twins are Coming' and I grinned. Then she moved and sat under a sign that said, 'Logan's Liniment will reduce the swelling,' and I had to smile. Then she placed herself under a deodorant sign that said, 'William's Big Stick Did the Trick,' and I could hardly contain myself. BUT, Your Honor, when she moved the fourth time and sat under a sign that said, 'Goodyear Rubber could have prevented this Accident' . . . I just lost it."

"CASE DISMISSED!"

This is the fairy tale that should have been read to us when we were little:

Once upon a time in a land far away, a beautiful, independent, self-assured princess happened upon a frog as she sat contemplating ecological issues on the shores of an unpolluted pond in a verdant meadow near her castle.

The frog hopped into the princess' lap and said: "Elegant Lady, I was once a handsome prince, until an evil witch cast a spell upon me. One kiss from you, however, and I will turn back into the dapper, young prince that I am and then, my sweet, we can marry and set up housekeeping in your castle with my mother, where you can prepare my meals, clean my clothes, bear my children, and forever feel grateful and happy doing so."

That night, as the princess dined sumptuously on lightly sautéed frog legs seasoned in a white wine and onion cream sauce, she chuckled and thought to herself: I don't think so.

School Answering Machine

This is the message a High School staff voted unanimously to record on their school telephone answering machine.

The outgoing message:

"Hello! You have reached the automated answering service of your school. In order to assist you in connecting to the right staff member, please listen to all the options before making a selection: To lie about why your child is absent—Press 1. To make excuses for why your child did not do his work—Press 2. To complain about what we do—Press 3. To swear at staff members—Press 4. To ask why you didn't get information that was already enclosed in your newsletter and several flyers mailed to you—Press 5. If you want us to raise your child—Press 6. If you want to reach out and touch, slap or hit someone—Press 7. To request another teacher, for the third time this year—Press 8. To complain about bus transportation—Press 9. To complain about school lunches—Press 0. If you realize this is the real world and your child must be accountable and responsible for his/her behavior, class work, homework and that it's not the teacher's fault for your child's lack of effort: Hang up and have a nice day!

After 35 years of accident free driving I finally had a wreck. I am fine, but it was one of those stupid rear end collisions, where it could have been avoided. It was really nobody's fault.

To my surprise, the guy I hit was a dwarf and he stormed out of his car, stomped back to my car and shouted at me, "I AM NOT HAPPY!"

So I asked him, "Well, which one are you?"

Learned one thing about dwarfs . . . they don't have a sense of humor.

A man walked into the produce section of his local supermarket and asked to buy half a head of lettuce. The boy working in that department told him that they only sold whole heads of lettuce. The man was insistent that the boy ask his manager about the matter.

Walking into the back room, the boy said to the manager, "Some asshole wants to buy half a head of lettuce." As he finished his sentence, he turned to find the man standing right behind him; so he quickly added, "And this gentleman kindly offered to buy the other half."

The manager approved the deal, and the man went on his way. Later the manager said to the boy, "I was impressed with the way you got yourself out of that situation earlier. We like people who think on their feet here. Where are you from, son?"

"Kansas, sir," the boy replied.

"Well, why did you leave Kansas?" the manager asked.

The boy said, "Sir, there's nothing down there but whores and football players."

"Really?" said the manager. "My wife is from Kansas."

"No joke," replied the boy. "Who'd she play for?"

There will only be 49 contestants in the Miss Black America Contest this year because no one wants to wear the banner that says "IDAHO."

A son asked his mother the following question:

"Mom, why are wedding dresses white?"

The mother looks at her son and replies, "Son, this shows your friends and relatives that your bride is pure."

The son thanks his Mom and goes off to double-check this with his father. "Dad why are wedding dresses white?"

The father looks at his son in surprise and says, "Son, all household appliances come in white."

A man appeared before St. Peter at the Pearly Gates.

"Have you ever done anything of particular merit?" St. Peter asked. "Well, I can think of one thing," the man offered. "On a trip to the Black Hills of South Dakota, I came upon a gang of bikers who were threatening a young woman. I directed them to leave her alone, but they wouldn't listen. So, I approached the largest and most heavily tattooed biker and smacked him in the face, kicked his bike over, ripped out his nose ring, and threw it on the ground. I yelled, 'Now, back off, or I'll kick the crap out of all of you!' "

St. Peter was impressed. "When did this happen?"
"Couple of minutes ago."

Brian invited his mother over for dinner. During the course of the meal, Brian's mother couldn't help but notice how beautiful Brian's roommate, Jennifer, was. Brian's Mom had long been suspicious of a relationship between Brian and Jennifer, and this had only made her more curious. Over the course of the evening, while watching the two interact, she started to wonder if there was more between Brian and Jennifer than met the eye. Reading his mom's thoughts, Brian volunteered, "I know what you must be thinking, but I assure you Jennifer and I are just roommates." About a week later, Jennifer came to Brian saying, "Ever since your mother came to dinner, I've been unable to find the can opener. You don't suppose she took it, do you?"

Brian said, "Well, I doubt it, but I'll send her an e-mail just to be sure." So he sat down and wrote: "Dear Mom: I'm not saying that you 'did' take the can opener from the house; I'm not saying that you 'did not' take the can opener. But the fact remains that it has been missing ever since you were here for dinner. Love, Brian."

Several days later, Brian received an e-mail back from his mother that read: "Dear Son: I'm not saying that you 'do' sleep with Jennifer, and I'm not saying that you 'do not' sleep with Jennifer. But the fact remains that if Jennifer is sleeping in her own bed, she would have found the can opener by NOW! Love, Mom."

LESSON OF THE DAY—NEVER LIE TO YOUR MOTHER

As you may already know, it is a sin for a Taliban male to see any woman other than his wife naked, and that he must commit suicide if he does. So, this Saturday at 4 p.m. Eastern Time, all American women are asked to walk out of their house completely naked to help weed out any neighborhood terrorists.

Circling your block for one hour is recommended for this anti-terrorist effort.

All men are to position themselves in lawn chairs in front of their house to prove they are not Taliban and to demonstrate that they think it is okay to see nude women other than their wife and to show support for all American women.

And, since the Taliban also does not approve of alcohol, a cold 6-pack at your side is further proof of your anti-Taliban sentiment.

The American government appreciates your efforts to root out terrorists and applauds your participation in this anti-terrorist activity.

God Bless America.

A woman went into a bar in Austin and saw a cowboy with his feet propped up on a table. He had the biggest feet she'd ever seen. The woman asked the cowboy if it's true what they say about men with big feet.

The cowboy grinned and said, "Sure is, little lady! Why don't you come on out to the bunk house and let me prove it to you?"

The woman wanted to find out for herself, so she spent the night with him. The next morning she handed him a $100 bill. Blushing, he said, "Well, thank ya Ma'am. I'm real flattered. Ain't nobody ever paid me fer mah services before."

The woman replied, "Don't be flattered. Take the money and buy yourself some boots that fit."

A blonde young woman in New York was so depressed that she decided to end her life by throwing herself into the ocean. She went down to the docks and was about to leap into the frigid water when a handsome young sailor saw her tottering on the edge of the pier, crying. He took pity on her and said, "Look, you have so much to live for. I'm off to Europe in the morning, and if you like, I can stow you away on my ship. I'll take good care of you and bring you food every day."

Moving closer, he slipped his arm round her shoulder and added, "I'll keep you happy, and you'll keep me happy."

The girl nodded yes. After all, what did she have to lose? Perhaps a fresh start in Europe would give her life new meaning.

That night, the sailor brought her aboard and hid her in a lifeboat.

From then on, every night he brought her three sandwiches and a piece of fruit, and they made passionate love until dawn.

Three weeks later, during a routine inspection, she was discovered by the captain.

"What are you doing here?" the captain asked.

"I have an arrangement with one of the sailors," she explained. "I get food and a trip to Europe."

The captain said, "Lady, this is the Staten Island Ferry."

Everyone seems to be wondering why Muslim terrorists are so quick to commit suicide.

Let's see now . . . No Jesus, No Wal-Mart, No television, No cheerleaders, No baseball, No football, No basketball, No hockey, No golf, No tailgate parties, No Home Depot, No pork BBQ, No hot dogs, No burgers, No lobster, No shellfish, or even frozen fish sticks, No gumbo, No jambalaya.

More than one wife.

Rags for clothes and towels for hats. Constant wailing from the guy next-door because he's sick and there are no doctors. Constant wailing from the guy in the tower.

No chocolate chip cookies.

No Christmas.

You can't shave. Your wives can't shave. You can't shower to wash off the smell of donkey cooked over burning camel dung.

The women have to wear baggy dresses and veils at all times.

Your bride is picked by someone else. She smells just like your donkey, but your donkey has a better disposition.

Then they tell you that when you die it all gets better!

I mean, really, IS THERE A MYSTERY HERE!!!

Wanda's dishwasher quit working so she called in a repairman. Since she had to go to work the next day, she told the repairman, "I'll leave the key under the mat. Fix the dishwasher, leave the bill on the counter, and I'll mail you a check. Oh, by the way, don't worry about my dog Spike. He won't bother you. But, whatever you do, do NOT, under ANY circumstances, talk to my parrot! I MUST STRESS TO YOU: DO *NOT* TALK TO MY PARROT!!!"

When the repairman arrived at Wanda's apartment the following day, he discovered the biggest, meanest looking dog he had ever seen. But, just as she had said, the dog just lay there on the carpet watching the repairman go about his work.

The parrot, however, drove him nuts the whole time with his incessant yelling, cursing and name calling. Finally, the repairman couldn't contain himself any longer and yelled, "Shut up, you stupid, ugly bird!" To which the parrot replied, "Get him, Spike!"

See—Men just don't listen!

Once upon a time there were three little pigs .The straw pig, the stick pig, and the brick pig.

One day this nasty old wolf came up to the straw pig's house and said, "I'm gonna huff and puff and blow your house down." And he did!!!

So the straw pig went running over to the stick pig's house and said, "Please, let me in, the wolf just blew down my house." So the stick pig let the straw pig in.

Just then the wolf showed up and said, "I'm gonna huff and puff and blow your house down." And he did!!!

So the straw pig and the stick pig went running over to the brick pig's house and said, "Let us in, let us in, the big bad wolf just blew our houses down!"

So the brick pig let them in just as the wolf showed up. The wolf said, "I'm gonna huff and puff and blow your house down." The straw pig and the stick pig were so scared! But the brick pig picked up the phone and made a call.

A few minutes passed and a big, black Caddy pulled up.

Out stepped two massive pigs in pin striped suits and fedora hats. These pigs came over to the wolf, grabbed him by the neck and beat the living heck out of him, then one of them pulled out a gun, stuck it in his mouth and fired, killing the wolf, then they tied cement blocks around his feet and threw his sorry ass into the creek. Then they got back into their Caddy and drove off.

The straw pig and stick pig were amazed!!! "Who the hell were those guys?" they asked.

"Those were my cousins . . . the Guinea Pigs."

A truck driver is driving along on the freeway. A sign comes up that reads "Low bridge ahead."

Before he knows it, the bridge is right ahead of him and he gets stuck under the bridge. Cars are backed up for miles. Finally, a police car comes up. The cop gets out of his car and walks around to the truck driver, puts his hands on his hips and says, "Got stuck, huh?"

The truck driver says, "No, I was delivering this bridge and ran out of gas."

An older gentleman was on the operating table awaiting surgery and he insisted that his son, a renowned surgeon, perform the operation. As he was about to get the anesthesia, he asked to speak to his son.

"Yes, Dad, what is it?"

"Don't be nervous, son; do your best and just remember, if it doesn't go well, if something happens to me . . . your mother is going to come and live with you and your wife . . ."

Murphy applied for an engineering position at an Irish firm based in Dublin. An American applied for the same job and both applicants having the same qualifications were asked to take a test by the Department manager. Upon completion of the test both men only missed one of the questions. The manager went to Murphy and said.

"Thank you for your interest, but we've decided to give the American the job."

Murphy: "And why would you be doing that? We both got the nine questions correct. This being Ireland and me being Irish I should get the job!"

Manager: "We have made our decisions not on the correct answers, but on the question you missed."

Murphy: "And just how would one incorrect answer be better than the other?"

Manager: "Simple, the American put down on question #5, 'I don't know,' and you put down, 'Neither do I.' "

A group of 3rd, 4th and 5th graders, accompanied by two female teachers, went on a field trip to the local racetrack, to learn about thoroughbred horses.

When it was time to take the children to the bathroom, it was decided that the girls would go with one teacher and the boys would go with the other.

The teacher assigned to the boys was waiting outside the men's room when one of the boys came out and told her that none of them could reach the urinal.

Having no choice, she went inside, helped the boys with their pants, and began hoisting the little boys up one by one, holding on to their "wee-wees" to direct the flow away from their clothes. As she lifted one, she couldn't help but notice that he was unusually well endowed. Trying not to show that she was staring the teacher said, "You must be in the 5th grade."

"No, ma'am," he replied. "I'm riding Confidence Man in the seventh race, but I appreciate your help."

It was many years ago since the embarrassing day when a young woman, with a baby in her arms, entered his butcher shop and confronted him with the news that the baby was his and asked what was he going to do about it? Finally he offered to provide her with free meat until the boy was 16. She agreed.

He had been counting the years on his calendar, and one day the teenager, who had been collecting the meat each week, came into the shop and said, "I'll be 16 tomorrow."

"I know," said the butcher with a smile. "I've been counting too, tell your mother, when you take this parcel of meat home, that it is the last free meat she'll get, and watch the expression on her face."

When the boy arrived home he told his mother.

The woman nodded and said, "Son, go back to the butcher and tell him I have also had free bread, free milk, and free groceries for the last 16 years and watch the expression on his face!"

A rather attractive woman goes up to the bar in a quiet rural pub. She gestures alluringly to the barman who comes over immediately. When he arrives, she seductively signals that he should bring his face close to hers. When he does so, she begins to gently caress his beard which is full and bushy.

"Are you the landlord?" she asks, softly stroking his face with both hands.

"Actually, no" he replies.

"Can you get him for me—I need to speak to him?" she asks, running her hands up beyond his beard and into his hair.

"I'm afraid I can't" breathes the barman—clearly aroused. "Is there anything I can do?"

"Yes, there is. I need you to give him a message" she continues huskily, popping a couple of fingers into his mouth and allowing him to suck them gently.

"Tell him that there is no toilet paper in the ladies room."

At Duke University, there were four sophomores taking Organic Chemistry. They were doing so well on all the quizzes, midterms and labs, etc., that each had an "A" so far for the semester.

These four friends were so confident that the weekend before finals, they decided to go up to the University of Virginia and party with some friends there. They had a great time, but after all the hearty partying, they slept all day Sunday and didn't make it back to Duke until early Monday morning.

Rather than taking the final then, they decided to find their professor after the final and explain to him why they missed it. They explained that they had gone to UVA for the weekend with the plan to come back in time to study, but unfortunately, they had a flat tire on the way back, didn't have a spare, and couldn't get help for a long time. As a result, they missed the final.

The professor thought it over and then agreed they could make up the final the following day. The guys were elated and relieved. They studied that night and went in the next day at the time the professor had told them. He placed them in separate rooms and handed each of them a test booklet, and told them to begin.

The, looked at the first problem, worth five points. It was something simple about free radical formation. "Cool," they thought at the same time, each one in his separate room, "this is going to be easy." Each finished the problem and then turned the page.

On the second page was written: (For 95 points): Which tire?

As he was quietly watching television at home, the man heard a sound on the roof of his house and rushed out to investigate. Seeing it was a fair-sized gorilla tearing the shingles off his home, he promptly called up the local zoo authorities to inform them one of their animals had escaped. He was reassured that a gorilla recovering unit was on the way and to remain calm. A few minutes later, an old beat up truck, displaying the gorilla recovery unit logo on its side, pulled up to the house. The elderly driver proceeded to recover from the back of the truck, a chihuahua dog, a pair of handcuffs, a ladder, a baseball bat, and a 12-gauge shotgun.

Puzzled on how this lone elderly man was to solve the problem of this gorilla that had by now torn half the roof apart, the chap asked him how he would go about doing this. As he handed him over the 12-gauge shotgun, the zoo employee explained the plan:

"First I'll climb up there with the ladder. Then I'll approach the gorilla and knock him off the roof using the baseball bat. As soon as the gorilla hits the ground, the specially trained chihuahua will attack its private parts. When I get back on the ground, the gorilla will have lowered its hands to its groin area to protect itself thus making it easy for me to slip on the handcuffs. Then, I lead him to the truck, lock him up and take him back to the zoo . . ."

Amazed at the procedure, the somewhat startled house owner asked why he was handed the 12-gauge shotgun?

"Well," explained the experienced gorilla retriever, "It's just a precaution should things not go exactly as planned. In the unlikely event that once on the roof, the gorilla knocks me off with the bat, shoot the dog."

A lawyer returns to his parked BMW to find the headlights broken and considerable damage to the hood. There's no sign of the offending vehicle but he's relieved to see that there's a note stuck under the windshield wiper.

"Sorry, I just backed into your Beemer. The witnesses who saw the accident are nodding and smiling at me because they think I'm leaving my name, address and other particulars. But I'm not. Sorry."

Grandmother died in 1985, but her birthday is coming up, and that always causes me to reminisce. The long walks we used to take to the store, the quarters she gave me for meaningless jobs like pulling weeds or washing the sidewalk . . . Those gems were all good, but the one I remember most, the jewel in the crown of grand motherly advice, occurred when I was only about 10. We were sitting in a park having just finished collecting some 40 soda bottles for the deposit money on a beautiful spring day. She told me that one day, I would find a wonderful woman and start my own family. "And remember always this thing," she said. "Be sure you marry a woman with small hands."

"How come, Grandma?" I asked her.

She answered in her soft voice . . . "Makes your dick look bigger."

Becky, who belonged to a synagogue group devoted to visiting and helping the sick members of her congregation, was out making her rounds visiting homebound patients when she ran out of gas. As luck would have it a gas station was just a block away.

She walked to the station to borrow a gas can and buy some gas. The attendant told her the only gas can he owned had been loaned out but she could wait until it was returned.

Since Becky was on the way to see another patient and behind schedule, she decided not to wait and walked back to her car. She looked for something in her car that she could fill with gas and spotted the bedpan she always had handy for needy patients. Always resourceful, she carried the bedpan to the station, filled it with gas, and carried the full bedpan back to her car which was decorated with many Hebrew decals and bumper stickers. As she was pouring the gas into her tank, two men watched from across the street. One of them turned to the other and said, “If it starts, I'm turning Jewish.”

Yesterday I was burying a large bag of Purina dog chow for Athena the wonder dog at Wal-Mart and was about to check out. A woman behind me asked if I had a dog.

On impulse, I told her that no, I didn't have a dog, and that I was starting the Purina Diet again Although I probably shouldn't, because I'd ended up in the hospital last time, but that I'd lost 50 pounds before I awakened in an intensive care ward with tubes coming out of most of my orifices and IVs in both arms.

I told her that it was essentially a perfect diet and that the way that it works is to load your pants pockets with Purina nuggets and simply eat one or two every time you feel hungry and that the food is nutritionally complete so I was going to try it again. (I have to mention here that practically everyone in the line was by now enthralled with my story.)

Horrified, she asked if I ended up in intensive care because the dog food poisoned me. I told her no, I stepped off a curb to sniff an Irish Setter's ass and a car hit us both.

A man takes the day off work and decides to go out golfing. He is on the second hole when he notices a frog sitting next to the green. He thinks nothing of it and is about to shoot when he hears, “Ribbit 9 Iron.” The man looks around and doesn't see anyone. Again, he hears, “Ribbit 9 Iron.” He looks at the frog and decides to prove the frog wrong, puts the club away, and grabs a 9 iron. Boom! He hits it 10 inches from the cup. He is shocked. He says to the frog, “Wow, that's amazing. You must be a lucky frog, eh?”

The frog replies, “Ribbit Lucky frog.” The man decides to take the frog with him to the next hole. “What do you think frog?” the man asks. “Ribbit 3 wood.” The guy takes out a 3 wood, and Boom! Hole in one. The man is befuddled and doesn't know what to say. By the end of the day, the man has had the best game of golf in his life and asks the frog, "Ok where to next?" The frog replies, "Ribbit Las Vegas."

They go to Las Vegas and the guy says, "Ok frog, now what?" The frog says, "Ribbit Roulette." Upon approaching the roulette table, the man asks, "What do you think I should bet?" The frog replies, "Ribbit $1000000, black 6." Now, this is a million-to-one shot to win, but after the golf game the man figures what the heck. Boom! Tons of cash comes sliding back across the table.

The man takes his winnings and buys the best room in the hotel. He sits the frog down and says, "Frog, I don't know how to repay you. You've won me all this money and I'm forever grateful."

The frog replies, "Ribbit Kiss Me." He figures why not, since after all the frog did for him, he deserves it. With a kiss, the frog turns into a gorgeous 15-year-old girl. "And that your honor, is how the girl ended up in my room. So help me God."

John, a University student, was on the side of the road hitchhiking on a very dark night and in the midst of a storm. The night was rolling on and no car went by. The storm was so strong he could hardly see a few feet ahead of him. Suddenly, he saw a car slowly coming towards him and stopped. John, desperate for shelter and without thinking about it, got into the car and closed the door, only to realize there was nobody behind the wheel and the engine wasn't on!!

The car started moving slowly. John looked at the road ahead and saw a curve approaching. Scared, he started to pray, begging for his life. Then, just before the car hit the curve, a hand appeared through The window and turned the wheel. John, paralyzed with terror, watched as the hand repeatedly came through the window, but never touched or harmed him.

Shortly thereafter John saw the lights of a pub appear down the road, so, gathering strength, he jumped out of the car and ran to it. Wet and out of breath, he rushed inside and started telling everybody about the horrible experience he had just had. A silence enveloped the pub when everybody realized he was crying and . . . wasn't drunk.

Suddenly, the door opened, and two other people walked in from the stormy night. They, like John, were also soaked and out of breath. Looking around, and seeing John sobbing at the bar, one said to the other, "Look Paddy . . . there's that idiot that got in the car while we were pushing it!!!"

Health Question and Answer Session

Q: I've heard that cardiovascular exercise can prolong life. Is this true?

A: Your heart is only good for so many beats, and that's it. Don't waste them on exercise. Everything wears out eventually. Speeding up your heart will not make you live longer; that's like saying you can extend the life of your car by driving it faster. Want to live longer? Take a nap.

Q: Should I cut down on meat and eat more fruits and vegetables?

A: You must grasp logistical efficiencies. What does a cow eat? Hay and corn. And what are these? Vegetables. So, a steak is nothing more than an efficient mechanism of delivering vegetables to your system. Need grain? Eat chicken. Beef is also a good source of field grass (green leafy vegetables). And a pork chop can give you 100% of your recommended daily allowance of vegetable products.

Q: Should I reduce my alcohol intake?

A: No, not at all. Wine is made from fruit. Brandy is distilled wine . . . that means they take the water out of the fruity bit so you get even more of the goodness that way. Beer is also made out of grain. Bottoms up!

Q: How can I calculate my body/fat ratio?

A: Well, if you have a body and you have body fat, your ratio is one to one. If you have two bodies, your ratio is two to one, etc.

Q: What are some of the advantages of participating in a regular exercise program?

A: Can't think of a single one, sorry. My philosophy is: "No pain . . . good."

Q: Aren't fried foods bad for you?

A: YOU'RE NOT LISTENING!!! Foods are fried these days in vegetable oil. In fact, they're permeated in it. How could getting more vegetables be bad for you?

Q: Will sit-ups help prevent me from getting a little soft around the middle?

A: Definitely not! When you exercise a muscle, it gets bigger. You should really only be doing sit-ups if you want a bigger stomach.

Q: Is chocolate bad for me?

A: Are you crazy?! HELLO . . . Cocoa beans—another vegetable!! It's the best feel-good food around!

Q: Is swimming good for your figure?

A: If swimming is good for your figure, explain whales to me.

Q: Is getting in shape important for my lifestyle?

A: Hey! "Round" is a shape!

For decades, two heroic statues, one male and one female, faced each other in a city park, until one day an angel came down from heaven.

"You've been such exemplary statues," he announced to them, "That I'm going to give you a special gift. I'm going to bring you both to life for thirty minutes, in which you can do anything you want." And with a clap of hands, the angel brought the statues to life.

The two approached each other a bit shyly, but soon dashed for the bushes, from which shortly emerged a good deal of giggling, laughter, and shaking of branches. Fifteen minutes later, the two statues emerged from the bushes with grins on their faces.

"You still have fifteen more minutes," said the angel, winking conspiratorially.

Grinning even more widely the female statue turned to the male statue and said, "Great! Only this time you hold the pigeon down and I'll shit on its head."

An old farmer went to town to see a movie. The ticket agent asked, "Sir, what's that on your shoulder?" The old farmer said, "That's my pet rooster Chucky; wherever I go Chuck goes."

"I'm sorry, sir," said the ticket agent. "We can't allow animals in the theater."

The old farmer went around the corner and stuffed the bird down his pants. He returned to the booth, bought a ticket and entered the theater. He sat down next to two old widows, Mildred and Marge. The movie started and the rooster began to squirm. The old farmer unzipped his pants so Chucky could stick his head out and watch the movie.

"Marge," whispered Mildred.

"What?" said Marge.

"I think the guy next to me is a pervert."

"What makes you think so?" asked Marge.

"He unzipped his pants and he has his thing out," whispered Mildred.

"Well, don't worry about it," said Marge. "At our age we've seen 'em all."

"I thought so too," said Mildred. "But this one's eatin' my popcorn!!"

Two Arabs boarded a flight out of London. One took a window seat and the other sat next to him in the middle seat. Just before take off, an American sat down in the aisle seat. After takeoff, the American kicked his shoes off, wiggled his toes and was settling in when the Arab in the window seat said, "I need to get up and get a coke."

"Don't get up," said the American, "I'm in the aisle seat. I'll get it for you." As soon as he left, one of the Arabs picked up the American's shoe and spat in it. When he returned with the coke, the other Arab said, "That looks good. I'd really like one, too." Again, the American obligingly went to fetch it. While he was gone the other Arab picked up his other shoe and spat in it.

When the American returned, they all sat back and enjoyed the flight. As the plane was landing, the American slipped his feet into his shoes and knew immediately what had happened. "Why does it have to be this way?" he asked. "How long must this go on? This fighting between our nations? This hatred? This animosity? This spitting in shoes and pissing in cokes?"

I was in the express lane at the store quietly fuming. Completely ignoring the sign, the woman ahead of me had slipped into the check-out line pushing a cart piled high with groceries. Imagine my delight when the cashier beckoned the woman to come forward looked into the cart and asked sweetly, "So which six items would you like to buy?"

Wouldn't it be great if that happened more often?

The reason congressmen try so hard to get re-elected is that they would hate to have to make a living under the laws they've passed.

Three friends from the local congregation were asked, "When you're in your casket, and friends and congregation members are mourning over you, what would you like them to say?"

Artie said: "I would like them to say I was a wonderful husband, a fine spiritual leader, and a great family man."

Eugene commented: "I would like them to say I was a wonderful teacher and servant of God who made a huge difference in people's lives."

Al said: "I'd like them to say, 'Look, he's moving!"